Father Peter John De Smet

THE OKLAHOMA WESTERN BIOGRAPHIES
RICHARD W. ETULAIN, GENERAL EDITOR

Father Peter John De Smet

JESUIT IN THE WEST

By Robert C. Carriker

UNIVERSITY OF OKLAHOMA PRESS : NORMAN AND LONDON

Published with the assistance of the National Endowment for the Humanities, a federal agency which supports the study of such fields as history, philosophy, literature, and language.

Library of Congress Cataloging-in-Publication Data

Carriker, Robert C., 1940–
  Father Peter John de Smet : Jesuit in the West / by Robert C. Carriker.
    p. cm. — (The Oklahoma western biographies ; v. 9)
  Includes bibliographical references and index.
  ISBN: 0-8061-2750-3 (cloth : alk. paper)
    1. Smet, Pierre-Jean de, 1801–1873. 2. Indians of North America—
  Missions—West (U.S.) 3. Jesuits—Biography. 4. Missionaries—West
  (U.S.)—Biography. 5. Jesuits—Missions—West (U.S.) I. Title. II. Series.
  E78.W5S622 1995
  266'.2'092—dc20
  [B]   95-11891
                                                                            CIP

Father Peter John De Smet: Jesuit in the West is Volume 9 in *The Oklahoma Western Biographies.*

All maps were drawn by Antoinette C. Smith.

The paper in this book meets the guidelines for permanence and durability of the Committee on Production Guidelines for Book Longevity of the Council on Library Resources, Inc. ∞

1 2 3 4 5 6 7 8 9 10

*This book is dedicated to the Carriker women,
Eleanor, Alba, Jackie, and Anne*

Contents

List of Illustrations	*page* ix
List of Maps	xi
Series Editor's Preface	xiii
Preface	xv
1. The Education of a Missionary, 1801–1840	3
2. Missionary to the Flatheads, 1840–1842	31
3. De Smet's Greatest Adventure: The Third Trip to the Rocky Mountains, 1843–1846	63
4. New Challenges, 1847–1851	107
5. Chaplain and Peacemaker, 1852–1859	138
6. While the Nation Fought a War, 1860–1865	166
7. Peacemaking during the Sioux War, 1866–1868	198
8. "A Saint, but a Saint According to His Own Way," 1869–1873	229
Bibliography	245
Index	251

Illustrations

 1. Youthful portrait of Father De Smet in the 1830s   *page* 24
 2. *St. Mary's among the Flatheads*, 1841   54
 3. *Oregon Missions and Travels over the Rocky Mountains, in 1845–46*   112
 4. Portrait of De Smet, October 1858   154
 5. *Coeur d'Alene Mission of the Sacred Heart of Jesus*   158
 6. De Smet with Indian chiefs   161
 7. Steamboat *Florence*, used by De Smet   172
 8. *On the Trail in the Coeur d'Alene Country*, 1860s   180
 9. Portrait of De Smet in 1864   195
10. *Fort Benton*, 1860s   204
11. *Father De Smet in Council with the Sioux*, 1868   224
12. Portrait of De Smet in 1872   234

Maps

1. The Education of a Missionary, 1821–1839   *page* 6
2. Journey to the Oregon Country, 1840–1842   32
3. The Rocky Mountain Mission, 1841–1846   74
4. The Missouri River Country, 1853   117

Series Editor's Preface

IN this exceptionally thorough and detailed biography of Father
Peter John De Smet, Robert Carriker assembles the full story of
the numerous western missionary travels and diplomatic journeys
of his important subject. Now we can follow, year by year and
crisis by crisis, the central parts the Belgian priest played in the
mid-nineteenth-century northern West.

Of major importance here is De Smet's important role as a
culture broker. Clearly no ignorant fundamentalist of dogmatic
stripe, De Smet was fully acquainted with several Indian groups
and thus could serve as a go-between for religious, governmental,
and military institutions interested in communicating with Indians and possibly winning their approval of European and American beliefs and actions. Indeed, few if any persons were as intimately acquainted as De Smet with the varied tribes of the
Northern Rockies and Plains. As Carriker notes, Father De Smet,
although embedded in his times, was no racist bigot demanding
attitudes and actions that would superimpose white ways and re-
duce Indians to third-class peoples.

Carriker's biography achieves several other major goals. Not only
has he provided a straightforward, smoothly written account of a
significant early western figure, but he also elucidates De Smet's
religious, diplomatic, and cultural roles in tension-filled middle
grounds between Indian and non-Indian peoples. These discussions help explain the seering impact of dramatic changes forced
on Indians from the 1840s through the 1860s.

Overall, Carriker views De Smet as a wonderfully positive influence on the pioneer West. As peacemaker, as indefatigable
worker, as a fearless and courageous man brimming with energy,
Carriker's De Smet built bridges of understanding among warring Indians in addition to soliciting priests and nuns to oper-

ate and raising money to finance Catholic missions in the Pacific Northwest, Rockies, and plains. Throughout his life, De Smet gained the respect, even love, of Native Americans in frontier areas that other whites feared to enter. Clearly, western Indians had confidence in De Smet's words and actions.

In short, this biography admirably carries out the goals of volumes in this series. It is a full and engrossing portrait of an important westerner and the insightful and revealing story of a frontier figure who did much to illuminate and shape western history for more than a generation.

RICHARD W. ETULAIN

University of New Mexico

Preface

THE life of Father De Smet is, in many ways, the simple story of a man who fell in love with America and its native inhabitants. Brash and reckless as a youth, Peter John De Smet grew to manhood in his native Belgium in the loving care of wealthy, socially prominent parents who attempted to place parameters on the lives of their children by maintaining a strict Catholic household. An indifferent student, Peter John early on reserved his passions for outdoor enterprises. "May God protect him! He will either be a soldier or a great traveler, but he will never be able to lead a quiet life!" Josse De Smet once exclaimed about his thirteen-year-old son. Indeed, old Josse's prediction came true a few years later when, in 1821, the youth left his home in Belgium, journeyed to America, and became both a soldier and a great traveler. To everyone's great surprise Peter John chose to become not a uniformed man-at-arms, but a soldier of Christ, a black-robed Jesuit missionary armed with a crucifix. Though it would have been unthinkable even to whisper such a thought in the mid-nineteenth century, especially after he became the best known Jesuit missionary in America and Europe, it is true that De Smet became a missionary among the Indians of the frontier essentially because the idea appealed to his sense of adventure.

After making his formation in the Society of Jesus as a novice, scholastic, and tertian, De Smet experienced a conversion to the religious life. No matter that his reasons for joining the Society of Jesus were more related to adventure than to ecclesiastical devotion, once he assumed a life of prayer and preparation for the Catholic priesthood, De Smet's faith deepened, and his desire to convert others to the sacred mysteries of Christianity thereafter dominated his life. Besides consoling Catholics and non-Catholics of all races, he devoutly read the prayers in his breviary every day, said daily Mass, and personally beseeched God and Saint Anthony to protect him on his wilderness journeys. His life's work, he believed, was to Christianize, civilize, and educate Native Americans, and he pursued that goal with a single mind for four decades.

De Smet took his ecclesiastical training at the Jesuit houses at White Marsh, Maryland, and Florissant, Missouri. When only a young and relatively inexperienced priest, he opened Saint Joseph's Mission for the Potawatomi Indians at a site near present-day Council Bluffs, Iowa. To be sure, De Smet looked upon his assignment as a great opportunity. He would ascend the Missouri River, see for himself the Great Plains, and visit native inhabitants. But his tenure at the Potawatomi mission proved to be an unsatisfying experience. Establishing the mission proved to be easy; in contrast, nothing he could do with the tribe spiritually could obscure the reality that with the arrival of each annuity check from the federal government the tribe grew more dependent upon strong drink and less motivated to receive Christianity.

Just when De Smet despaired that the Potawatomi mission would ultimately fail, in September 1839 two Indian emissaries bearing important information beached their canoe at Saint Joseph's Mission. These two travelers comprised the fourth delegation sent by the Flathead Indians, a tribe living an isolated existence in the Rocky Mountains, to find a Jesuit priest ready to live with them. De Smet knew immediately he must be the one to answer the call.

Inquisitive and, at the same time, visionary, De Smet thrived in the fertile mission field of the Rocky Mountains. He opened contact with a dozen tribes in the Oregon country besides establishing permanent missions for the Flatheads, Kalispels, and Coeur d'Alenes. To prepare for future expansion of the missions, he applied a proven design used in the seventeenth century by Jesuits in Paraguay. And all the while he tested out new routes between his missions, blazing a system of trails that ultimately benefited all pioneers to the Oregon country. An indefatigable traveler, in one year alone De Smet logged sixty-five hundred miles by foot, horseback, canoe, and steamboat as he snowshoed to the summit of the Rocky Mountains, floated the unrestrained

Columbia and Missouri Rivers, and hiked across the Canadian
prairies and the Yellowstone Desert. In the course of his wandering De Smet baptized thousands of Indians, renewed the religion
of countless white pioneers, and counseled peace between the
two races. Too bad, then, that he left the Rocky Mountain Mission in 1846 under a cloud of accusations.

In addition to being a Jesuit missionary and a world traveler,
Peter John De Smet also became a businessman and publicist.
Combining a natural talent for financial figures, something he no
doubt inherited from his successful businessman-father, with a
flair for writing, De Smet spent the majority of his life—a period
stretching from 1847 to his death in 1873—managing accounts for
the Society of Jesus in Saint Louis and raising money and recruits
for Jesuit Indian missions in the trans-Mississippi west. Six Jesuit
historians have examined the life of Father De Smet in the twen-
tieth century, and all of them have concluded, by one line of
reasoning or the other, that De Smet's contribution was absolutely essential to the success of the nineteenth-century Jesuit
Indian missions in America.

In order to revisit the Indian missions, De Smet sometimes
agreed to be an Indian commissioner, or special peace envoy, for
the federal government. Thus, in 1851, 1859, 1864, 1867, and 1868
he roamed the upper Missouri River country bringing messages
of peace to warring tribes and consoling the neutral Indians
caught in the middle of the Sioux Wars. De Smet loved living the
life of a missionary, especially the dangers on the trail and in the
camps. He advised younger Jesuits that "a fast of a day or two
gives zest to appetite. Should a storm keep one awake, one sleeps
better the following night. The sight of the enemy lying in wait to
take one's life teaches more confidence in God; teaches one to
pray well." And, he explained, there are compensations even beyond the salvation of souls: "Sleeping on the snow and in the open
may sound uncomfortable to those accustomed to soft mattresses
and warm rooms, but never was there a greater mistake," he
asserted. "Come and breathe the pure air of the mountains," he
urged, "where coughs and cold are unknown, and where con-
diments are not needed to excite the appetite! Come and try a

nomad's life and see how the fatigues of a long day's journey are forgotten; come and experience the joy of health and sound sleep, wrapped in a buffalo hide, lying upon pine branches beside a crackling fire!''

Prematurely gray by middle age, De Smet nevertheless wore his years well. Though slightly overweight, he exhibited unusual physical endurance, as his numerous escapades on foot and astride a mule demonstrate. A lifetime on the trail did, however, leave him with several prominent scars. One resulted from a tussle with a bear; most he earned by breaking a trail through thick forests. Once De Smet emerged from a mountain traverse with black eyes and torn cheek, noting that at any place but the American frontier such an appearance "would have laid me open to suspicion as being a highwayman from the Black Forest, rather than a missionary in search of souls." The cruelest scar of all, he lamented, resulted when a powderhorn exploded in his face, scorching him severely, completely stripping the skin from his nose, cheeks, and lips. The real pain came later, he said, when strangers mistook him for a raw-faced tenderfoot. In later life De Smet suffered deafness in one ear (the result of a tooth extraction) and the ordinary maladies of threescore years of life (as the remedy for which Saint Louis physicians curiously prescribed that he let his beard grow long). De Smet ultimately died of complications arising from Bright's disease, a kidney ailment.

Like his friends the Indians, De Smet appreciated the harmony of nature in the constantly changing western landscape. A constant desire to see for himself Mother Nature's next miracle farther up the trail in part fueled his penchant for travel. In his lifetime De Smet traveled 180,000 miles. He treated each journey as an adventure, an odyssey which he delighted in describing to his family and friends in long, tightly written letters that could squeeze twelve hundred words onto a page meant to hold less than a quarter of that number. His correspondence regularly appeared in Catholic magazines, where it enjoyed great popularity. Periodically De Smet would gather together the best of his letters and publish them in book form. As a result, he became in the minds of his contemporaries—Native Americans, Americans, and

Europeans—the epitome of a Catholic missionary among the Indians.

The popularity of the four books he wrote made it easier for De Smet to raise money and recruits for the Indian missions. He ultimately begged an amount estimated to be the equivalent of more than a million dollars in today's currency and enrolled close to one hundred recruits for the Saint Louis Jesuits. The books also established De Smet's reputation as an amateur botanist, frontier geographer, and recorder of Indian customs.

When De Smet passed away on May 23, 1873, an obituary in the *Missouri Republican* saluted him as one of the "world's most enterprising missionaries of Christian civilization." Thousands of Saint Louis citizens honored Father De Smet by joining in a city-wide funeral procession. Fatefully, the steamer *De Smet*, named for the man who had blessed it just two days earlier, spread the word of the passing of Black Robe to the upper Missouri Indian camps on its maiden voyage.

Certain persons have greatly furthered my education on Jesuit missionaries in general and Father De Smet in particular. None of them, however, should share the blame for my errors and omissions. Father William Lyle Davis, S.J., introduced me to Father De Smet in 1967 when I first arrived at Gonzaga University. At that time Father Davis was writing a biography of Father De Smet that he had begun a quarter of a century earlier. I knew something about De Smet, the building that housed the history department at Saint Louis University, my alma mater, being named for him, but not enough to help Father Davis finish his book before he died in 1973. Father Wilfred P. Schoenberg, S.J., admired De Smet less than did Father Davis, but he knows considerably more than anyone else in the world about the Oregon country missions established by the great Black Robe and his successors. No one has been a bigger influence in my life than Father Schoenberg. A collector of Jesuitica, founder of the Oregon Province Archives of the Society of Jesus, and a generous colleague, Father Schoenberg forced me to think of historical figures with Roman collars as real men and the institutions they founded as more than mere buildings.

Along the way other Jesuits helped me too: Gerald McKevitt, S.J., at the University of Santa Clara; Fredric Schlatter, S.J., and Anthony P. Via, S.J., at Gonzaga University; Thomas Connolly, S.J., at De Smet Mission, Idaho; and Cornelius M. Buckley, S.J. Non-Jesuits likewise assisted me in stitching together the many aspects of De Smet into a single narrative: Sharon Prendergast at Gonzaga University's Foley Library provided research assistance; Cole Hanford of the Gonzaga University School of Education provided necessary technical support for my hard drives and software; Professor Richard W. Etulain at the University of New Mexico read the entire manuscript and asked the questions I needed to hear; Dr. Jackie Peterson gave me the benefit of her amazing insight into the contact period between missionaries and Indians on several occasions; Christine Reilly provided the opportunity to take my De Smet concepts on the road in the Missouri Chautauqua; Andrew Carriker tried to teach me grammar; and David Smyth of Parks Canada provided useful maps and information in a prompt manner. Antoinette Cook Smith, a former student and professional cartographer, prepared the maps for this book, and for that I am deeply grateful. I am also indebted to John Drayton, editor-in-chief at the University of Oklahoma Press, for never giving up on the project. No one gave up more personal time to this life of De Smet than did Eleanor R. Carriker, my behind-the-scenes coauthor and spouse. Gonzaga University again proved itself to be a patient and supportive employer by providing money for research, computers for writing, and a protective attitude toward the hundreds of thousands of pages of original Jesuit documents it administers in the Oregon Province Archives of the Society of Jesus.

ROBERT C. CARRIKER

Spokane, Washington

Father Peter John De Smet

CHAPTER I

The Education of a Missionary, 1801–1840

"HOW can it be that Napoleon found millions of men ready to sacrifice their lives to ravage a nation and aid him to conquer the world, while I cannot find a handful of devoted men to save an entire people and extend the reign of God?" The question begged for an answer, yet the audience of young Belgians enrolled in the preparatory seminary at Mechelin, future candidates for the Catholic priesthood, remained silent. Father Charles Nerinckx waited patiently for a response. The American missions desperately needed young men with a vocation to the priesthood, not only in the emerging cities of Boston, Baltimore, and Philadelphia but also in the frontier provinces of western Maryland and Kentucky and the new Louisiana Purchase territory. Most of the seminarians in the audience that day had grown to manhood during the Napoleonic wars; they knew firsthand the appeal of the Little Corporal, who had met his final defeat not many miles away at Waterloo. Indeed, Father Nerinckx posed a difficult question to answer.

Peter John De Smet listened in rapt attention as an America of rustic cities, rugged mountains, free-spirited rivers, and dusky natives emerged from Father Nerinckx's talk. The vision was irresistible—not just the part about converting whole nations of Indians to Christianity, but also the prospect that he could explore new lands. He liked the idea of daring to be different. As a youth Peter John managed to break away from the regimented household established by his successful father to become something of a gadabout on the docks of Termonde, now Dendermonde in East Flanders, present-day Belgium. Known as Samson to his chums because of his barrel chest and muscular upper body, Peter John enjoyed abundant free time and used it to tempt fate on the wharves where his father's company outfitted military and commercial vessels with arms and equipment. He could always be counted on to participate in any games of war, roughhouse, or impromptu sport. His sister once described him as "a kind of Hercules, a terror to his school fellows, impetuous in the extreme, disputatious, and always in trouble." His brother characterized him simply as "hardy, adventurous, and indifferent to danger."

Peter John's penchant for audacious action, in fact, prompted the patriarch of the De Smet family to exile his daredevil son to a Catholic boarding school in Ghent at the age of thirteen. There the boy would be expected to learn proper manners. But Ghent became only the first of several junior seminaries and colleges at which the young De Smet willfully challenged rules. Dendermonde, East Flanders, even all of Europe had limits for Peter John's imagination and ambition. The young De Smet's life changed on the day in 1821 when he heard Father Charles Nerinckx's eloquent appeal for clergymen in America.

Within a matter of days following Father Nerinckx's presentation, Peter John De Smet and another young man from the seminary in Mechelin volunteered to join the Catholic missionary corps in America. Together with seven other men similarly enticed away from their studies at other schools, they hastened toward Amsterdam, their embarkation point for the New World. The students that Father Nerinckx accepted for the American clergy feared their parents' fault-finding with their decision, not to mention the probable disapproval of the anti-Catholic government of the Kingdom of the Netherlands if it learned that Father Nerinckx plotted to take minor boys out of the country, so they decided to leave Europe silently, without seeking parental approval. "To have asked the consent of our parents would have been to court a certain and absolute refusal," De Smet later explained.

Nerinckx's plans for a secret departure, however, hit a snag. Old Josse De Smet learned of his son's plans to go to America, so he empowered another son, Charles, with the parental authority to find Peter John, prevent his departure, and return him to Dendermonde, by force if necessary. The De Smet family had lived at the confluence of the Dendre and Scheldt Rivers for more than three hundred years, they enjoyed great prestige in their town of ten thousand persons, and Josse had intended for Peter John to join him someday in the family business almost from the moment the boy and his twin sister, Collette, had entered the world on January 30, 1801, as the fifth and sixth children of Josse's second wife, Marie-Jeanne Buydens. Fate chanced to bring the two De Smet boys together on the streets of Amsterdam, and in the confidential conversation that followed, Charles realized the earnestness of his would-be missionary sibling. Weeping with emotion, Charles withdrew his arguments, and he even donated a large sum of money to his brother. It became the first of many purses De Smet opened in a lifetime of begging.

Two weeks later, on August 15, 1821, Peter John boarded an American brig, prophetically named the *Columbia,* and set sail for America without benefit of a reconciliation with his father. Josse De Smet, meantime, did not accept his son's conduct with quiet resignation to God's will. In spite of a thoughtful letter of apology in which Peter John told his father how he suffered cruelly because he left home without benefit of a parental blessing, anger turned to sorrow and then bitterness for the eighty-five-year-old patriarch. He even refused to permit the reading of his disobedient son's letters in the family home. In time the two De Smets would be reconciled, but they would never see each other again; Josse De Smet died in 1827, six years before Peter John returned to Europe.

Of the young men Father Nerinckx brought to America that year, two elected to become diocesan priests once the ship docked in Philadelphia, but the other seven, including Peter John De Smet, chose to continue on to Georgetown College in the District of Columbia, where, on October 3, they enrolled in the Society of Jesus. Father Anthony Kohlmann, S.J., proudly reported to the father general of the society in Rome that his new recruits were both physically robust and properly schooled in syntax, Latin, poetry, rhetoric, and logic.

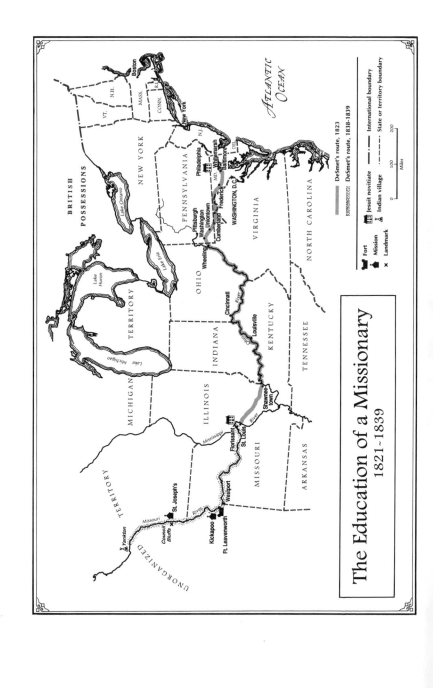

The Education of a Missionary
1821–1839

The novitiate at White Marsh, Maryland, twenty-four miles from Georgetown and fifteen miles west of Annapolis, housed the future of the Society of Jesus in the United States. There, petitioners to the society received their first instructions in the *Spiritual Exercises* of Saint Ignatius and, at the same time, learned the history and constitution of the order. Founded by Ignatius Loyola as a "charismatic fellowship," his company of religious men began as itinerant preachers of the catechism. Known popularly as Jesuits, the Society of Jesus received formal recognition from Pope Paul III in 1540. The order had a structure unique for the times. A father general, elected for life, sat in Rome. Beneath him were various provincials and superiors who coordinated the activities of priests, who administered six sacraments, and brothers, who assisted the priests. All Jesuits wore the same garb, a black robe; they followed the same schedule of training; and they bound themselves to the religious life by the three vows of poverty, chastity, and obedience. No monastic or choir obligations should impede their mobility, nor would they allow appointment to the hierarchy of the church to distract them from their work, which, after an early period of improvisation, generally favored education and the missions.

Early on, the Jesuits displayed such energy in seeking new souls for Christ that even before the death of Ignatius in 1556 they operated missions in Africa, Asia, and America. In North America they fanned out into the possessions of New Spain, New France, the Mississippi Valley, and, briefly, even the English colonies of Maryland and Pennsylvania. Jesuit missions at once became the envy of other religious orders and a thorn in the side of Bourbon monarchs in Europe. As a result, in 1773, Pope Clement XIV, a politic man, yielded to anti-Jesuit influences and dispersed the order. Only a few Jesuits, principally those at isolated outposts in Russia and Prussia, avoided the suppression, while all other elements of the society—twenty-three thousand Jesuits, 670 colleges, twenty-four universities, and 273 missions—lost their ecclesiastical status within the Catholic Church. A year later Clement died, and his pontifical successor, Pius VII, unobtrusively began to restore the Jesuits to their former status.

American Jesuits operated under normal conditions as early as 1805, when two dozen survivors of the order gathered in Maryland to rebuild their lost libraries, schools, and missions. A suspicious political climate in the new republic, unfortunately, made the restoration in America especially difficult. Thomas Jefferson, for example, no advocate of organized religion, considered the resurgence of the Jesuits "a retrograde step from light toward darkness."

But if Jefferson had no use for the Jesuits, an American bishop, the Right Reverend Louis Du Bourg, bishop of Upper and Lower Louisiana, did. He needed priests for the vast Louisiana Purchase that spread to the west beyond the new state of Missouri. Bishop Du Bourg knew from personal contact with Archbishop Ambrose Maréchal of Baltimore that unpaid debts of the society, thin soil at White Marsh, and a legal dispute over title to the Maryland plantation placed the Jesuit novitiate in a precarious position.

Even novices solicited funds from their families in order to keep the place open. "My passage here is not yet paid for, and the society's means are not sufficient to maintain us," De Smet pleaded in one letter to his father asking for two thousand florins. Letter followed letter, each asking for money, black cloth, books, vestments, and so on. Receiving no answer after more than a year of waiting, the young De Smet retained a Flemish lawyer to help him extricate funds from his mother's estate. We do not know how Josse De Smet reacted to that, but eventually he forgave his son for his rude leave-taking and shortly thereafter opened the family treasury for the benefit of the society.

By 1823 the superior of the Maryland Jesuits contemplated dissolving the novitiate and dismissing the twenty young men. At that moment Bishop Du Bourg offered the Jesuits 250 arpens (212 acres) of prime land on the outskirts of Saint Louis, plus four thousand dollars with which to build a new novitiate. The bishop needed priests for his Indian frontier, lest that field be abandoned to Protestants, and the Jesuits needed a new novitiate. On March 25, 1823, the two parties signed a letter of intent: Jesuit missionaries would evangelize the Indian tribes of Missouri and the Louisiana country, and the bishop would provide the Jesuits with land and building expenses for a western headquarters.

Father Charles Van Quickenborne, S.J., superior of the new mission, chose six Belgian novices, two priests, and three brothers to assist him in Missouri; the group included Peter John De Smet. Not just De Smet, but all the novices felt little sadness when they left White Marsh on April 11, 1823. When the Belgians came to America they believed they would be trained for a missionary career to the Indians, but in eighteen months they had met no Native Americans in Maryland. The prospect for Indians and great adventures seemed assured on the Missouri frontier. So, with high hopes De Smet and the other Belgians set out on the journey that would take them to Saint Louis by way of the Ohio River. Nicholas Biddle's narrative *Expedition under the Command of Captains Lewis and Clark*, first published in 1814, had developed quite a following among the privileged, literate families of Europe about the time the young Peter De Smet entered boarding school, so he knew that the captains' great adventure had begun in Pittsburgh, followed the Ohio River, and proceeded up the Mississippi River to a point opposite Saint Louis. Now it would be Peter John's turn to retrace their route to his new home in Missouri.

Even with the assistance of three black married couples, it took the Jesuits eighteen days to journey from Baltimore to Wheeling on the Ohio River via the National Pike. Traveling without funds, they literally begged their way across western Pennsylvania, sleeping in outbuildings and imposing on the generosity of Catholic families along the way. At Wheeling, Father Van Quickenborne allowed three days' rest while he exchanged the party's wagons for two broadhorns, or river-running flatboats. Unable or unwilling to hire a navigator, Father Van Quickenborne instead purchased a copy of the *Riverman's Guide to the Ohio River*, a do-it-yourself instruction pamphlet for self-confident emigrants. In an act of faith in God's mercy, Van Quickenborne lashed the two flatboats together and shoved off from the shore with most of his order's possessions—and future priests—on board. The eventful voyage that followed more than satisfied the imaginative Peter John's lust for adventure. Father Van Quickenborne, for example, frequently tried to lengthen the day by continuing to float on after dark in spite of the fact that his makeshift barge bore no lights. Numerous logs and snags, some of them of hull-bursting size, bristled from the water's surface, menacing the fragile Jesuit craft day and night. High winds impeded progress, several times forcing the floating monastery to scurry to shore for safety.

Except for a three-mile portage around the falls of the Ohio at Louisville, Father Van Quickenborne permitted no stops until May 22, when Shawneetown, Illinois, came into view. Knowing that the unwieldy scow he piloted down the Ohio would not go easily up the mighty Mississippi, Van Quickenborne sold his vessel and used the money to consign his order's trunks, boxes, and parcels the rest of the way to Saint Louis on a steamer. The Jesuits themselves would have to walk the rest of the way, 150 miles, "staff in hand," according to the terminology of the day. That the staff sank half a foot into slimy mud or that spring rains bloated streams neck-deep did not deter the clergymen, and they reached their objective on the final afternoon of May after a fatiguing eight-day march. Father Van Quickenborne, anxious to be about his work in establishing a new novitiate, delayed only slightly, in Saint Louis, before he ushered his tiny Jesuit community the final fifteen miles to their new property at the Franco-Spanish village of Saint Ferdinand de Florissant.

Once in Missouri, the Maryland Jesuits worked diligently to establish a new novitiate. The convent and school of the Ladies of the Sacred Heart, a group of sisters who came from France to Saint Louis in 1818, occupied one corner of the bishop's farm at Florissant; the parish church of Saint Ferdinand filled another section; and the Jesuits took possession of the largest area. As the Jesuit house of studies at Florissant slowly took form, both in buildings and in the cultivation of fields, the novices continued to progress in orderly fashion through their academic courses. On September 23, 1827, having successfully completed examinations in logic, metaphysics, philosophy, and theology, Peter John De Smet and three of his classmates received the sacrament of

Holy Orders at Saint Ferdinand Church. Henceforth, Peter John De Smet would be called Father De Smet.

Now began a period of "third probation" within the society, a time for personal spiritual development rather than academic study. As part of his training in the practical work of ministry, Father De Smet visited six small communities and parishes within a 150-mile radius of Florissant to say Mass and offer religious instruction. Ever curious about the unique environment of the Missouri Valley, De Smet energetically accepted this assignment, since it allowed him to travel widely. He became adept at saying Mass in roofless churches where the altars dripped alternately with wax from melted candles in summer and icicles in winter. In long letters to his sister Rosalie, De Smet described the exhilaration he and his fellow fledgling priests felt at finally becoming active advocates of Christianity and civilization, seeking Catholics "like lost sheep, often at the peril of our lives." During the day he frequently passed through woods alive with bears and wolves; he mostly spent nights in abandoned huts, his cassock serving as both bed and cover. "We cross rivers," he wrote, "sometimes on horse-back, at other times by a log, or again, in a bark canoe. Now and then we eat at six o'clock in the evening, at other times we put off eating until the following day. Believe me, this reduces corpulence."

The heavyset De Smet, who weighed nearly 220 pounds but stood only five feet, seven inches tall, seemed always to be conscious of his stocky physique. His bulk made him appear slow of foot, but the reverse was more true. In fact, De Smet possessed considerable agility, and he thrived on the strenuous aspects of frontier travel. He enjoyed excellent health as a young man, save for an annoying skin rash that surfaced every so often—an eczema that caused an irresistible itch when it covered his body with sores and scabs.

In contrast to his rotund body, De Smet's temperament tended to be light or pixieish rather than pious or scholarly. He displayed, a colleague once commented, "transparent integrity." His broad, round face seemed always to be happy, his blue eyes shining as if he were just looking for an opportunity to demonstrate his subtle sense of humor with some wry, ironic observation. On the other hand, De Smet could also be deeply introspective and pensive. Anxious to please, De Smet felt rejection or unkindnesses deeply. "It does not require much to make him imagine that he has lost the confidence of his Superiors, that he is made little of by them and looked upon as an entirely useless member," a superior noted. Then he added, "I don't know what he might do in such depression of spirits." At such times De Smet normally sought solace in writing long, discursive letters to his family and friends. Reflective correspondence provided him with a sense of accomplishment; it made his spirits soar.

During the course of De Smet's studies at Florissant the Jesuits opened Saint Francis Regis Seminary, a school for Osage Indian boys. Father Van Quickenborne believed that the presence of thirty or so Indian children would benefit his young missionaries by familiarizing them with the habits and language of the western tribes. At the same time, the school would develop a cadre of young natives who could later serve as guides and interpreters when missionaries reached their tribes. Besides, an act of Congress in 1819 had created a "civilization fund" that offered up to ten thousand dollars per year to all groups that worked for the betterment of the Indian tribes living adjacent to the frontier, so that fund provided a further incentive, though the Jesuits seldom received more than four hundred dollars during any one year that the school remained open.

Native Americans fascinated De Smet. At first their unique costume, stately appearance, and independent manner attracted him to them. Later, when they became his students, he further recognized in them an innate goodness, a purity of soul. He also saw in them a great potential for Christian living. In this judgment, however, De Smet sometimes held a minority opinion in his own order.

In 1831 the Missouri Mission separated administratively from the Maryland Province, and in one of its first independent decisions it closed Saint Regis Seminary. In part the federal government precipitated the decision when it moved several Missouri tribes to the Indian Territory beyond the western border of the state. Seven years of financial drain also were a negative influence on the decision to keep or to close the school, as were philosophical differences of opinions among the Missouri Jesuits. True, Bishop Du Bourg had invited the Society of Jesus to Missouri to evangelize the Indians, but by the beginning of the 1830s a large number of Jesuits at Florissant believed that no great results would ever be possible among peoples whom they viewed as indolent and wandering. Indians monopolized the priests' time and resources, they complained, while the white population, which needed consolation and education every bit as badly as the natives, strayed to Protestant sects.

De Smet personally wished to maintain the Indian school at Florissant, and he deeply regretted its closure. If the Indians could no longer come to Florissant, then, in his opinion, the Jesuits should go to them, establishing missions for individual tribes. In this suggestion both Father Van Quickenborne and General William Clark, superintendent of Indian affairs for the western territories, supported De Smet. But always, it seemed, money, or the lack of it, influenced decisions. Unfortunately, most of Van Quickenborne's plans, and De Smet's recommendations, died for want of funds.

Ministering to the white settlers did not require the same drain on the manpower and financial resources of the Missouri Jesuits as did ministering to the Indians, so the order continued to expand in that area. First, it extended its parish work to the most remote outlying areas of Missouri. Second, it accepted responsibility for Saint Louis College, a school begun by Bishop Du Bourg in 1818 as the Saint Louis Academy. Ironically, De Smet, who wished to continue to work with the Indians, became an integral part of the school for young white men. Simultaneously he served as treasurer, prefect of men, and, in a tribute to his Americanization, professor of English language at the college.

Increased activity in parish work, plus a mushrooming debt at Saint Louis College, vexed the Missouri Jesuits. Liabilities that began modestly at three hundred dollars escalated to ten times that amount in just three years. De Smet told his sister his "cashbox is as empty and smooth as the palm of my hand, and yet from every side I am besieged for this thing and that, and, lacking the means to satisfy these demands, am called stingy." The Missouri Jesuits, he said, needed to make long-range plans to bring their obligations into alignment with their financial resources. And that is exactly what his superiors had in mind.

In view of Father De Smet's family connections with some of the wealthiest and most influential people in Belgium—Josse De Smet's investments during the Napoleonic wars had made him the nineteenth-century equivalent of a millionaire—the superior of the Missouri Mission decided to send De Smet to Europe to raise money and, if possible, attract new recruits to the society. De Smet could also use this opportunity to clear up the matter of the inheritance from his father's estate, a potentially significant sum that he had received upon the elder De Smet's death in 1827 but which subsequently had become entangled in legal formalities. Coincidentally, for some time De Smet had suffered a flareup of his eczema, the source of which baffled Saint Louis physicians, and this trip would also be an excellent opportunity for him to consult European doctors. Somewhat ominously, Father Peter Verhaegen, S.J., informed the father general that some other consideration besides anxiety over health seemed to be affecting De Smet at the moment: "He appeared to be restless and in a somewhat unsettled state of mind as to his future."

Delaying his departure from Saint Louis long enough to take out naturalization papers as an American citizen in September 1833, De Smet reached Belgium at the beginning of the new year. He had been absent from his homeland for fourteen years, yet during the next nine months he raised nearly sixty thousand francs (eleven thousand dollars) from fifty prominent Catholic families in northern Europe, a sizable amount for those times. People treated him as if he had never left his father's social circle. From convents, colleges, and seminaries he procured additional funds, vestments, altar furniture, paintings, and scientific instruments destined for the classrooms of Saint Louis College. He also purchased books, including the entire library of a former Augustinian monastery. Some of this De Smet paid for in cash with money he received in settlement of his father's estate. At the same time, he encouraged five Jesuit scholastics to join the Missouri Mission. Gratified by the results of his effort, in November 1834, De Smet crated his booty into fifty trunks and booked passage on a ship bound for America.

The North Sea turned violent that fall, and as the brig *Agenoria* inched its way up the Kentish coast of England, De Smet, who had fully recovered from his skin rash, suddenly fell gravely ill with a new ailment. The ship's captain became so alarmed by De Smet's condition that he altered course long enough to seek medical assistance at the coastal port of Deal. There, doctors diagnosed De Smet's illness as an internal rupture of some sort, probably induced by violent vomiting as a result of seasickness. They prescribed a month of complete rest, so, sadly, De Smet relinquished his authority over the five recruits and ordered them to sail on without him. It was, in De Smet's estimation, "a set-back without parallel," one that left him "in a condition of depression and complete discouragement."

During his lengthy convalescence De Smet searched for God's meaning in this untimely change of plans. Perhaps he had only joined the Society of Jesus to further his romantic notions about faraway lands and aboriginal people, and this was God's way of punishing him for his selfishness. But should the Missouri Mission also suffer for his insincerity? Realizing that his continued medical treatment would place an additional burden on the already debt-ridden Jesuit community in Saint Louis, De Smet convinced himself that he should withdraw from the Society of Jesus but still honor his vows as a priest. He would live the remainder of his life in Belgium as a parish priest. With genuine regret, Father General John Roothaan, S.J., accepted De Smet's resignation on March 31, 1835, three months after he tendered it. No matter what his state of health, Roothaan informed De Smet, "never would I agree to dismiss you against your will, never, never. . . . But since you ask for your dismissal, I give my consent."

When Abbé De Smet's release from the Society of Jesus became official, the bishop of Ghent assigned him to an orphanage. Meanwhile, Father General Roothaan urged De Smet to initiate a correspondence with the Missouri Mission as a way of easing

16   FATHER PETER JOHN DE SMET

his feelings of remorse for having abandoned his brothers in
Saint Louis. He did and felt relieved when he experienced no
rancor from his friends in America. After the exchange of several
letters he even volunteered to assist the Missouri Jesuits as a
purchasing and fiscal agent in Europe. De Smet's diocesan duties
were modest, essentially preaching in an orphanage and serving
as a chaplain for a convent of Carmelite nuns, so he had time to
spare for the Americans. He not only raised money on their behalf, but he also borrowed funds for them, once even securing a
loan of 125,000 francs (approximately $23,000) from the Baroness
de Ghyseghem, a resident of Termonde. Meanwhile, his health
rebounded.

Although his life as a diocesan priest provided De Smet with a
certain measure of satisfaction, two years after his decision to
leave the Society of Jesus he experienced a change of heart and
wished to be reinstated to the order. His life as a secular priest
seemed incomplete without the frontier, and he longed to return
to the Jesuits. Any abbé could serve as a chaplain to orphans and
nuns; he felt he could do so much more with his talents in America. He knew from personal experience that the growing settlements of Missouri required additional priests and that entire nations of Indians waited for the word of God in remote villages
and camps, and he reproached himself for being weak, for having
left the society in a moment of temporary adversity. Timidly, De
Smet petitioned for reinstatement to the Society of Jesus, and, to
his great relief, Father General Roothaan permitted this extraordinary step.

Had De Smet not maintained his contact with the Missouri
Mission—and if the American missions had not been in such
desperate need of manpower—the answer would certainly have
been different, but in 1837 the timing was right, and De Smet
hesitated not at all when he received permission to join four Jesuit
recruits waiting for passage to America at Le Havre. He packed
a variety of gifts he had collected for the Missouri Jesuits into
thirteen trunks, secured sixty thousand francs in his money belt,
and booked passage to New York. Interestingly, for the second
time in as many leavings De Smet decided not to inform his

family of his departure for America. Only later did he write to his brother Francis, "My departure from Belgium will no doubt have grieved and perhaps even angered you." He did what he did, he said, because "I could not find rest and interior peace except by doing my duty."

Upon his return to Saint Louis, neither the city, which had doubled in population to fifteen thousand, nor the Missouri Mission looked the same as when he left for Europe four years earlier. The Missouri Mission now totaled sixty-one Jesuits— there had been only sixteen when De Smet left in 1833—but with growth there came responsibility. The College of Saint Louis operated now as a fully chartered university, twenty-six novices were being trained at Saint Stanislaus Seminary, and the burgeoning city of Saint Louis necessitated a corresponding increase in the number of Jesuit parishes. In addition, about the same time De Smet had departed for Europe in 1833, the Second Baltimore Council of the Catholic Church had formally asked the pope to assign to the Society of Jesus responsibility for all of the Indian missions in the continental United States west of the Mississippi River and north of Mexico. After due deliberation, the Holy See acceded to the request, and the father general of the society in turn delegated to the Missouri Jesuits the task of reaching the western Indians. Clearly, there would be an open slot for an able volunteer.

For several reasons the Catholic hierarchy in America considered the Jesuits to be the most suitable religious order to convert the Indian tribes of the trans-Mississippi West. Part of the rationale had to do with the order's rigid discipline and rigorous academic formation, training that infused Jesuits with a soldier-like dedication to tasks. Just as certainly the recommendation in Baltimore stemmed from the commonly held notion that the society had unusual access to the moneyed families of Europe, thereby ensuring the necessary resources to accomplish their assignment. Historically, the Jesuits could point to a record of successful missions, those of New France being a conspicuous example. These were triumphs based, in large measure, upon the judicious use of the order's principle of accommodation.

Jesuits were free, within the rules of their order, to bend themselves to live in compliance with the natives' cultures, not only to adopt their languages, but also to embrace their life-styles. From this position the Jesuits could adapt Christian teachings accordingly. This principle of accommodation reinforced for the natives the seriousness of the Jesuits' commitment to them, actions speaking louder than mere words. Thus, at mission locations in the Far East, India, and elsewhere Jesuits not only learned a difficult language—they also mastered the etiquette, customs, skills, attitude, and sometimes even the appearance of the native people. This affinity for native culture opened the Jesuits to criticism at times, for it shocked large segments of the European public. But it also made the Society of Jesus the most successful missionary order in the world.

Many Missouri Jesuits swallowed hard when they learned they would be responsible for missionary work among the western Indians. President Andrew Jackson's Indian removal policy, begun in 1830, they pointed out, could potentially relocate as many as two hundred thousand Indians from Indiana, Michigan, Wisconsin, Illinois, Georgia, and Mississippi to the Indian Territory adjacent to Missouri. Still, as requested by the American bishops and required by the father general of the society, in 1836 the Missouri Mission established its first Indian mission, a small settlement for the rebellious Kickapoo tribe eight miles north of Fort Leavenworth and just west of the Missouri border.

About that same time, in December 1835, an Iroquois Indian named Ignace la Mousse led his two sons to Saint Louis and there delivered an eloquent appeal to ecclesiastical authorities, pleading with them to send a missionary priest to his adopted tribe in the Rocky Mountains, the Flatheads. Actually, a Flathead delegation had arrived in Saint Louis four years earlier. Unfortunately, the arrival of the Indians in 1831 had directly coincided with the decision of the Missouri Jesuits to close Saint Francis Regis Indian School at Florissant, so, at that particular moment, the society showed little interest in beginning a new missionary enterprise in a remote and distant corner of the continent. Now, four years later, the Jesuit superior at Saint Louis wished to honor the Flatheads' request, but all of his available manpower for missionary outreach had already been scheduled for the Kickapoo mission. New entities must wait, however painful that decision might be for the Flatheads.

Neither the Jesuits nor the bishop of Saint Louis, apparently, fully comprehended the significance of the Flatheads' request. Shortly after the War of 1812 several dozen Iroquois canoeist had accompanied brigades of North West Company fur traders to the Oregon country, and they had become, by a twist of fate, the first apostles of Christianity to the natives of that region. Baptized by French Jesuits at missions along the Saint Lawrence River, Iroquois paddlers like Ignace la Mousse subsequently took up residence with the Flatheads and, over the course of time, introduced them to Christianity, Catholicism, and the Society of Jesus. Several Iroquois men even assumed the duties of a catechist, or religious leader, instructing their adopted tribe in rudimentary prayers and the sign of the cross. The ritual splendor of Christianity, even translated secondhand, soon gripped the imagination of the Flatheads, and they yearned to know more about the white man's religion. More importantly, the white man's Master of Life offered a feeling of hope to the Flatheads during a turbulent time of significant internal and external changes.

The introduction of the horse to the intermontane tribes of the Columbia Plateau in about 1720 had produced the first of three shock waves to affect the Flatheads. Domesticated horses radically altered normal patterns of hunting and gathering for the Flatheads, but, at the same time, the herds also allowed their tribal enemies to greatly extend the circle of war. Not long after the introduction of the horse a second, equally important, change took place in the Rocky Mountains when Canadian fur traders bartered guns to certain tribes, most notably the Blackfeet. Arming the Blackfeet put peaceful tribes such as the Flatheads at a major disadvantage when trying to protect their villages and hunting grounds. A third influence that had rocked the complacency of the Flatheads occurred in the 1790s when seafarers on the North Pacific Coast, so-called Boston men, infected tribesmen at the mouth of the Columbia with a series of diseases, including smallpox and malaria. "Fever and ague" decimated entire Chinookian villages on the lower Columbia and then traveled silently upriver, borne by unsuspecting native canoeists. Not every contagious disease brought by whites to the Pacific Northwest reached epidemic proportions, but the Flathead tribe experienced enough deaths and witnessed enough sorrow in other tribes to properly fear all of the white man's infections.

Many tribes in the intermontane West felt the strong force of change in their lives by these signal events, but only the Flatheads attempted to solve their problems by seeking favors from the white man's Master of Life. The Iroquois told the Flatheads emphatically that the same Jesuits who had changed the lives of their people in the Saint Lawrence Valley could work similar wonders for the Flatheads, implying that certain blessings rebuffed not only smallpox and cholera but bullets as well. Jesuits could also make Flathead warriors spiritually more powerful than their better-armed enemies. Little wonder, then, that by 1831 the Flatheads sent their first emissaries to Saint Louis requesting Jesuit missionaries.

Although the Flathead appeal in 1831 went unanswered by the Catholic hierarchy in Saint Louis, Protestant missionary groups answered the Indians' call immediately and decisively. A letter in the March 1, 1833, *Christian Advocate and Journal of New York* detailed the plea of the Flathead delegation and created a minor sensation among Protestant churches, several of which acted. The Methodists took the field first, dispatching Jason Lee and his nephew Daniel, both ordained ministers, to the Pacific Northwest the next year. The Lees, however, changed plans once they reached Fort Vancouver, and they ultimately located their mission in the Willamette Valley, hundreds of miles from the Flathead villages, though conveniently near to the Hudson's Bay Company post. The next year the American Board of Commissioners for Foreign Missions followed the Methodists' lead and sent Dr. Marcus Whitman and Samuel Parker to the Rocky Mountains. But the American Board missionaries similarly forsook the Flatheads. They selected one site in the Walla Walla Valley and another adjacent to the Snake River.

The Jesuits of Saint Louis never knew until years later that in 1837 a third delegation of Flathead emissaries had attempted to reach Saint Louis. That group, unfortunately, fell into an ambush by Sioux warriors at Ash Hollow Creek, Nebraska, and never made it to the Missouri River. In the meantime, the Missouri Jesuits decided to establish a second Indian mission, this one at Council Bluffs, the new reservation home for the Potawatomi tribe.

Only as an afterthought did Father Verhaegen, superior of the Missouri Mission in Saint Louis, select Father De Smet to open the Potawatomi mission at Council Bluffs. Although De Smet was initially passed over because rules of the society required that anyone reentering must begin again as a novice, a sympathetic adviser to the superior resurrected De Smet's name from the pool of applicants. Thus, almost by accident De Smet realized his ambition to be an Indian missionary. In retrospect, it seems odd that De Smet's name did not immediately spring to the top of the list. Everyone knew he stood ready to commit himself to the life of an Indian missionary, frequently repeating his novice master's dictum that "to come to America to teach in a college or to be a missionary to the whites, is child's play in comparison to the Indian Mission." Moreover, he had experience teaching Indian boys at Saint Regis School in Florissant. In any case, De Smet got the assignment, and Father Verhaegen waived certain reentry requirements because of special circumstances.

From the moment the *Howard* pulled away from the Saint Louis levee on May 2, 1838, all of De Smet's dreamy notions about steamboat travel on the Missouri River evaporated as quickly as the puffs of steam that emitted from the boat's smokestacks. Twice the steamboat's engines broke down, and once the engineer ordered the ship back to Saint Louis to repair the defective part. Later, sandbars, sawyers, and hulls of sunken ships dangerously clogged the main channel of the river. The unregulated buildup of steam in the malfunctioning boilers, De Smet told his brother, made the situation an absolute flirtation with total body dismemberment. He would sooner cross the ocean ten times, he decided, debilitated by seasickness, than repeat his first trip up the mighty Missouri. After switching passage to the *Wilmington* at Fort Leavenworth, De Smet felt more secure and soon became a devotee of steamboat travel.

The boilers on Missouri River steamboats daily consumed multiple cords of wood, so the vessels made frequent stops on the trip upriver. At such moments De Smet went ashore to stretch his legs. The missionary enjoyed a reunion with a former student, now an Iowa chief, at one stop, but not every Indian village left him with the same feeling of satisfaction. At an Oto village he walked along a path lined by the most dismal, vermin-filled mud dwellings he had ever seen. Sullen, disfigured native women, looking for all the world like abused slaves, peered at him from their shabby huts while the men lounged around outside.

Beckoned into the chief's cabin, De Smet entered and seated himself upon a deerskin pad he thought fairly "glittering with dirt." Unceremoniously, the wife of the chief stepped forward to hand him a wooden dish and roughly carved spoon, neither of which, De Smet thought, had been washed since they were made. Next the woman served food, a "mysterious ragout," the recipe of which, De Smet decided, must have been of her own concoction. The very sight of the blend made him nauseated; his stomach rebelled. As best he could tell, his plate swam with a mixture of buffalo tongue, wild sweet potatoes, and thick bear fat gravy. It was a crucial moment of decision for the young priest. Just how badly did he want to be a missionary? "Oh well," he finally reasoned, "this is no place for style. We are not in Belgium. Let us seriously begin our apprenticeship; and since we are in the woods, let us with good will howl with the wolves." With that he faced down a dozen hungry hounds, each with eyes fixed on his plate, and swallowed his objections. Much to his relief, De Smet actually found the frontier fricassee delicious. So much so, he politely returned the plate to his hostess cleaner than when she had given it to him.

Invigorated by this trial by food in a real Indian camp, De Smet disembarked at Council Bluffs feeling confident of his ability to be an effective Indian missionary. "Nearly 2,000 savages, in their finest rags and carefully painted in all sorts of patterns, were awaiting the boat at the landing," he informed Verhaegen; "I had not seen so imposing a sight nor such fine-looking Indians in America: the Iowas, the Sauks and the Otoes are beggars compared to these." Alas, the Indians showed their enthusiasm not for him, it turned out, but for the shipment of whiskey traditionally secreted in the hold of arriving steamboats. Too late the Indians discovered that the *Wilmington* carried no booze. Too late, also, De Smet discovered that the alcoholism of the Potawatomis would be the major disappointment of his first missionary assignment.

De Smet completed the first order of business, establishing a residence for himself, Father Felix Verreydt, S.J., and Brother John Mazelli, S.J., rather quickly. Four unfinished log cabins suited that purpose for the time being, and a former blockhouse, once used by Colonel Stephen Watts Kearney, became Saint Joseph's Mission church. The second task occupied more of De Smet's time. During the next several weeks De Smet mingled freely with the Indians, learning all he could about their wants and needs.

It took two weeks to discover a single Catholic Indian in the tribe. Even so, in his initial appraisal of the Potawatomis De Smet found much to admire in his charges. "The Potawatomies are very gentle and tractable by nature," he reported to Verhaegen, "They do not lack spirit and never appear timid; they recognize neither rank nor dignity among themselves; they have no expression to blaspheme the name of the Lord; their most injurious term is 'dog.'" Moreover, so quickly did the tribe learn the basic tenets of Christianity that by mid-August De Smet had baptized twenty adults, including the wife of the head chief. De Smet christened her with the baptismal name of Rosalie, a tribute to both his sister and the Indian woman. The very idea so tickled De Smet that he continued the practice for the rest of his life, expanding his list of names to include other family members: Francis, Charles, Anthony, Peter, Jeannette, Marie, Sophie, and Teresa.

But De Smet soon learned that the Potawatomi people also possessed a dark side, one so profound that he could not overcome it no matter how diligently he worked. He could counsel

Portrait of the youthful Father De Smet, missionary to the Potawatomi in 1838. Courtesy of Oregon Province Archives of the Society of Jesus, Gonzaga University.

them against idleness, gambling, polygamy, and superstition, but when they were drunk, he said, "all their good qualities vanish, they no longer resemble men; all must flee before them; their yells and howls are fearful; they hurl themselves upon each other, they bite off each others' noses and ears and mutilate each other horribly." For months De Smet struggled to combat the alcoholic affliction of the tribe. The opening of a school for thirty children, twice daily instructions for adults, and the formation of a forty-voice tribal choir that sang hymns in English, French,

Latin, and Potawatomi, however, all failed to obscure the reality
that with each passing day the tribe grew more dependent upon
strong drink. As the tribe staggered toward destruction, barrels
of whiskey spread as much death as if they had been fully loaded
artillery pieces:

> Fifty large cannons have been landed, ready charged with the most
> murderous grape shot, each containing thirty gallons of whiskey,
> brandy, rum or alcohol. The boat was not as yet out of sight when the
> skirmishes commenced. After the fourth, fifth and sixth discharges,
> the confusion became great and appalling. In all directions, men,
> women and children were seen tottering and falling; the war-hoop,
> the merry Indian's song, cries, savage roarings, formed a chorus.
> Quarrel succeeded quarrel. Blows followed blows. The club, the toma-
> hawk, spears, butcher knives, brandished together in the air. Strange!
> Astonishing!

Naturally, De Smet sought to prohibit the whiskey traffic that
flowed so easily on the Missouri River, and to that end he demanded legal action from the secretary of war in a letter filled
with righteous indignation. After witnessing two more drunken
orgies, the priest drafted a second letter, this time denouncing the
illegal liquor traffic as not only illegal but immoral as well. Unfortunately, the Missouri Jesuits depended on a modest federal sub-
sidy to help them maintain the Indian missions, so De Smet's
superiors toned down his letters and ordered him to clear all future business correspondence through society officials. De Smet
wrote the secretary of war several times more from Council Bluffs,
but his sanitized letters failed to bring the reforms he desired.

In addition to what he considered to be a lack of administrative
support, De Smet experienced two additional frustrations during
his eighteen-month sojourn with the Potawatomis: the absence
of regular supplies and the paucity of outside communication.
Once, in April 1839, a steamboat carrying thousands of dollars in
provisions for Saint Joseph's Mission struck a snag in the Missouri and sank before De Smet's unbelieving eyes. He could
salvage only a saw, a plow, and a pair of boots among five hundred dollars' worth of supplies. "Providence is still kind to us,"
he noted wryly to his brother: "The plow has enabled us to sow a

good crop of corn. Thanks to the saw, we can now build a better house, and with the boots I can tramp the prairies and woods without fear of being bitten by snakes." He found no humor, however, in the fact that his confreres in Saint Louis failed to send him letters at least as regularly as did his family in even more distant Belgium. In six months he received but five lines from the Saint Louis Jesuits. "We who are at the end of the world, far from friends and fellow-priests, in the midst of strangers and infidels, suffering privations and daily witnessing revolting scenes," he lashed out, "look forward to letters as a real treat." By nature, De Smet required the constant approval of his fellow Jesuits and to deny him regular communication made him feel exiled and unappreciated.

Although Potawatomi leaders should have feared the utter destruction of their tribe by the ravages of alcohol, they did not. In their view, the atrocities committed by the Yanktons, a middle tribe of the Sioux, threatened them more. This judgment piqued De Smet's natural curiosity, and he decided to view for himself this tribe that lived several hundred miles up the Missouri. If he could not halt the whiskey traffic at Council Bluffs, perhaps he could negotiate a durable peace between these two tribal enemies.

To accomplish this goal, De Smet boarded the *St. Peter,* an American Fur Company steamer, buying passage as far as the Vermilion River. By good fortune, among the passengers already on board were a number of notable westering men, including the well-known explorers Joseph Nicollet and John C. Frémont. Nicollet, whose current scientific interest focused on the upper Missouri River, asked as many questions of De Smet as the priest did of him. Together they formed a pact each to take a series of scientific calculations on the Missouri River during the next four months and then to compare notes. To seal the bargain, Nicollet presented De Smet with a barometer, a compass, several thermometers, and an instrument designed to calculate the height of landmarks.

Charles A. Geyer, a distinguished German botanist, happened also to be on board, and from him De Smet developed an appreciation for the unique flora and fauna of the Missouri River basin. In the interests of science they took several field trips on shore looking for minerals and rare plants. The most tangible result of their expeditions, however, turned out to be an abundant supply of onions, thumb-sized asparagus, strawberries, gooseberries, plums, and various other wild fruits for the passengers of the *St. Peter*. Never one to remain idle, De Smet smugly congratulated himself for having made the most of what could have been a monotonous twelve-day river trip: "This study has great attraction for me, and the hours I have spent tramping over hill and dale with a friend are among the most agreeable of my life."

The Yankton Sioux camp welcomed Father De Smet as they would any important visitor. That meant a feast in his honor, and from earlier experiences with the Pawnees and Omahas at Council Bluffs, De Smet knew he could not decline. Entering the chief's buffalo hide tent, the priest took a seat in a circle and waited stoically while the women delivered huge slabs of venison. After the men had eaten, and each had rubbed his belly with the obligatory sign of satisfaction, the headmen invited their guest to speak to them.

Using all of the personal charm at his disposal, De Smet spoke extemporaneously to the chiefs about the reason for his visit. Peace between the Yanktons and the Potawatomis, he told his listeners, would make fast the friendship of two great nations. Tribal relationships should not be marked by stealing, warfare, and the cries of widows and orphans, but by honor. His words came out clumsy, labored, he feared, for he did not know the Sioux language and he had not yet mastered the art of speaking through an interpreter. Still, the Yankton headmen seemed to grasp the gist of his remarks, for they frequently nodded in unison.

At length, the chiefs agreed to smoke the pipe of peace with the Potawatomis. But they would not immediately, they explained, because they expected to follow the buffalo herds west very soon. As a sign of their sincerity, however, they agreed to "cover the dead"—that is, to distribute presents to Potawatomi orphans, children of their past victims. De Smet considered these tokens a signal triumph of his diplomacy, for he was too inexperienced in such matters to know that while the intentions of the Yanktons were genuine, peace agreements among the Missouri River tribes seldom lasted beyond a season. Eager to report his triumph to the Potawatomis, De Smet decided not to wait for the next steamboat going downriver and accepted an offer by two Yankton paddlers to take him back to Council Bluffs in a canoe.

The peace pact with the Yanktons, De Smet predicted, boded well for the future of the Potawatomi mission. Yet what would it matter if the tribe continued to abuse itself with alcohol? "What can we do in the midst of 2000 drunks?" he asked rhetorically. Before leaving Saint Louis to come to Council Bluffs, De Smet had worried that he might not have enough patience, the one quality necessary to be an apostle to the Indians. At the time, however, he consoled himself that God would provide him with sufficient strength to overcome his weaknesses. Now he was not so sure. Murders and mutilations continued unabated at Saint Joseph's while he counseled with the Yanktons; brutalizations now approached the awful total of one hundred since his arrival at Council Bluffs. There seemed to be neither respite nor security at the mission, and De Smet considered even his own life to be in danger.

> The savages drink and gamble so long as there remains to them a half a farthing. The love which they have for drink is truly inconceivable. It is necessary to see it to form any idea of it. It is to them a veritable tarantula. When they are soused, all their blood is inflamed in their veins. They become lustful for more alcohol. Obtaining some, they continue to cry "More, more!" until consumed by firewater they fall dead drunk. No sooner have they regained their senses than their first and only exclamation is always: "Whisky, whisky, whisky," as if life and death depended on it.

Reluctantly, De Smet arrived at the inescapable conclusion that the Potawatomi mission would ultimately fail. He realized now that he truly desired a missionary career, a life of unselfish Christian service to needy neophytes. Yet that prospect dimmed with each day at Council Bluffs. Then, miraculously, his fading heart resuscitated on September 18, 1839, when Pierre Gaucher and Young Ignace la Mousse beached their canoe at Saint Jo-seph's Mission. These two Catholic Indians comprised the fourth delegation sent by the Flatheads to Saint Louis to seek a Jesuit priest. When De Smet learned the objective of their mission (and they spoke in French, no less), his heart leapt.

Oh, if only he could return to the Rocky Mountains with these men! There lived the sincere, uncorrupted tribe of Indians he longed to convert, natives worthy of a life dedicated to others. Hastily, De Smet prepared letters of introduction for the natives to carry to Father Verhaegen, knowing full well how important it would be for his name to be associated with the latest Flathead appeal. Even now the fathers in Saint Louis must be discussing the future of the Potawatomi mission, and if anyone should be assigned to a new Flathead mission, he must be that person.

By the close of 1839 the small Jesuit community at Saint Jo-seph's Mission teetered between staying and leaving. De Smet personally toyed with the idea of abandoning the mission as early as August, even before the Flatheads stopped to confer with him. In February of 1840 he unexpectedly announced an emergency situation at the mission and then cheerfully volunteered to jour-ney to Saint Louis, even in the dead of winter, to gather further instructions and needed supplies. In addition, he said, he needed medical attention for an undisclosed ailment. That he followed the two Indians to Saint Louis was merely coincidental—or so he tried to convince his confreres at Saint Joseph's Mission.

Accompanied by a single companion, De Smet traveled on foot across an icy wilderness toward Saint Louis. Constant expo-sure to a chilling wind not only froze his cheeks and nose, but also penetrated deep into his lungs, making it difficult for him to breathe by the time he reached the Jesuit residence. If De Smet thought he needed to see a physician before he left Council Bluffs, he certainly required medical attention by the time he arrived in Saint Louis on February 20. "I was put under the care of a physician—I who fear American doctors as I do the pest," De Smet lamented to his family, and "this one hastened to employ the entire resources of his apothecary: bleeding and leeches were the first prescription, then followed baths, powders, pills, plasters, and ever, known tisane, sweet, bitter, hot, cold, and tepid; added to which a strict regimen was ordered. Complete rest quickly restored my health and I immediately set about getting out of the hands of the doctor, who would soon have had all the flesh off my bones."

While he recuperated, De Smet subtly inquired among the Jesuits as to the fate of the Flatheads who had preceded him to Saint Louis. He knew well that for some time Father General Roothaan endorsed in principle Father Verhaegen's desire to begin a Jesuit presence among the Rocky Mountain tribes. Verhaegen, in fact, made tentative plans as early as November 1839 to send two Jesuits to the Flatheads, but the program fell through because of a lack of funds. The arrival of yet another Flathead delegation merely reinforced Verhaegen's resolve, and he promised the two young Indians firmly that in the spring of 1840 he would send a priest to their nation.

Young Ignace and Pierre Gaucher received Verhaegen's pledge with whoops of joy. Eager to relay the announcement to their tribe, they decided that Pierre Gaucher should depart immediately for the mountains, while Young Ignace would stay the winter with the Jesuits and return to the mountains with the missionary in the spring. They would reunite at the Green River fur trade rendezvous in late June.

Meanwhile, Verhaegen informed De Smet that he had assembled a shipment of provisions, church vestments, clothing, and tools for him to take back to Council Bluffs. Saint Joseph's Mission would not close, nor would De Smet be reassigned to the Rocky Mountains. Then, just before De Smet pushed off, Verhaegen reversed himself and permitted De Smet to accompany Young Ignace back to the Rocky Mountains. What changed his mind? "He manifested such eagerness and ardent zeal for the work," Verhaegen wrote to the father general: "He possessed, moreover, such remarkable qualities, that it was hardly possible for us to make another choice."

CHAPTER 2

Missionary to the Flatheads, 1840–1842

NOW in his fortieth year, Father De Smet approached his first journey to the Rocky Mountains with boyish enthusiasm. His primary objective, officially, was to honor the Flathead request—four times sent and three times received between 1831 and 1839—for a Jesuit missionary. In addition, Father Verhaegen authorized him "to sound out the dispositions of the Indians and to see what success we could promise ourselves from the establishment of a mission in their midst." He should contact as many Indian tribes as possible and attempt to learn the natives' aptitude for Christian teachings, all with an eye toward costs to the society in manpower and money, of course. De Smet's primary interest, personally, was to reinvigorate his vocation as a missionary after his recent, unfulfilling experience among the Potawatomis. He also expected to satisfy his growing curiosity about the far West. This would be an exploring expedition in the broadest senses of the term.

By prearrangement, the American Fur Company agreed to allow De Smet and Young Ignace, who had spent the winter at the Jesuits' Kickapoo mission in Kansas, to join their annual wagon train to the Green River rendezvous in present-day southeastern Wyoming. De Smet needed only to take a steamboat 390 miles to Westport, Missouri, link up with Young Ignace and be ready to leave in April.

Nothing De Smet had ever done before in his life prepared him for the rigors of an overland passage across the Great Plains. Andrew Drips, captain of the American Fur Company brigade, advised De Smet to purchase four horses and three mules to carry his equipment, but beyond that he could do little to ready

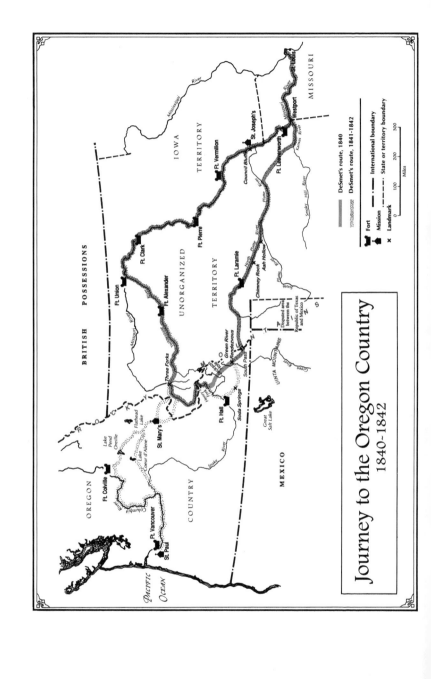

Journey to the Oregon Country
1840-1842

the priest for the difficulties of an extended journey. The caravan got under way on the last day of April: fifty men, an equal number of two-wheeled carts, and sixty pack mules. Almost immediately De Smet learned why frontiersmen referred to the Kansas plains beyond Westport as the "Great American Desert."

Hot, capricious winds swept over the caravan incessantly from the start. On most days an oppressive, sticky heat also hung heavy in the air. During daylight hours bright sunshine ricocheted shimmering heat waves off the hard-baked plains soil, but at night temperatures plummeted. During the first ten days De Smet struggled to maintain the eighteen-mile-per-day pace. Overcome by heat exhaustion, burning with fever, he developed a reoccurring, retching cough. Sympathetic companions urged the priest to return to Westport, but the memory of his personal weakness in the face of an illness along the coast of England in 1834 goaded De Smet onward. He took refuge in the rear of a cart, but he rested little, as each jolt in the road flailed his nearly unconscious body between boxes and bundles. The fever never completely left De Smet during the next four months.

By the time Drips's pack train reached Grand Island on the North Platte River, De Smet sufficiently recovered from his illness to fully appreciate the beauty of springtime on the Great Plains. He adored the colorful spring flowers, but nothing overwhelmed him quite as much as the uncountable numbers of grazing buffalo spread across the lush countryside. Beyond the North Platte the trail passed briefly through an arid land of naked rocks and brown grass, but after that De Smet sighted the Rocky Mountains. "You think you have before your eyes the ruins of a whole world covered with the eternal snows as with a shroud," he rhapsodized about his first sighting. Anxious to share his experiences vicariously with his brothers and sisters in Belgium, De Smet jotted down detailed descriptions of everything he saw. The same letter, with slight revisions, might also be recast for Father Verhaegen in the form of a preliminary progress report. And in some cases De Smet composed another, nearly identical, letter for the benefit of the father general in Rome.

On June 4 the caravan's line of march across the Laramie

River intercepted a small party of Northern Cheyenne Indians. The traders shied away from the Indian camp, but De Smet could not contain his curiosity and hovered close by until someone invited him to a feast. The affair began with a short introduction by the chief, after which several women entered the lodge bearing food. Three dogs, the chief proudly informed De Smet, had been slaughtered in his honor. Social convention required a guest to eat all the food placed before him, in this case two thighs, a paw, and a rack of ribs. De Smet actually liked the flesh of dogs, considering it "very delicate and extremely good," but the amount easily exceeded his appetite. So in order to avoid disgrace, he imitated the conduct of others and excused himself by activating a Cheyenne custom that allowed a person to pass his dish to another with an accompanying gift of tobacco. After dinner De Smet spoke briefly to the Indians about the Ten Commandments, a sermon that the Indians received with such signs of respect that it led him to believe that a zealous missionary would have good success in converting this tribe to Christianity.

Weeks passed, but never in boredom for the priest. Just keeping up with the fur traders required all of his concentration. Snow enveloped the pack train on June 24, but even so, on the following day the men and animals pushed over South Pass, the legendary trail across the Continental Divide. Finally, on June 30, two months after leaving Westport, the American Fur Company brigade reached the Green River, site of the annual fur trade rendezvous. The trade fair buzzed with excitement. There was enough drunkenness and debauchery in progress to embarrass any man of the cloth, but De Smet hardly noticed because, as he had hoped and prayed for many months, Pierre Gaucher and an escort of nine young men waited for him. In a touching moment, the young men of the escort greeted De Smet as would "children who, after a long absence, run to meet their father. I wept for joy embracing them, and with tears in their eyes they welcomed me with tenderest expressions." The main camp of Flatheads, Gaucher informed De Smet, waited for him many days' ride away at a place called Pierre's Hole.

Giddy with excitement, yet suddenly feeling the effects of his overland travel, De Smet told the Flatheads he needed to rest for a few days before continuing on to Pierre's Hole. He occupied part of this recuperative period by visiting among the Indians attending the rendezvous, mostly Shoshones and Utes. He also preached to the American and French-Canadian hunters who came to sell their furs at the Green River. On one such occasion De Smet met Jean-Baptiste de Velder, a former grenadier in Napoleon Bonaparte's Grand Army and now a fourteen-year veteran of the beaver fur trade in the Rocky Mountains. De Velder felt an immediate friendship to the Belgian priest and offered him his assistance as an interpreter. De Smet could hardly refuse, for Indian languages totally mystified him.

The path to the main Flathead camp at Pierre's Hole, though rugged and dangerous, became for De Smet a spiritual journey of appreciation for God's creation. Setting a course north and west along the Green River on July 6, De Smet, De Velder, the Flatheads, and ten French-Canadian fur trappers along for part of the trip found themselves sometimes clinging to a mountainside and sometimes picking their way through a narrow defile until finally they reached flat ground in the small valley called Jackson's Little Hole. From there the trail sidled across "mountains of almost perpendicular cliffs that rise to the region of perpetual snow," but it was the only way to reach the other Jackson's Hole and the Snake River. Following the turbulent Snake River into the high mountain country required numerous crossings, events De Smet seldom looked forward to: "Its roaring waters rushed furiously down and whitened with their foam the great blocks of granite which vainly disputed the passage with them. The sight intimidated neither our Indians nor our Canadians; accustomed to perils of this sort, they rushed into the torrent on horseback and swam it. I dared not venture to do likewise. To get me over, they made a kind of sack of my skin tent; they then put all my things in and set me on top of it."

A seemingly uninterrupted chain of mountain passes and cascading rivers awed De Smet daily until, on July 12, at the far end of Pierre's Hole, a twenty-five-mile long valley lying along the

western base of the Teton Mountains, he spied the main camp of
sixteen hundred Flathead, Pend Oreille, and Nez Percé Indians
who had traveled more than eight hundred miles to see the Jesuit
priest Pierre Gaucher had said would come in the summer. Chief
Big Face of the Flatheads stepped forward to welcome the priest
as he entered the camp. Tribal elders stood in silent awe, but
young men expressed their satisfaction by leaps and shouts of happiness. "Black Robe speak!" Big Face commanded, "We are all
your children. Show us the path we must follow to reach the
place where abides the Great Spirit. Our ears are open, our hearts
will heed your words! Speak, Black Robe! We will follow the
words of your mouth!" For De Smet, it was a triumphant, defin-
ing moment. After years of self-doubt in Europe and a discourag-
ing introduction to the missionary life at Council Bluffs, he truly
felt like a missionary.

During the next four days De Smet tirelessly preached to the
Flatheads, gently instructing them in Catholic beliefs and practices. So eagerly did the tribe accept De Smet's message that
during the course of his brief stay he baptized, by his own estimation, several hundred Indians, including two chiefs. "Black Robe,"
a term once used to identify missionaries in general or Jesuits in
particular, now became a special designation reserved exclusively
for De Smet. Henceforth there could be no other Black Robe for
the Flatheads. Eventually other tribes picked up the sobriquet,
and for the next thirty years tribesmen from Saint Louis to the
San Juan Islands knew De Smet by the same name. Even De Smet
took to referring to himself in his letters and journals as "Black-
robe," or sometimes "Black-gown," in either case preferring a
hyphenated version of the term.

Several days after De Smet reached Big Face's camp, the chief
pulled up stakes and moved his indefensibly large camp to safer
territory at the headwaters of the Missouri River. The buffalo
hunting season approached, and the Flatheads needed to lay in a
supply of meat and robes before winter set in. The march began
on July 16 and ended three weeks later. Traveling at a pace of nine
to ten miles per day, the route passed up Henry's Fork of the
Snake River, surmounted the Continental Divide at a spot be-

tween Henry's Lake and Red Rock Lake, followed Red Rock Creek to the Beaverhead River near present-day Dillon, Montana, and from there transferred to the Jefferson River, one of the three forks that comprise the headwaters of the Missouri River.

Meriwether Lewis and William Clark had reached the Three Forks in 1805, the first Euro-Americans to do so, but for generations before and after their arrival one of the truly great Indian trade fairs in the West took place there each summer. Each August the flat, well-watered grasslands surrounding the Three Forks attracted a large number of plains and plateau tribes. They came principally to hunt buffalo, but also to barter and exchange information, safe in the knowledge that their large numbers kept sinister Blackfeet raiders at a distance. With De Smet as a witness, the Flatheads killed more than five hundred bison in 1840 at Three Forks, an event the priest vividly re-created for Father Verhaegen in several detailed letters. But De Smet had more serious business to consider on Father Verhaegen's behalf than mere buffalo hunts during his seventeen-day stay at the Three Forks.

Mainly, De Smet asked himself if the initial piety shown by the Flatheads justified the establishment of a permanent mission. To that question De Smet answered a resounding yes. He thought the Flatheads the most pious and eager group of potential converts he had ever come across. Among them, he testified, honesty prevails, slander is unknown, and everyone is "polite, always of a jovial humor, very hospitable, and helpful to one another in their duties." Moreover, "they share one another's sufferings, give help in time of need, and care for the orphans. They are well-mannered, gay, and very hospitable; their tent is open house; key and locks are unknown. Often I said to myself, 'There are the people that civilized men dare to call barbarians!'" Unlike the Potawatomis, the Flatheads did not yet know the crippling vices of white frontiersmen. Their only character flaw, De Smet reported, involved gambling, but tribal leaders abolished even that after they learned it violated the Ten Commandments. "It is a great error to judge the Indians of the interior by those of the frontier," De Smet instructed Verhaegen: "These last have learned the vices of the white men, whose insatiable greed of gain is served by corrupting the Indians, and whose bad example leads him into vicious habits." Verhaegen should act immediately to establish a permanent mission for these inviting neophytes.

Having decided the content of his report to Father Verhaegen, De Smet turned to ecclesiastical protocol. Using a makeshift desk, he penned a letter of introduction to Fathers Francis Norbert Blanchet and Modeste Demers, resident priests in the Willamette Valley near Fort Vancouver. Blanchet and Demers had come to the Oregon country in 1838 at the request of the bishop of Quebec. Great Britain and America jointly occupied the Oregon country after 1818, so Canadian bishops had as much right to preach in the Pacific Northwest as did American missionaries. To De Smet's knowledge, Blanchet and Demers constituted the entire Catholic clergy in the Pacific Northwest besides himself. In his letter he explained the nature of his trip to the mountains, commented upon the faith of the Flatheads, and implied that he would soon return with more Jesuits.

Toward the end of August, when the Flatheads made preparations to leave Three Forks and return to their homelands farther west, De Smet explained to Big Face that he, too, must soon leave. He must reach Saint Louis before winter snows sealed off the travel routes. But, he promised, he would return in the spring. Because De Smet knew it would be impossible, at that late time, for him to rejoin the American Fur Company's caravan retracing its steps to Saint Louis from the Green River rendezvous, he decided to use the route taken by the Flathead envoys in the 1830s. In addition to exploring new lands, he could also establish contact with the traders at the American Fur Company posts scattered along the Yellowstone and Missouri Rivers. A council of Flathead elders deputized an armed escort of twenty warriors to guide and protect De Smet on his journey east. "Long before sunrise all the Flatheads had assembled to say good-bye," De Smet remembered about August 27, 1840; "No word was spoken, but sadness was written on every countenance. The only thing that consoled them was a formal promise to return the following spring, with a reinforcement of missionaries."

The first part of De Smet's route, to the Yellowstone River, followed an ancient buffalo trail through a gap in the mountains, a passage later known to gold seekers as Bozeman Pass. De Smet knew from an earlier reading of Nicholas Biddle's *History of the Expedition under the Command of Lewis and Clark* (1814) that if he followed the Yellowstone it would take him directly to the Missouri River. Fort Union, a major American Fur Company outpost located at the confluence of those two rivers since the early 1830s, would provide a convenient resting spot. Unfortunately, the Yellowstone Desert, a barren stretch of irregular gulches and ravines, posed a problem. Travel would be slow and tiresome. The Yellowstone also passed through the land of the Crow Indians, a fierce, possessive tribe not always at peace with the Flatheads—or any visitors, for that matter.

One can never relax when crossing the lands of a powerful tribe such as the Crows, De Smet observed: "Right here I will remark that in these solitudes, though the howling of wolves, the hissing of venomous serpents and the roaring of the tiger and grizzly bear are capable of freezing one with terror, this fear is nothing in comparison with that which fresh tracks of men and horses can arouse in the soul of the traveler." De Smet prayed that he and his escort might pass unnoticed the entire length of the Yellowstone River, but eventually his Flathead scouts spotted a hunting party of Crows, and the Crows saw them in return. The two tribes, momentarily friends and allies, approached each other cautiously, then settled down for a council.

De Smet saw in this impromptu meeting an opportunity to widen his circle of Indian friends. For two days the tribesmen traveled together before the Crows veered away to hunt alone. Almost immediately they were replaced by a second band of Crows, this one a full village containing upward of one thousand persons, at the confluence of the Yellowstone and Bighorn Rivers. They had already heard from scouts and others about the Black Robe traveling along the Yellowstone with his Flathead escort, so they came forward in peace. As before, De Smet appreciated the interruption. Moreover, he liked the Crows—admired them, even—especially for their honesty and humor. On one occasion he spoke to the headmen about religion, and at their insistence he depicted in colorful adjectives the torments of hell, proclaiming that the Great Spirit retained such a place for those who broke sacred laws. This prompted one of the chiefs to reply: "I think there are only two in all the Crow nation who will not go to that hell you speak of; those are the Otter and the Weasel; they are the only ones I know who have never killed, nor stolen, nor been guilty of the excesses which your law forbids. Still, I may be mistaken about them, and in that case we will all go to hell together."

De Smet sighted no new bands of Indians in the time it took for him to travel from the Crow camp to Fort Alexander, an American Fur Company trading post at the mouth of the Rosebud River. There he released his faithful Flathead attendants. It might be more dangerous for him to continue with the Flatheads than without them, De Smet reasoned, inasmuch as some tribes might mistake his peaceful guard for invaders and launch an attack. If the Crows knew about Black Robe, so too would other tribes, and it seemed to De Smet that he and de Velder would probably be safer without an escort.

Still, traveling without protection frightened De Smet. He later looked upon the last leg of the journey to Fort Union as a religious experience, the constant danger bringing him closer to God:

> Upon awakening one morning I saw, about a quarter of a mile distant, the smoke of a big fire, which turned out to be the camp of a party of savages. Being separated from them by only a point of rock, we hurriedly saddled our horses and galloped off. That day we made about fifty miles without stopping, arriving at camp two hours after sunset. Fearing the savages had seen our trail and might pursue us, we dared not light a fire, and went to bed supperless. I rolled myself in my blanket, lay down on the grass, and recommended my soul to God. My brave grenadier soon began to snore like a steam-engine under way, sounding all the notes of the gamut and ending in a deep sigh which harmonized with the prelude, while I tossed from one side to the other and spent a sleepless night.
>
> The next morning at daybreak we were off. Toward noon, another alarm. A buffalo had been killed scarcely two hours before at the place we were then passing; his tongue, marrow bones, and several other tidbits had been taken out. Providence provided us with a supper of what was left. We traveled in an opposite direction from the

Indian tracks, and the following night camped in the midst of some rocks, once the lair of panthers and wolves. There, I slept well, undisturbed by my companion's music.

The twinkling lights of Fort Union, "the vastest and finest of the forts that the [American] Fur Company has upon the Missouri," provided a welcome sight for De Smet and de Velder when they detected its glimmer in the evening gloom of September 20. Graciously welcomed to the post by the bourgeois (chief trader), James Kipp, De Smet remained for three days, enjoying good food, clean quarters, and gentle companionship. Kipp advised De Smet to proceed the rest of the way to Saint Louis by canoe, a distance he estimated at about two thousand miles. He even volunteered the assistance of the post carpenter to construct a skiff for De Smet and his companion. But since neither De Smet nor de Velder felt confident in maneuvering a small, frail vessel in swift-moving water, they decided to continue their journey on horseback, at least as far as Fort Vermilion, no matter that it might take twice as long.

Although the journey to Council Bluffs proved to be tedious and slow, De Smet used it to his advantage. Along the way he visited several bands of Indians, including the Mandans, Arikaras, and Blackfeet Sioux, a tribe different and unrelated to the Blackfeet of the Rocky Mountains. He also introduced himself to fur trade officials at Forts Clark, Pierre, and Vermilion. De Smet's experience at Fort Union taught him that the bourgeois, though sometimes brusque, nevertheless possessed a vast store of information about the Indians, a cache of erudition he intended to tap someday when it came time for him to place an Indian mission on the upper Missouri.

De Smet's emotional return to the Potawatomi mission at Council Bluffs ran the spectrum between exhilaration and depression. It pleased him greatly to be reunited with his fellow Jesuits, Fathers Verreydt and Christian Hoecken, but it hurt him to be reminded of the adverse influence white men have on Indians. Barely fifty Potawatomi families still remained in the vicinity of Saint Joseph's Mission, and De Smet could not help but be reminded again how truly blessed the Flatheads were as a tribe to be so wonderfully isolated from white man's "civilization."

The day following De Smet's arrival at Council Bluffs, the Missouri River froze solid, halting all traffic. De Smet , however, remained undeterred in his determination to reach Saint Louis. No matter what privations might be encountered, he must report to his superiors and plead the case for a permanent Flathead mission. On December 14 the subzero temperatures let up slightly, and De Smet and de Velder took to the saddle once again. Fortunately, they met neither obstacles nor accidents along the route to Westport, where they exchanged their mounts for a ticket on a stagecoach bound for Saint Louis. In a dramatic gesture, De Smet entered the Jesuit residence at Saint Louis University on New Year's Eve, 1840. "Would you believe it," he boasted about his passage of 249 days and nearly five thousand miles, "Not the least accident happened to me. On the contrary, [sixteen tribes of] Indians most feared and mistrusted have everywhere received me with demonstrations of the greatest joy."

Although the faculty at Saint Louis University welcomed De Smet home warmly, financial conditions in the Missouri Vice-Province, which had been upgraded in status within the Society of Jesus, prevented Father Verhaegen from sharing in De Smet's enthusiasm for a new Indian mission in the Rocky Mountains. De Smet recounted the incident for his brother:

> On my arrival at St. Louis I gave an account to my superior of my journey and of the flattering prospects which a mission beyond the Rocky Mountains held out. You will easily believe me when I tell you that my heart sank within me on learning from him that the funds at his disposal for missionary purposes would not enable him to afford me scarcely half of what was necessary for the outfit and other expenses of an expedition. The thought that the undertaking would have to be given up, that I would not be able to redeem my promise to [return to] the poor Indians, pierced my very heart and filled me with the deepest sorrow. . . . One of my friends encouraged me to appeal to the zealous and learned coadjutor of Philadelphia and to his indefatigable clergy. I immediately acted upon the thought. I did appeal, and with what success.

On his way back to Saint Louis from Philadelphia, De Smet continued to beg for funds in Catholic churches on both sides of the Ohio River. A parish in Pittsburgh provided $140, the pastors of Kentucky gave $300, and so it went until his treasury for the Flathead mission totaled about $2,000. New Orleans raised an additional $1,000 in cash, plus six boxes of useful articles for the missions. Verhaegen assisted De Smet by printing a pamphlet entitled *The Indian Missions in the United States of America, under the Care of the Missouri Province of the Society of Jesus*, which could be used as a tangible reward to donors. Twenty-four of the thirty-four pages of the booklet contained two letters written by Father De Smet, one in which he summarized his experiences at the Potawatomi mission at Council Bluffs, and another in which he recounted his 1840 journey to the Rocky Mountains. De Smet liked the idea of being published and prepared additional material which he sent to *The Annals of the Propagation of the Faith,* a French publication with an English-language outlet for American Catholics.

The charity of the American Catholic community persuaded Verhaegen to reconsider his earlier reluctance to establish a Jesuit mission for the Flatheads, and in January 1841 he approved De Smet's request. Verhaegen designated the project the Rocky Mountain Mission, and he appointed De Smet its superior. He then assigned forty-two-year-old Father Nicolas Point, S.J., to accompany De Smet on his return to the Oregon country. Later, he added Father Gregory Mengarini, S.J., a recent arrival to America from Italy and a specialist in languages, medicine, and music. Three coadjutor brothers—Charles Huet, a tinsmith; Joseph Specht, a carpenter; and William Claessens, a blacksmith—completed the community. De Smet, as leader of this diverse crew, used the money at his disposal to purchase tickets on the steamboat *Oceana* as far as Westport and to buy general supplies, four small carts, one wagon, and several horses and mules for his community.

De Smet had four goals for the Rocky Mountain Mission. Primarily he intended to establish a permanent mission among the Flatheads. Second, he planned to write a series of "edifying" letters. His superiors, in fact, requested it of him. These letters should be the same kind of descriptive dissertations he had written during the 1840 journey, only this time with an eye to future publication and fund raising. Ignatius Loyola, the founder of the Society of Jesus, viewed letter writing both as a means to unify the hearts of his Jesuits and as a principle of public relations. His own seven thousand letters, in fact, are the largest extant correspondence of any sixteenth-century figure, so De Smet considered it an honor to comply with his superior's request. Third, De Smet desired to establish communication with both Father Blanchet and the Hudson's Bay Company, the dominant ecclesiastical and political authorities, for all practical purposes, in the jointly occupied Oregon country. Finally, De Smet hoped to identify travel routes between the mission he established and the Hudson's Bay Company posts at Forts Vancouver, Walla Walla, and Colville.

In 1841, unlike 1840, De Smet had to make his own arrangements to reach the Green River rendezvous, the American Fur Company having informed him that they could not accommodate six Jesuits and five fully loaded vehicles in their fast-moving brigade. This worried De Smet, but, happily, once he reached Westport he struck an agreement with Thomas Fitzpatrick, a highly regarded frontier scout, to act as a guide at least as far as the Green River rendezvous. Fitzpatrick furnished a hunter to supply food for the six Jesuits and teamsters to drive their vehicles. "The caravan was composed of a curious collection of individuals," De Smet informed Father Verhaegen: "In my little band of eleven were men of eight different nationalities." Meanwhile, other wagons bound for California and Oregon began to pull out of Westport during the first week in May.

Separately and in pairs, a few days after leaving Westport nearly all the wagons bound for the Oregon country reassembled along the Kaw River at Sapling Grove, just below present-day Topeka, Kansas. There they halted to form a wagon train, elect officers, and draw up a set of governing rules. By the time De Smet's party reached Sapling Grove, nearly seventy persons had already formed the Western Emigration Society under the leadership of John Bidwell. None of them, however, knew much about the trail west, so when De Smet and his party of experienced mountain men arrived, the Western Emigration Society expressed a willingness to merge with the Jesuits. "It will be understood," twenty-one-year-old John Bidwell committed to paper, "that Fitzpatrick was captain of the missionary party and pilot of the whole," while John Bartleson would be captain of the Western Emigration Society. The remaining pioneers promised to maintain their own wagons, keep up with the group, and share the camp duties. Only De Smet and Fitzpatrick received official exemptions from taking their turn at guard duty.

Coordinating travel with such a large group took some getting used to—mules ran away, horses became ill, wagons got stalled in mud—but in time the twenty wagons in the Bidwell-Bartleson train established a daily regimen and thereafter remained monotonously on course day after day. As before, De Smet took careful notes on all that he observed and later wrote long letters to his family and friends. The lush beauty of the Kansas prairies; a terrifying tornado; the shallow, shadowy Platte River; the majestic Rocky Mountains; and South Pass all became worthy subjects for his pen.

When at last the immigrant train reached the Green River on July 24, De Smet found to his dismay that the fur traders had long since deserted the rendezvous. A party of disenchanted pioneers on their way back to the states temporarily occupied the site. This unexpected development shocked De Smet, but only until he realized that the small party at the rendezvous site also included a young Flathead man who waited patiently for Black Robe to return. While the two immigrant groups sorted out the relative merits of continuing on to California or not, De Smet queried the Flathead youth about Chief Big Face. All was well with the chief and his tribe, Francis Xavier, son of Old Ignace, informed De Smet; the tribe waited for Black Robe in a valley with plentiful game and ripe berries. Francis Xavier would lead the way.

Although De Smet had the utmost confidence that Francis Xavier knew the route, after he learned that Fitzpatrick and the Bidwell-Bartleson families intended on staying together through at least Soda Springs on the Bear River, he reasoned it might be better to remain with the wagon train just a little longer. The wagon train provided a certain measure of security, for example, when crossing rivers and ascending mountains. In truth, his Jesuit colleagues found it difficult to adapt to the rigors of frontier travel. Thus far Father Mengarini had fallen off his horse six times and Father Point nearly as often. Moreover, the apprenticeship of the brothers as mule skinners did not go well. "Our Brothers, forced by circumstances to take the reins," De Smet observed, "would often find themselves, one on a mule's neck, another on his hind quarters, and a third under the fore feet of the animals, not knowing how they got there."

The route to Soda Springs tested the resolve of the travelers, though everyone came through unharmed. At that point Bidwell and the California colonists turned to the south; the remaining immigrants, thirty-two others, branched to the north, heading for the Willamette Valley of the Oregon country. Fitzpatrick had business elsewhere and went off alone. In the interval, while the immigrants separated themselves into groups, De Smet and Francis Xavier struck out for Fort Hall, the Hudson's Bay Company post on the Snake River. They reached it on De Smet's 115th day out of Saint Louis; the Oregon-bound immigrants and the Jesuits followed in a few days. And so, too, did Bravest of the Brave, a noted Flathead horseman, and twenty of his warriors. Bravest of the Brave announced that when De Smet and the other Jesuits felt sufficiently rested he would lead them to the main Flathead camp.

Anxious to reach the Flathead camp, yet appreciative of the luxuries at Fort Hall, De Smet busied himself for a few days at the post by mending his equipment and replenishing his supplies. Frank Ermantinger, the chief factor, treated the Jesuits with great kindness, even selling them goods at cost or a liberal discount, a generous consideration inasmuch as it was a thousand miles to the next supply outlet. Father De Smet appreciated Ermantinger's obliging attitude, though Father Mengarini scoffed at the "bargains." In his judgment the chief factor inflated prices excessively and could therefore afford to offer a discount. Mengarini also denigrated the quality of Ermantinger's goods, noting that "toro," his freshest product and a "luxury not sold in civilized markets," merely combined portions of buffalo meat, grease, and berries.

Just before the Jesuits' leave-taking at Fort Hall, on August 18 the mood at the fort turned somber when news arrived that the Bidwell command had suffered an Indian attack on their way to California. Interestingly, word of this attack spread so quickly, and so widely, that it even reached Saint Louis. When he heard the news, Father Verhaegen drew the erroneous conclusion that his cadre of zealous missionaries had all perished. Actually they were on their way to the main camp of the Flatheads.

Led by Bravest of the Brave, the priests and Indians traveled north to Henry's Fork of the Snake River, crossed the Continental Divide above Henry's Lake, and then made their way west to the Beaverhead River. There, in that protected valley, on August 30, almost a year to the day since he had left the Flatheads at Three Forks, De Smet rejoined his tribe of pious converts. When Big Face saw the Jesuits approaching in the distance, he mounted a horse and came forward to personally escort De Smet the final two miles. "The tribe had the appearance of a flock crowding with eagerness for their shepherd," De Smet remembered; "This evening was certainly one of the happiest of our lives. We could truly say that we had reached the peaceful goal. All previous dangers, toils and trials were at an end and soon forgotten."

During the next week De Smet introduced his small Jesuit community to life in an Indian camp. He also reacquainted himself with his Flathead converts. With childlike simplicity the Indians told Black Robe of the ways in which they had practiced their faith during his absence. Twice on weekdays and three times on Sundays the entire tribe assembled to say prayers in common. The box of vestments De Smet left with them the previous summer they carried everywhere, reverently holding them on high every time the camp moved. When emergencies arose, the catechist baptized the sick and dying. One young girl, the Indians reported to De Smet in reverential tones, even received an apparition of the Blessed Virgin Mary. Had there ever been a more saintly tribe? De Smet asked himself.

When snow from the higher elevations began to encroach on the Flathead camp, Big Face announced that his tribe must return to their own territory. This time De Smet would go with them, live with them. Following a route that twice crossed the Continental Divide, in mid-September the Indian caravan passed through Hell Gate, the graphically named mountain defile near present-day Missoula, Montana, that the Blackfeet used so effectively to inhibit would-be trespassers from invading their buffalo hunting lands on the plains adjacent to the Missouri River. A little farther on, the entourage entered the Bitterroot Valley, and there, on September 24, in a long meadow twenty-eight miles down the Bitterroot River, at a spot near present-day Stevensville, De Smet ordered his Jesuits to halt their wagons. Erecting a cross in the center of the camp, De Smet anointed the site as the location of the first Jesuit Indian mission in the Pacific Northwest. He named it Saint Mary's Mission.

During the course of the next month Brothers Huet, Specht, and Claessens began the physical construction of Saint Mary's Mission while Fathers De Smet, Point, and Mengarini reinforced the theological education of the Flatheads. "Whilst I am writing these lines," De Smet informed his superior, "I hear the joyful voices of the carpenters, re-echoing to the blows on the smith's anvil, and I see them engaged in raising the house of prayer." As buildings rose around him, De Smet dreamed of what the future could bring in this location, and he chose as his model for the Rocky Mountain Mission the seventeenth-century Jesuit reductions in Paraguay, South America.

For a century and one-half beginning in 1607 the Jesuit missionaries in Paraguay, and to a lesser extent in Argentina, Uruguay, Chile, and Bolivia, enjoyed unprecedented success among the native peoples of New Spain. With native assistance they laid out as many as one hundred autonomous townlike missions, which they called reductions, each containing from 350 to 7,000 native converts. All nonnatives were excluded, except for the Jesuits. Assisted by missionaries, natives administered the civil government, staffed an army, and managed the communal economy. European-style homes, workplaces, small hospitals, schools, and farms made each community self-sufficient. Enlightenment scholar Charles Louis de Secondat, Baron de Montesquieu, extolled the virtues of these "forest utopias" in numerous writings, but the

Spanish crown exhibited considerably less enthusiasm for the independent native communities. Sycophants in the royal Spanish court, fearful of diminished New World patronage, accused the Jesuits of manipulating the Indians, suggesting that they encouraged the natives to resist imperial policies. Eventually the Spanish crown accepted the conclusions of the detractors and expelled the Jesuits from their South American colonies. A general suppression of the society followed in 1773, and after that the great experiment in Paraguay died a death of no resurrection.

De Smet believed that the Rocky Mountains in general and the Bitterroot Valley in particular exhibited many of the same basic elements that first made the Paraguayan reductions a success. The high mountains surrounding the Bitterroot Valley compared favorably to the impenetrable jungles of Paraguay in forming a natural barrier to isolate Saint Mary's Mission from the distracting influences of white pioneers. In addition, within four or five days' journey from Saint Mary's lived numerous large tribes of Indians—the Pend Oreilles and the Nez Percés to name two—all of them offering thousands of potential converts to Christ. De Smet, in fact, envisioned two hundred thousand potential new Christians in the Pacific Northwest. A possible defect of the Bitterroot Valley site, De Smet admitted, might be its proximity to the Blackfeet, "the only Indians of whose salvation we would have reason to despair, . . . for they are murderers, thieves, traitors, and all that is wicked." He would have to think about how to deal with them. "From what has hitherto been said," De Smet reiterated, "we may draw this conclusion, that the nation of the Flatheads appear to be a chosen people—'the elect of God;' that it would be easy to make this tribe a model for other tribes."

Father Point had some familiarity with reductions—he had modified the idea to suit his situation at Westport before joining the Rocky Mountain Mission community—and he shared De Smet's enthusiasm for a renewal of the concept. Point, who lagged behind on the journey west, melancholy over perceived wrongs done to him at an earlier assignment in Louisiana, warmed to his Rocky Mountain Mission appointment once De Smet gave him some of the responsibility for shaping the new reduction. A natural architect and planner, Point dedicated himself to the task. In 1837, Father Point had founded the Jesuit college at Grand Coteau, Louisiana, and he chose for his inspiration the "Fribourg Plan" for Jesuit schools. Point liked models, and now he adapted the Paraguayan plan to Saint Mary's Mission. First to be built would be a great church with homes and fences; farms and livestock would come next; storehouses, mills, schools, and an infirmary took third place on the list of priorities.

De Smet envisioned a grand system of ten or more reductions for the Oregon country, each one branching out from the hub at Saint Mary's. Natives would benefit from a full program of religious training and education in the European tradition. To obliterate paganism and replace it with the attributes of Christianity and western civilization was, after all, the measure of success for missionary activity in the nineteenth century. The Jesuit principle of accommodation provided a certain latitude in allowing the natives to maintain elements of their own culture, but the final goal would always be the conversion of the Indians to the twin principles of Christianity and civilization.

The second part of Point's plan for the Bitterroot Valley reduction called for the planting of crops and the introduction of domestic animals. Fort Colville, the Hudson's Bay Company post on the Columbia River, would likely have oat and wheat seeds suitable for the Pacific Northwest climate; they would also have tools and, possibly, even a few head of cattle to spare. With the building program at Saint Mary's Mission progressing so well, De Smet decided in late October to visit Fort Colville with a shopping list. Besides, by that time De Smet had an insatiable desire to see even more of the Oregon country. That Fort Colville was more than two hundred miles distant, or that the mountains overshadowing the Bitterroot Valley already glistened with snow, invigorated, rather than deterred, the adventurous nature of De Smet.

Guided by ten veteran warriors, De Smet rode out of Saint Mary's Mission on the afternoon of October 28, 1841. Large flakes of snow covered the trail on the second day out, but the priest refused to turn back. When the greenish blue Bitterroot River merged with the swift-flowing Clark Fork River, the trail became even more intimidating. Several times the steep trail above the Clark Fork seemed to jut out over the water, four to six hundred feet straight down, causing De Smet to say that though he had seen landscapes of "awful grandeur" before in the Rocky Mountains, this path "certainly surpassed all others in horror." Fortunately, De Smet's mule, Lizette, remained unfazed by the danger and leaped adroitly from one rocky precipice to another while De Smet, his eyes closed tight, held on for dear life. At other moments, such as when the path pushed uphill through dense cedar and pine forests, De Smet dismounted, commended himself to God, grasped the tail of his docile mule, and followed meekly behind. Committing himself to God, in fact, became part of De Smet's daily routine, as he told a fellow Jesuit: "Certainly the life of a missionary has its trials and dangers; yet, however great these may be, he guards the serenity of his soul by centering his mind upon God."

On Sunday, November 7, De Smet paused to rest at a Kalispel Indian camp on a bay of Lake Pend Oreille. To his surprise, another party of travelers, eight men paddling two boats, joined him. Squinting into the haze, De Smet recognized one of the canoeists as Charles, a Flathead who had assisted him as an interpreter in 1840. Charles, it turned out, now worked for the Hudson's Bay Company, and he carried two messages for De Smet from Dr. John McLoughlin, the chief factor at Fort Vancouver. McLoughlin's letters, written in late September, invited De Smet to visit him at Fort Vancouver at his earliest convenience.

This was all very curious. How could the Hudson's Bay Company know so much about him and his location? And why would they care? It was simple, really. In August, as De Smet and his cadre of Jesuits departed Fort Hall on the last leg of their journey to the main Flathead camp, Frank Ermantinger dutifully alerted officials at Fort Vancouver of the arrival of the Jesuits and their intentions in the Oregon country. As soon as he heard the news, McLoughlin acted. Unlike some traders, McLoughlin viewed Hudson's Bay Company interests broadly. He envisioned a new society forming in the Pacific Northwest, and he believed that Christianity would play a pivotal role in its development. Educational institutions and Indian missions were, in his opinion, necessary foundations for civilization. And to underscore his sincerity, he offered as a gift the supplies heaped aboard the two canoes. McLoughlin's letters did not hint that he was contemplating a return to Catholicism, but he was, and within the next two years he would rejoin the Roman Catholic Church. At De Smet's request, Charles continued on his way to Saint Mary's Mission by way of the Clark Fork River to deliver the supplies. De Smet and his Indian entourage, meanwhile, continued on to Fort Colville. The mission still needed seeds and livestock.

It took another full week to reach Fort Colville. Along the way, De Smet stopped for three days to visit more camps of Kalispels. By that time, De Smet had mastered the techniques necessary to instruct large numbers of Indians in a short time. The Kalispels, like most of their neighbors, respected the oral tradition, and De Smet knew how to tell a good story. Assisted by an interpreter, he began by regaling his listeners with lively narratives of personal valor during the campaigns of Napoleon Bonaparte, stories he had heard as a youth. Then he moved on to the kind of stories from the Old Testament that would impress warriors: Noah's ark and the deluge, the life of Samson, David's battle against Goliath, and so. Finally, he arranged to have the Lord's Prayer, the Hail Mary, the Ten Commandments, and the acts of faith, hope, and charity translated into the native tongue. Placing his pupils in a circle, he assigned to each Indian, in order, a specific line of a prayer or commandment. As each recited his part in turn, all enjoyed the benefits of the repetition until everyone in the circle knew the full components. The first to know all of the prayers by heart received a medal. The missionary also used music—De Smet played the clarinet—and artwork prepared by Father Point to further convey concepts of salvation in the Catholic faith. With slight variations, De Smet continued to use these techniques for the rest of his time in the Oregon country.

The Hudson's Bay Company had established Fort Colville in 1825 on the shores of the Columbia River above thundering Kettle Falls. Archibald MacDonald, the chief agent for the company, had already heard through the grapevine about De Smet's new mission in the Bitterroots, and he welcomed the interruption when Black Robe and his escort straggled in on November 15 in the midst of a snowstorm. For the next three days De Smet exchanged information with the local French-Canadians, conversed with the chief of the Kettle Indians, and purchased from MacDonald the seeds for which he had come. Unfortunately, MacDonald could provide no livestock for Saint Mary's; he did, however, secretly place within De Smet's pack of provisions complementary extras such as sugar, coffee, tea, chocolate, butter, crackers, flour, poultry, ham, and candles.

De Smet's return to Saint Mary's followed the same path that he took to Fort Colville. Ironically, though the packs carried by his mules contained elegant foods, De Smet did not know it at the time and believed it necessary to subsist on toro, the Hudson's Bay Company concoction he had first tasted several months earlier at Fort Hall. He supplemented his diet with a thick soup the Indians made from cakes of pine moss. "It could be eaten," he joked, but only "if seasoned with a good appetite and a prolonged absence of other nourishment."

On December 8, after an absence of forty-two days, De Smet returned to his flourishing Christian colony on the Bitterroot River. By this time the diligence of Brothers Huet, Specht, and Claessens had transformed Saint Mary's from a temporary outpost into a permanent village. Fences now defined the fields, and a palisade bristling with three thousand stout stakes enclosed and protected the mission buildings. The chapel interior, constructed with no tools other than an ax, saw, and auger, accommodated an altar, balustrade, choir, seats, and columns. Father Point, who liked things orderly, had placed the entire village on a regular schedule. In the morning the chief or a suitable elder awoke the tribesmen and called everyone to morning prayers and Mass. Adults received religious instructions after the morning meal, men and women in separate sodalities; at 2:00 P.M. the children assembled for their own classes in the catechism. The entire tribe repeated evening prayers at sunset. On Sundays and holy days the

This drawing by Father Nicholas Point, S.J., in 1841 shows the progress of the Flathe
reduction that took place during De Smet's brief trip to Fort Colville. The illustratic
first appeared in De Smet's first edition of *Letters and Sketches with a Narrative of*
Year's Residence among the Indian Tribes of the Rocky Mountains (Philadelphia, 184
Courtesy of Oregon Province Archives of the Society of Jesus, Gonzaga University.

schedule expanded to include several more services. "I preached
regularly four times a day, and each time they ran eagerly to secure
good places," De Smet told his fellow Jesuits. Virtually every person in the Flathead nation declared the intention to be baptized.

De Smet naturally saw in the faith of the Flatheads the hand of
God. He simply could find no earthly explanation for what he
called their "avidity" to hear the gospel of Jesus Christ. But there
were earthly reasons. Although De Smet early on recognized that
the fearsome Blackfeet intimidated the Flatheads, he did not yet
comprehend that the Flatheads expected the Jesuits to save them
from their enemies. The Jesuits, the Flatheads assumed, would
protect them from raids and attacks, bullets and arrows. If the
Black Robe wished them to learn prayers, sing hymns, and par-
take in Christian rituals, they considered it a small price to pay for
invincibility. Besides, participating in the Black Robe's ceremonies could be both agreeable and satisfying. The two cultures

actually converged in several ways. Baptism, marriage, the Mass, and other Catholic liturgy appealed to the Flatheads' sense of drama and color. Jesuits talked about miracles from the hand of the Blessed Mother and a lexicon of saints; the Indians sought their favors from natural spirit helpers. The crucifix, holy medals, and rosaries paralleled sacred charms and other "medicines" used by the Indians. Gregorian chants sung by the priests resembled tribal prophesy songs. The incense burned at Mass seemed closely related to the smoke of sage and tobacco that carried the Indians' own prayers skyward.

By the spring of 1842 the need for more supplies and, no doubt, an acute curiosity to see Fort Vancouver pulled De Smet away from Saint Mary's a second time. Charles, who had spent the winter at Saint Mary's after delivering McLoughlin's supplies, recommended that De Smet retrace his steps of the previous fall to Fort Colville and from there ride the Columbia River to Fort Vancouver in a Hudson's Bay Company barge. It sounded like a workable plan, so De Smet concurred. De Smet also liked Charles's idea because en route he could visit other tribes of Indians, and so he did. One night he shared an elk dinner with Kootenai Indians on the Saint Regis River. Later he spent some time with the Kalispels on the Pend Oreille River. And at the request of an envoy from the Coeur d'Alene tribe, De Smet made a detour to their village on the banks of the Spokane River.

Such digressions greatly satisfied De Smet, but they also delayed his arrival at Fort Colville. In fact that did not matter, because when he reached Kettle Falls the chief trader told De Smet that all boat traffic on the Columbia, even the Hudson's Bay Company's twelve-man barges, was halted until the spring runoff in the Columbia River subsided. Thus the river journey to Fort Vancouver did not begin until May 30. Peter Skene Ogden, the legendary explorer of the Snake River country and the Great Basin, honored De Smet with a seat in the vessel under his command. For the first hour or so the two men entertained each other with timely "bon mots" on the peculiarities of frontier travel. But the celebrated rapids, falls, and cascades of the middle

Columbia River soon jostled the men into pensive reflection. On the second day out the barge approached a particularly rough "dalle," a rock-lined trough in the bed of the river where giant waves rebounded off the canyon walls in no predictable rhythm. De Smet elected to walk along the bank and rejoin his companions down below.

> I had gone ashore and was walking along the bank, scarcely thinking what might happen; for my briviary, papers, bed, in a word, my little all, had been left on the barge. I had proceeded about a quarter of a mile, when seeing the bargemen push off from the bank and glide down the stream with an easy, careless air, I began to repent having preferred a path along the river's side, so strewn with fragments of rocks that I was compelled at every instant to turn aside or clamber over them. I still held on my course, when all at once the barge is so abruptly stopped that the rowers can hardly keep their seats. Regaining, however, their equilibrium they ply the oars with redoubled vigor, but without any effect upon the barge. They are already within the power of the angry vortex; the waters are crested with foam; a deep sound is heard which I distinguish as the voice of the pilot encouraging his men to hold on to their oars—to row bravely. The danger increases every minute, and in a moment more all hope of safety has vanished. The barge, the sport of the vortex, spins like a top upon the whirling waters—the oars are useless—the bow rises—the stern descends, and the next instant all have disappeared.

Motionless with shock, De Smet waited as if held in suspended animation. Suddenly the whirlpool spewed out oars and poles, then the barge and some of the supplies. In another moment Charles and some of the other men popped to the surface, De Smet mentally pulling them to shore with his prayers. Five men from the boat drowned in the river that day, forging a never-to-be-forgotten memory for De Smet.

Fort Vancouver in 1842 may have been the most sophisticated village west of Santa Fe, with the possible exception of Monterrey, California. The Hudson's Bay Company operated a shipyard, gristmill, dairy, orchard, and farm in addition to the headquarters post. Situated on a floodplain adjacent to the north bank of the Columbia River, Fort Vancouver's bristling stockade fence of stout cedars and brooding bastions made it appear at first sight to be a military post. But once inside the wide, beckoning front gates, De Smet realized that commerce, not combat, occupied the principal interest of this fort. The magnitude of the physical setting overwhelmed the priest. Inside the enclosure nestled a hospital, thirty or more small houses for engagés, storehouses, a blacksmith shop, and numerous buildings where patrons bought, sold, or traded furs. All of the buildings seemed diminutive compared to the baronial residence of the chief factor for all of the Columbia Department, Dr. John McLoughlin. Making good on his earlier invitation, McLoughlin ushered De Smet into his home, treating him like an honored guest. A giant of a man at six feet, four inches, with a large head of gray-white hair and a beard to match, McLoughlin reveled in his reputation as an astute businessman and a host of legendary proportions. The two men formed an instant friendship.

Besides conducting his business at Fort Vancouver—that is, persuading McLoughlin to provide supplies for Saint Mary's Mission on credit—De Smet also contacted Fathers Francis Norbert Blanchet and Modeste Demers. These two representatives of the bishop of Quebec lived twenty or so miles up the Willamette Valley, where they maintained Saint Paul's Mission, a Catholic church for French-Canadians. Blanchet exercised the ecclesiastical authority of an acting vicar general, meaning that he had jurisdiction over all of the Oregon country situated west of the Cascade Mountains. Principally, De Smet wished to know from Blanchet his intentions with regard to the interior tribes.

Blanchet and De Smet shared much in common as clergymen and pioneers. De Smet felt immediately at ease, and the two men spoke frankly. Blanchet disclosed his personal commitment to make Saint Paul's Mission the headquarters of the Catholic Church in all of the Oregon country. He expressed his hope that De Smet would establish a similar headquarters for the Society of Jesus in the Willamette, and perhaps someday a college. De Smet divulged his own plans for a series of self-sufficient, Paraguayan-style reductions for the interior Indians, commenting that only when he considered the project well on its way would he agree to expand the Rocky Mountain Mission into the Willamette Valley

or the lower Columbia or Puget Sound. At this point he mainly
needed more missionaries. De Smet explained: "In so extensive a
field we are but few, and beset with so many dangers, that at the
dawn of day we have often reason to doubt whether we will live to
see the sun go down. It is not that we have anything to fear from
the climate; far from it—for, if here death came only by sickness,
we might indeed count upon many years, but water, fire, and the
bow, often hurry their victims off when least expected." Together
the two priests decided that De Smet should return to Saint Louis,
seek his superior's approval, and then sail to Europe in search of
money and recruits for his Oregon country missions. They further
agreed that the pope must be persuaded to provide a bishop for
the Oregon country, though De Smet immediately declared his
personal lack of interest in such a post.

His business complete, De Smet returned to the Columbia
River, gathered up a modest quantity of provisions, tools, and
clothes, and, accompanied by Charles, departed Fort Vancouver
on the last day of June. With wind filling the sails and sailors
putting their backs into the oars, the Hudson's Bay Company
barge on which they traveled reached Fort Walla Walla without
incident in just short of two weeks' time. At that point De Smet
decided to explore a new, overland route to Saint Mary's Mission. Charles explained that an ancient Indian trail proceeded
from Fort Walla Walla to the Snake River and thence crossed the
Spokane Desert to the southern end of Lake Coeur d'Alene. The
path then followed a small stream (the Saint Joe River) that
ended abruptly in mountains. Saint Mary's Mission would be on
the other side of the mountains. Charles told De Smet the truth,
and in fact on July 27 they did reach Saint Mary's Mission safely.
But, as De Smet later explained to his confreres, not only did the
mountainous part of the trail thwart his progress and lengthen
the journey by several days, but the steep rocks and dense forests
he encountered also threatened his life. "I could scarcely believe
that any human being had ever preceded us over such a road," he
concluded. Readers of his letters could easily read between the
lines and tell that he loved every exasperating moment.

Father Mengarini alone remained at Saint Mary's when De

Smet returned, Father Point having left ten days earlier to accompany the Flatheads on their summer buffalo hunt to the Three Forks. Mengarini had assigned Point to act as a chaperone lest the natives return to their old ways in regard to superstition and religion. It took De Smet five days to recuperate from his overland trip, but as soon as he did, he went in search of Point and the Flatheads. He had many things to tell Father Point.

Instead of going north down the Bitterroot River to Hell Gate and then proceeding east to Three Forks, De Smet allowed Charles to show him yet another traditional Indian route across the mountains. This time Charles led De Smet up the Bitterroot River, not down it, to its source at Ross's Hole. After cresting the mountains beyond at present-day Gibbon's Pass, the two men descended into the Big Hole River drainage system and from there worked their way east to Three Forks by way of the Beaverhead and Jefferson Rivers. One of the character traits the Indians most admired in De Smet was his appetite for adventure, his inquisitiveness about new country and ancient trails. Although De Smet complained to his friends and superiors, sometimes in mock humor, about the physical strains he experienced as an explorer, with the Indians he never showed any weaknesses, and for that they loved him all the more.

De Smet and Point exchanged much news when they met at the buffalo hunting camp about the first of August. Point asked De Smet to send him north to initiate contact with the Blackfeet and to open a mission for them. What better way to bring peace to the Rocky Mountains, he asked, than to Christianize the most elusive and dangerous tribe in the region? De Smet denied the request. Point, he said, should open a mission for the Coeur d'Alenes, not the Blackfeet. On his way to Fort Colville in May, De Smet had promised the Coeur d'Alenes a mission and missionary of their own, but he could not minister to them himself because he needed to go to Saint Louis. Father Mengarini should remain at Saint Mary's, so Point must go to the Coeur d'Alenes. Point protested, arguing that the future success of the Rocky Mountain Mission pivoted on a mission for the Blackfeet, but De Smet refused to alter his stance. De Smet had a grand plan for the

Oregon country, and Point, who once had failed as an administrator at Saint Charles College in Louisiana, would not now give him advice. If anyone could mollify the Blackfeet, the most fearsome tribe in the Pacific Northwest, it would be he. Someday.

De Smet's second farewell from the Flatheads took place with considerably less emotion than his departure in 1840, in large measure because now the tribe had its own mission and priests. Nevertheless, as before, an escort of Flathead warriors accompanied him. The missionary appreciated the escort, for he knew from past experience that the Yellowstone Desert could be dangerous, foreboding territory.

On the second day out from Three Forks De Smet intercepted a large band of Crows. Hearing that Black Robe had returned, three thousand Indians rushed out of their huts in what De Smet described as a wild, tumultuous scene.

> All the chiefs and about fifty of their warriors hastened around me, and I was literally assailed by them. Holding me by the gown, they drew me in every direction, whilst a robust savage of gigantic stature seemed resolved to carry me off by main force. All spoke at the same time, and appeared to be quarreling, whilst I, the sole object of all this contention, could not conceive what they were about. I remained passive, not knowing whether I should laugh or be serious. The interpreter soon came to my relief, and said that all this uproar was but an excess of politeness and kindness toward me, as every one wished to have the honor of lodging and entertaining the Blackgown. With his advice I selected my host, upon which the others immediately loosened their hold, and I followed the chief to his lodge, which was the largest and best in the camp.

De Smet considered the Crows "unquestionably the most anxious to learn; the most inquisitive, ingenious, and polished of all the savage tribes east of the mountains." In part De Smet respected them because their chiefs abhorred the use of liquor. Echoing De Smet's feeling as well as his own, a chief explained: "For what is this fire-water good? It burns the throat and stomach; it makes a man like a bear who has lost his senses. He bites, he growls, he scratches and he howls, he falls down as if he were dead. Your fire-water does nothing but harm—take it to our enemies, and they will kill each other, and their wives and children will be worthy of pity. As for us we do not want it, we are fools enough without it."

De Smet also favored the Crows because they exhibited a healthy curiosity about Euro-American culture, evidence in his mind that someday the tribe would accept both civilization and Christianity. On this occasion they plied him with questions about the numbers of white men who lived afar. "Count the blades of the grass in your vast prairie," De Smet told them, "and you will then have some idea of their number." Next he told them of the white man's great cities. Such marvels left them speechless, he reported, yet he continued by describing "moving tents drawn by a machine that vomited forth smoke and outdistanced the fleetest horse; boats that traversed the ocean, transporting in a few days the inhabitants of an entire village from one country to another; men rising in the air and soaring in the clouds like mountain eagles." Astonished, the Indians clasped their hands over their mouths to conceal squeals of surprise. "The Master of Life is great," said the chief at last, "and the white men are his favorites." It was exactly the impression De Smet hoped to leave.

Upon leaving the Crows, De Smet dismissed the majority of his Flathead escort. Accompanied now by only Young Ignatius, a mixed-heritage Cree named Gabriel, and two Americans he met in the Crow camp, De Smet rode bravely across the arid plains to Fort Union in six days. Again, as in 1840, he rode from daybreak to sunset with only a single stop of an hour or two near midday. "After the evening meal, " De Smet explained, "in order to deceive the enemy, we built a big fire, hurriedly erected a cabin out of branches of trees, after which we got on our horses and rode until ten or eleven o'clock at night. We then dismounted and without fire or shelter rested as best we could."

This time, De Smet agreed with the chief factor at Fort Union that the use of a skiff would, in fact, be the most efficient manner for him to continue on to Saint Louis, so he, Ignatius, and Gabriel sold their horses and took to the water in a hand-carved dugout canoe. This decision, he later declared, proved most fortunate, for on the third day out the canoeists met a steamboat traveling upriver, and by happenstance four proprietors of the American Fur Company were on board the *Omega*. The company officers invited the priest and his companions to return with them to Fort Union, after which they would all go directly to Saint Louis. Their assertion that several Indian war parties waited in ambush along the river provided all the additional persuasion De Smet needed to join them.

Forty-six days later De Smet reached Saint Louis. By that time the steamboat had taken on the appearance of a skeleton, said De Smet, its keel having been pierced by submerged rocks in the low water, its sides rent by snags, and the pilothouse damaged in a windstorm. Nevertheless,

> On the last Sunday of October [1842], at twelve o'clock, I was kneeling at the foot of St. Mary's Altar in the Cathedral offering up my thanksgiving to God for the signal protection he had extended to his poor, unworthy servant. From the beginning of April I had traveled 5,000 miles. I had descended and ascended the dangerous Columbia River. I had seen five of my companions perish in one of those life-destroying whirlpools, so justly dreaded by those who navigate that stream. I had traversed the Willamette, crossed the Rocky Mountains, passed through the country of the Blackfeet, the desert of the Yellowstone, and descended the Missouri; and in all these journeys I had not received the slightest injury.

CHAPTER 3

De Smet's Greatest Adventure: The Third Trip to the Rocky Mountains, 1843–1846

"ALL our Fathers burn with the desire to accompany him thither next spring," Father Verhaegen informed Father General Roothaan after De Smet's return from the Oregon country. "The details he has given us about the Indians of the far away regions which have become the theater of his apostolic labors have filled our hearts with the sweetest consolations." But supporting a mission in the far-off Pacific Northwest would involve a serious commitment by the Missouri Jesuits, and Verhaegen made it clear to De Smet that at the moment he could spare only Fathers Peter De Vos, S.J., and Adrian Hoecken, S.J., plus Brother James B. MacGean, S.J., as reinforcements for Saint Mary's Mission.

Assigning men to the missions was something Verhaegen could do; providing the necessary funds for De Smet's projected chain of Rocky Mountain Mission reductions was something he could not do. De Smet therefore took that obligation for himself. He began by assembling some of the letters from his recent journey to the far western frontier. Experience told him that he would need to promote the missions before he could beg for them. In the tradition of explorers everywhere, De Smet disciplined himself to write an account of the day's events each evening, then during extended stays at rendezvous or forts or on long steamboat trips he transferred the accumulated notes into letters. It would be a relatively easy task for him to recopy a packet of letters and direct them to a publisher.

With the assistance of Father Verhaegen, whose command of

the English language exceeded his own, De Smet edited fifteen letters and sent them to a Philadelphia publisher, who issued them under the title *Letters and Sketches with a Narrative of a Year's Residence among the Indian Tribes of the Rocky Mountains*. Part one of the 252-page volume recapped the journey of 1840 in two letters; the second part detailed De Smet's experiences during 1841 and 1842 with epistles datelined from such exotic locations as the banks of the Platte River, Fort Hall, Big Face's camp, Hell Gate, Saint Mary's Mission, and Fort Vancouver. Sixteen pen-and-ink sketches by Father Point provided illustrations. The first edition of this book also contained a pull-out copy of De Smet's "ladder," a vertical-shaped visual device he used to explain to natives the progression of Christianity from Adam and Eve to the present. Catholic priests everywhere, it is said, eagerly acquired copies of *Letters and Sketches,* though not for its carefully measured prose—they wanted the ladder to use in their own work.

Now suitably armed with something he could present as a gift in return for a generous donation or, if need be, sell to the curious, De Smet embarked on a begging tour that began in New Orleans and continued on to Boston, Louisville, Cincinnati, Pittsburgh, Baltimore, Washington, Philadelphia, and New York City. Everywhere church groups received the missionary with enthusiasm, and before long he had five thousand dollars in his pocket for his Rocky Mountain Mission fund. These funds enabled De Smet to purchase needed supplies for the mission and also to outfit De Vos, Hoecken, and MacGean for a wagon train bound from Westport, Missouri, to the Oregon country. Two notable figures in the political formation of the Oregon Territory, Jesse Applegate and Peter H. Burnett, also registered for the same wagon train, as did Dr. Marcus Whitman, a Protestant missionary. De Smet excused himself from this trip; he needed to go to Europe to confer with the pope about the ecclesiastical status of the Oregon country.

De Smet's intentions in the Oregon country were, by this time, well known in Protestant missionary circles. Fearing a Catholic buildup in the previously Protestant domain of Oregon,

Dr. Whitman informed a friend that "two papal priests and their lay-helpers are along, and De Smet has gone back in order to go to Europe and bring others by ship." Several days later, Whitman advised another correspondent: "I want you to get Dr. Smith's [De Smet's] Indian Sketches [*Letters and Sketches*]. It can be found at the Catholic book Store. You will see what way the Society of Jesus do their missionary work and what we have to contend with in Oregon."

Dr. Whitman, like other Protestants, deeply resented what seemed to him a cavalier attitude toward baptism by the Catholic clergy. Protestants reserved baptism for persons who satisfactorily completed a conversion experience, often demanding the ability to read chapter and verse from the Bible. Catholics, by contrast, sought only an expression of good intentions from candidates and a minimum of instruction in the faith. Thus, while De Smet baptized hundreds of Indians in a matter of months, Jason and Daniel Lee, both ordained Methodist ministers, could not point to the conversion of even a single Indian in the Oregon country between 1834 and 1840. Dr. Whitman did only slightly better himself in five years at his mission in the Walla Walla Valley. It also bothered Protestants that Catholic priests had no family responsibilities and thus moved about freely among the Indians.

De Smet never learned of Whitman's uncharitable comment, but, it should be noted, he himself showed little patience with Protestant missionaries and exhibited toward them the same feelings of distrust and disrespect. De Smet admired no Protestant clergyman and often said so in private. He considered Protestant missionaries little more than charlatans, clever opportunists, or fanatics, and he derided them for the "millions of dollars" they spent on the Indians. In reality, he said, "all this money goes to enrich the missionaries with their wives and children, who always accompany them." On the trail De Smet would purposely detour around a Protestant mission.

The outpouring of interest in the Rocky Mountain Mission that De Smet received in Belgium and Holland, his destination immediately after seeing De Vos and the others off to the Oregon country, quite amazed him. His letters to Jesuit benefactors in northern Europe, particularly those recounting his adventures among the Flatheads and Crows, earned for De Smet a certain celebrity status, and with that came benefits. Prominent families vied for his attention at social gatherings and competed with each other to present him with the largest gift of money. Anxious to cultivate a growing list of charitable donors, yet having nothing suitable to give in return save a book written in English, De Smet arranged for a French edition of *Letters and Sketches* to be published at Malines for his European benefactors. So numerous were the demands on his schedule that he scarcely found the time to interrupt his begging tour and confer with Father General Roothaan and Pope Gregory XVI in Rome.

True to his arrangement with Father Blanchet, De Smet asked Roothaan to assign more Jesuits to the Oregon missions. The father general saw in De Smet's work a great opportunity to extend Christianity to New World natives, so he approved the missionary's request, even allowing him to solicit men from the Jesuit houses in Rome, Naples, Lyons, Spain, and Germany. Convincing the pope to designate a bishop for the Oregon country involved greater persuasion.

De Smet began his audience with Pope Gregory XVI by describing the diversity of tribal cultures and languages contained in the land between the Pacific Ocean and the Rocky Mountains. A growing number of whites also inhabited the region, he reported, and inevitably more would come. Politically the Oregon country operated under a unique joint occupation agreement between Great Britain and the United States. These two nations also furnished priests for the Oregon country: Blanchet and Demers came from Quebec, and the Jesuits came from Missouri. The French-Canadian priests sought to strengthen the faith of whites in the Willamette Valley, while the Jesuits worked among the Indians of the interior. The Oregon country needed a bishop, De Smet pleaded—someone to coordinate this flurry of ecclesiastical activity. Moreover, the Fifth Baltimore Council of American bishops, meeting in May 1843, endorsed the idea of a bishop for Oregon. De Smet did not say, though the pope already knew,

DE SMET'S GREATEST ADVENTURE   67

that the American bishops placed his name at the top of their list of candidates. He vigorously denied any personal interest in administrative positions beyond that of superior of the Rocky Mountain Mission. De Smet intended to remain an Indian missionary, and in this declaration he received the support of Father General Roothaan. The pope weighed these many factors and on December 11, 1843, agreed to form a separate Oregon apostolic vicariate under the authority of Father Blanchet. This pleased De Smet very much, for now he could continue to administer his Rocky Mountain Mission unrestrained by hierarchical responsibility.

After leaving Rome, De Smet spent the next several weeks working his way through France, Belgium, and Holland begging and recruiting. Benefactors continued to respond eagerly and generously to De Smet's sincere plea for financial support for the Oregon country Indian missions. So deftly did he open the pocketbooks of Europe that when he left Antwerp in December 1843 he carried with him a bank credit for more than 145,000 francs ($26,500), a princely sum for the times. In addition, eight Jesuit volunteers answered De Smet's call to be an American missionary. De Smet placed three of them on a ship bound for New York City but took the other five with him directly to Fort Vancouver. De Smet also persuaded six Sisters of Notre Dame du Namur to establish a convent and school in the Oregon country, and they, too, joined his traveling party.

Inasmuch as his authority now extended over a dozen persons and several tons of supplies, De Smet decided it would be more economical to charter a ship directly to Fort Vancouver than to break the voyage at New York, Saint Louis, Westport, and Green River. Besides, an extended sea voyage, even across two oceans, would be less strenuous than the rigors of an overland journey, especially for the religious women. The captain of the brig *Infatigable* agreed to make the voyage for eighteen thousand francs (thirty-three hundred dollars) as long as he could take along additional paying passengers and supplies; De Smet agreed to both terms.

The *Infatigable* surged into the billowing, stormy North Sea, wrote De Smet, "like a spirited steed released after being long

held in check." The ship shuddered, pitched, and rolled so con-
tinuously that before long De Smet's entire cadre lay incapaci-
tated with seasickness. De Smet likened one of his priests to
a green parrot, "clawing at benches, chairs, and the shoulders
of passengers" as he made his way to the upper deck where he
could, with relief, pay his tribute to King Neptune. The Atlantic
Ocean, like the North Sea, remained tempestuous all the way to
Cape Horn, the most southerly tip of South America, much to
the regret of De Smet and his landlubber associates.

Foul weather continued even when the ship passed into the
currents of the Pacific Ocean. For days on end gale-force winds
pushed against the vessel with mast-bending force, severely test-
ing the skill of the captain, the courage of the passengers, and the
obedience of the crew. "The waves rose in pyramids around us,
and masses of water torn off by the fury of the wind were hurled
upon us in floods and filled the deck with foam," De Smet
recorded in his journal; "The peril was great." As an afterthought he commented: "A tempest is truly a sublime spectacle:
the description is infinitely more agreeable than the reality. If
there had been less of the frightful about it, probably I should
have enjoyed it more." Happily, the danger diminished as the
ship proceeded up the coast of South America, and during the
first weeks of April the captain even permitted landings in Chile
and Peru. After Lima, however, the captain set a course directly
for the Columbia River, a destination he reached on July 28.

Sighting the Oregon Coast after seven long months at sea
greatly cheered the passengers. Within a short time, however, all
joy on board the *Infatigable* turned to despair. In order to enter
the estuary of the Columbia River the ship would have to pass
over the churning tides of the Columbia River bar, "the seven-
fanged horror of the Pacific," as some mariners called it, and the
captain of the *Infatigable* now confessed that he had been unable
to obtain a chart of the Columbia River before his departure
from Antwerp. He therefore knew nothing specific about the en-
trance to the river. The sailors on board knew by heart the names
of ships that had wrecked on the treacherous bar at the mouth
of the river, not the least being the *Peacock*, Captain Charles

Wilkes's flagship for the United States Exploring Expedition. After the *Peacock* ran aground in July 1841, Wilkes surveyed the entire length of the bar in another ship, reporting depths as shallow as twenty-five feet on one end and as deep as seventy-eight feet on the other. Without a chart, the captain of the *Infatigable* did not know which end of the bar to skirt, north or south, in order to reach the estuary.

After studying the rocky shoreline from a distance, the captain steered his vessel out to the open sea to spend the night. That evening De Smet paced the deck alone praying the rosary. Several times he stopped and peered across the open water to Cape Disappointment, wondering about the wisps of smoke he saw arising from campfires on shore. "This sight filled my soul with indescribable emotions," he mused in a moment of deep introspection; "It would be necessary to be placed in the same position, to understand fully what were then our feelings. Our hearts palpitated with joy as we gazed on those boundless regions, over which were scattered so many abandoned souls—the young, the aged—dying in the shades of infidelity, for want of missionaries; an evil which we were about to alleviate, if not for all, at least for a great number."

About ten o'clock the next morning the captain decided to approach the bar. Enormous breakers made him rethink the idea. About that time several passengers on the middle decks observed a demonstration on the distant northern shore; it appeared to be several men firing rifles. This alarmed the crew, and the captain, too, so he tacked about and spent the night in the less threatening open sea. On the morning of the third day the captain brought the *Infatigable* around again, this time hoping to estimate the depth of the water across the bar by calculating the velocity of the breakers. The captain himself took station at the topmast, but regrettably he could see nothing upon which a sound judgment could be made. "But just then, when everything seemed desperate," De Smet recalled, "a ship was espied in the distance, in Baker's Bay, making toward Cape Disappointment, and hope sprang up again at once in all hearts. 'Let us see how they come out, then we can go in by the same way,' was the unanimous expression." For an hour the possibility seemed real, as the captain followed the ketch with his spyglass. Then the vessel suddenly dropped out of sight. Next the captain sent the ship's second officer and four volunteers to reconnoiter the mouth of the river in a small boat. The bobbing craft disappeared as it approached the bar and did not return to ship that night.

July 31, Saint Ignatius' feast day in the calendar of the Society of Jesus, dawned bright and clear on a calm ocean. Twenty-one years earlier De Smet, then a mere scholastic, had celebrated the feast day of his society's founder by ceremoniously scooping a spade full of dirt from the foundation of Saint Stanislaus novitiate in Florissant; this day he and his fellow priests prayed five Masses, asking their patron to grant them safe passage across the Columbia River bar. After Mass most everyone scanned the waves looking for the dory carrying the second officer. When it finally appeared in the distance, "Our hearts beat hard: all were divided between hope and fear," De Smet confided; "All awaited uneasily the word which was about to decide our fate." The mate reported that close to midnight he had found the passage; it seemed to have at least five fathoms of water and no other obstacles. The captain needed only a moment to digest the news before deciding to make a run at crossing the bar. He knew that sometimes ships sat off the Columbia River for a month waiting for a suitable opportunity to cross, and this might be his best opportunity.

Taking command of the tiller, the captain unfurled all the sails and piloted the *Infatigable* directly toward the vortex of crashing waves. A serious attitude gripped the crew and passengers on the swaying ship, most of whom stationed themselves at the rail of the forward deck; the sisters, however, retired below to pray. As the *Infatigable* lurched forward to the point of no return, the waves crashing on the reef parted to reveal two clear channels in the brownish green water, one veering to the north, toward Cape Disappointment, and the other easing toward the opposite shoreline in the direction of Clatsop Spit. The captain instructed his navigator to set a course for the southern shore.

De Smet remembered the next few moments in intimate detail

for the rest of his life. A sailor tied himself to the outside of the vessel and began to count the depth of the water by casting a lead weight at the end of a line.

> The sounders had several times reported seven fathoms—soon six fathoms was heard—after that five then four and one half—presently four, and so it went, always growing less. Each cry was a shock that oppressed our hearts, and at the repeated cry of three fathoms all countenances were visibly discomposed, for that was the vessel's minimum draft; several of us thought that it was all over, that the ship was about to strike. . . . Soon the cry of four fathoms caused something of a revival of joy. But of the five miles of the bar we had as yet made only three. Suddenly a cry of "three fathoms" plunged us again into consternation—at the cry of two and one-half fathoms I felt, as it were, annihilated. I expected to see the anchor let go, and then a mad scramble for the boats.

But neither the anchor nor the lifeboats let go from the *Infatigable*, and the captain held his course. The next cast of the lead showed four fathoms, then five, and from that moment on the depth of the water beneath the *Infatigable* increased at every plunge until the cry of "no bottom" allayed all fears on board. Steadily the ship made its way into the wide, protected estuary of the Columbia River and set its anchor in Youngs Bay.

Later that afternoon, while the passengers and crew celebrated their triumph, a canoe carrying a dozen Clatsop Indians and a white man pulled alongside the *Infatigable* and requested permission to come on board. Using sign language, the Indians told the ship's officers that no previous ship had crossed the bar using the uncharted southern channel. James Birnie, superintendent of the Hudson's Bay Company post at Astoria, clarified the matter. When the Indians alerted him to the presence of a ship offshore, he said, he crossed the estuary to Cape Disappointment and attempted to illuminate the proper side by using fires, flags, and guns. Apparently, however, the *Infatigable* chose to ignore his advice. To the contrary, De Smet hastened to explain, "We had indeed observed all these signals, but seafaring makes people suspicious; it was feared that it was some ambush of the Indians, desirous of capturing the vessel," and therefore the captain favored the southern side. The captain believed luck carried his ship across the untested side of the Columbia River bar; De Smet believed that Saint Ignatius guided the ship to the estuary with divine power.

In the evening Superintendent Birnie returned to the *Infatigable* with fresh salmon and potatoes for the new arrivals. A band of Chinook Indians came along, but they provided only inquisitorial stares. De Smet's companions, seeing Indians up close for the first time, remarked at the natives' poor clothes, unkempt appearance, long hair, and sullen manner. De Smet hastened to explain that these tribesmen were not the same as his Rocky Mountain neophytes; Columbia River Chinooks, he remarked, tended to be lazy "because of the great ease with which they can procure fish and game. They live from day to day, and spend the greater part of the daytime stretched motionless in the sun." In time, he promised, the new Jesuits and the nuns would learn the idiosyncrasies of many tribes, not just these.

While the captain of the *Infatigable* negotiated for the services of a river pilot to take him through the maze of islands scattered across the lower Columbia River, De Smet set out for Fort Vancouver, a distance of approximately one hundred miles, in a canoe. Favored by a good wind and nine strong Indians at the paddles, De Smet reached his destination on the evening of the second day. Dr. McLoughlin, James Douglas, and the post physician, Dr. Forbes Barclay, greeted their priest friend warmly, secured him a place to stay, and dispatched a messenger to Saint Paul's Mission to inform Father Blanchet.

With his guest's comfort assured, Dr. McLoughlin sat down to report the good news he had of the interior missions. During De Smet's absence Fathers De Vos and Hoecken had arrived safely at Saint Mary's Mission from Saint Louis. De Vos now lived with the Kalispels while Father Point remained with the Coeur d'Alenes, and both missions appeared to be successful. McLoughlin also proudly announced that a year earlier he had openly professed his Catholicism, a decision that the bigoted element at Fort Vancouver subsequently used to explain his paternal attitude toward the Jesuit missions. True, McLoughlin discounted supplies to De Smet's missions as much as 50 percent, and he frequently provided free transportation on Hudson's Bay Company barges, but so, too, did the chief factors at Forts Walla Walla, Colville, and Hall. They did so not because they were sympathetic toward Catholics, but because London's policy courted the favor of all missionaries; assisting them helped business. De Smet added his own good news to the discussion, stating that as soon as the *Infatigable* reached Fort Vancouver, the Sisters of Notre Dame would establish a school in the Willamette Valley.

For eight glorious days after the *Infatigable* docked at Fort Vancouver, the Jesuits and the sisters basked in the effusive hospitality of Dr. and Mrs. McLoughlin. Even so, they willingly detached themselves from the comforts of the post when Father Blanchet arrived to guide them up the Willamette Valley, for they were anxious to set up housekeeping on property of their own. As they proceeded up the Willamette, Father Blanchet described for the sisters their nearly complete convent. He had built it approximately two miles from Saint Paul's Mission. The location for the Jesuit mission in the Willamette Valley, he said, waited for Father De Smet's approval.

Blanchet suggested that De Smet should consider the abandoned Methodist mission built a decade earlier by Jason and Daniel Lee. Rumor had it that the Methodists had spent a quarter of a million dollars on the property and improvements. But De Smet rejected the Methodist site after seeing it and decided on another location on a bend of the Willamette River nearer to Oregon City. De Smet preferred land crowded with large, healthy trees, a sign to him of rich soil and therefore of bountiful future harvests when the land was cleared and put into production with fruit trees and produce. Moreover, he saw no reason to purchase land from others, especially Methodists, when the rules governing land titles in Oregon changed with each revision of the governmental charters currently being debated by the American settlers in the Willamette Valley.

Under De Smet's direction workmen erected a fifteen-room, two-story house, three shops, and several other buildings. He named the complex Saint Francis Xavier Mission and intended

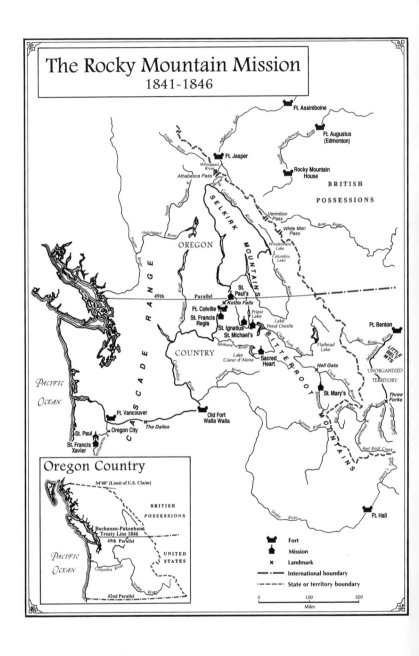

The Rocky Mountain Mission
1841~1846

Ft. Assiniboine

Ft. Augustus
(Edmonton)

Fraser River

Athabasca River

Saskatchewan River

Ft. Jasper

Whirlpool River

Athabasca Pass

Rocky Mountain House

BRITISH

POSSESSIONS

North Thompson R.

Wood R.

Columbia River

Vermilion Pass

White Man Pass

Bow River

Thompson River

OREGON

SELKIRK MOUNTAINS

Windermere Lake

Columbia Lake

Fraser River

Okanagan River

49th   Parallel

St. Paul's

Kettle Falls

Ft. Colville

St. Francis Regis

St. Ignatius

St. Michael's

Priest Lake

Lake Pend Oreille

Kootenay River

Clark Fork River

Flathead Lake

Ft. Benton

Sun River

LITTLE BELT MTS

CASCADE RANGE

COUNTRY

Spokane River

Lake Coeur d'Alene

Sacred Heart

Palouse River

Columbia River

BITTERROOT

Clark River

Hell Gate

UNORGANIZED TERRITORY

Missouri River

PACIFIC

OCEAN

St. Mary's

Three Forks

Ft. Vancouver

Old Fort Walla Walla

The Dalles

Salmon River

Big Hole Fork River

Beaverhead R.

Madison R.

Jefferson R.

Gallatin R.

St. Paul

St. Francis Xavier

Oregon City

Willamette R.

Red Rock Creek

Henry's Fork

Snake River

Ft. Hall

Oregon Country

54'40' (Limit of U.S. Claim)

BRITISH POSSESSIONS

Buchanan-Pakenham Treaty Line 1846

49th Parallel

PACIFIC

OCEAN

Columbia River

UNITED STATES

Snake River

42nd Parallel

Fort	
Mission	
×	Landmark
	International boundary
	State or territory boundary

0   100   200

Miles

for it to become the chief supply station, or "mother" mission, for the Jesuits in the Oregon country. Saint Mary's Mission in the Bitterroots, however, would continue to be the administrative headquarters for the reductions.

With the building program well on its way, De Smet readied himself to visit the interior missions. He was, after all, still the superior of the Rocky Mountain Mission of the Society of Jesus. First he sent a message to Saint Mary's Mission in the Bitterroots asking Father Mengarini to come to the Willamette and assist him in transporting the supplies he had brought from Europe to the interior missions. Second, he ordered Father De Vos, the acting superior of the Rocky Mountain Mission during De Smet's absence, to leave the Kalispel mission and take up permanent residence at Saint Francis Xavier in the Willamette.

Mengarini reached the Willamette mission first, three weeks after receiving the call. De Smet, meantime, fell ill from the "bloody flux," a contagious, flulike ailment that periodically swept up the Columbia River and the Willamette Valley. In 1844 hundreds of Indians died, and countless other persons were immobilized by the infection. Among the Catholic clergy, "three of the Sisters, were attacked by the pestilence; Reverend Father Accolti also experienced its terrible effects; for myself, I was obliged to keep my bed during fifteen long days, and to observe a rigorous diet." When the illness ran its course De Smet decided not to wait for De Vos to arrive at Saint Francis Xavier, because snow could close the mountain passes to Saint Mary's any day. He and Father Mengarini left Saint Francis Xavier on October 3, 1844. Fortunately, just as De Smet and Mengarini reached Fort Vancouver, an eight-oar Hudson's Bay Company barge prepared to leave for the interior. Dr. McLoughlin generously secured places for the priests and their baggage on board. In the few hours he had to spare at Fort Vancouver, De Smet hired Peter Biledot, a Canadian mechanic, to come along and install the grindstones De Smet had brought all the way from Belgium so that Saint Mary's Mission would have a flour mill.

It required several portages to bypass the five major chutes and falls on the Columbia River between Fort Vancouver and Fort

Walla Walla, and at one of those stops De Smet chanced to meet Father De Vos and Brother MacGean, who were on their way to Saint Francis Xavier. De Vos had come from Saint Mary's by way of the Kalispel village, where, together with Father Hoecken, he had laid out the site for the society's third reduction, Saint Michael's Mission. De Smet and De Vos, whose friendship extended back to youthful days in Belgium, spoke frankly about many things, including a dossier detailing grievances against Father Point. De Vos intended on forwarding the package to Saint Louis and Rome, but De Smet, using his authority as superior of the Rocky Mountain Mission, confiscated the documents and refused to return them.

There were, in fact, several loose ends for De Smet to investigate as he learned, little by little, the chaotic state of the Rocky Mountain Mission during his sojourn in Europe. When De Smet had put De Vos, Father Adrian Hoecken, and Brother MacGean on the wagon train at Westport in September 1843, he had placed De Vos in temporary charge of the Rocky Mountain Mission. It was, in retrospect, the wrong thing to do. Only now did De Smet realize the impact of this decision. Father Point, De Smet neglected to recognize, had clashed with Father De Vos several years earlier at the Jesuit college at Grand Coteau, Louisiana, a rupture so serious that it had resulted in Point's reassignment to the Rocky Mountain Mission. As if to add fuel to an already smoldering relationship, Father Verhaegen, the superior of the Missouri Vice-Province, told De Vos on the day before he left for Westport that "it would be good to seize and destroy the papers of Father Point which could compromise the society, if ever they fell into the hands of the public." The papers in question, apparently, had to do with some racial attitudes that offended Point during his tenure at Grand Coteau, and he refused to lay the matter to rest. De Smet, for example, noticed on the overland journey to the Rocky Mountains that Point occupied much of his time drafting formal letters to Father General Roothaan complaining about the Louisiana situation. De Smet disapproved of such acrimony, and, in an effort to encourage Point to make better use of his time, he appointed him the official Jesuit diarist for the journey. For a long period afterward Point said nothing more about the Grand Coteau affair.

Once settled in at Saint Mary's, Point became immersed in the round-the-clock responsibilities of establishing a reduction and warmed to his new life as an Indian missionary. Point genuinely loved the natives, of that there is no question, and to all appearances he seemed happy among the Flatheads. But he was not so with the Coeur d'Alenes. Point would have preferred to approach the Blackfeet, if he had to move from the Flatheads at all, so in July 1842 when De Smet ordered him to open a mission for the Coeur d'Alenes, he resented it. De Smet had promised the Coeur d'Alenes a mission, but Point wondered why he had to be the one to fulfill the pledge. Before De Smet left for Saint Louis, Point asked him to carry a letter addressed to Father Roothaan. De Smet presumed that the document belabored Point's grievances on the Grand Coteau affair yet again, but he accepted the letter anyway.

While De Smet conducted his business in Saint Louis and Europe, Point, Mengarini, and the Jesuit brothers struggled at two locations to satisfy the increasing demands of the Flatheads and the Coeur d'Alenes for priestly comfort and assistance. Point and Huet took station among the Coeur d'Alenes as ordered, selecting a site in November 1842 on the Spokane River, about a mile from the northern end of Lake Coeur d'Alene, for the second Rocky Mountain Mission reduction. Almost from the first, unfortunately, a chief named Stellam vexed Point because the chief felt threatened by the spiritual power of the Jesuits. Little by little, however, Point made progress. He sincerely believed that the Coeur d'Alene mission would be fully operational by the time De Smet returned in another year with needed supplies, tools, and additional men. But De Smet did not appear; De Vos did.

Much to Point's annoyance, De Vos ruled the Rocky Mountain Mission in De Smet's absence with a heavy administrative hand. Point did not take it kindly, for example, when De Vos, on his first visit to the Coeur d'Alene Mission of the Sacred Heart, relocated and renamed the mission. De Vos decreed that Sacred

Heart Mission should be repositioned at the southern end of
Lake Coeur d'Alene, about a mile up the Saint Joe River, and
henceforth it would be known as Saint Joseph Mission. Then he
reassigned Point, ordering him to accompany the Flatheads on
their fall buffalo hunt—not a choice assignment for a warm-
blooded Frenchman—an action the veteran priest greeted with
contempt. Father Joset later wrote that this "affected him [Point]
so much that his head seemed some deranged on that point, and
which at intervals, made his conversation very painful to his
Brother [Jesuits]." Even more offensive to Point was De Vos's
success in assembling a cache of Point's personal letters, material
which De Vos apparently thought subversive; the senior priest
placed them in a sealed envelope for Father Verhaegen in Saint
Louis. Such an invasion of privacy may have been odious, but it
was, nevertheless, implicit in the vow of obedience taken by
members of the Society of Jesus.

De Smet concluded his consultation with De Vos by promising
to examine the Point affair. De Vos doubted that; he felt that De
Smet would probably disregard the dossier on Point and never
make a formal inquiry. Miffed by De Smet's insensitivity to what
De Vos considered a crucial matter for the society, shortly after
the two men parted De Vos wrote a letter to Father General
Roothaan criticizing De Smet. In his opinion De Smet showed
more interest in establishing a chain of reductions—building
more buildings—than he did in mediating sensitive personnel
matters for the society. De Smet loved to start missions, but he
seldom remained in them long. He sought glamour by planning,
establishing, and publicizing the Indian missions.

De Smet and Mengarini, in the meantime, had resumed their
journey. When they reached Fort Walla Walla they transferred
their supplies from the barges to a string of twenty horses and
mules purchased for the duty. They also bought a few head of
cattle and hired two men to guide them across the Spokane
Desert to Fort Colville; from there De Smet would know his way
across the mountains to the Kalispel village on the Pend Oreille
River and, ultimately, Saint Mary's Mission. By coincidence, yet
another Jesuit traveler, Father Tiberio Soderini, S.J., one of five

priests who had left Westport in the spring of 1844 bound for
Saint Mary's Mission, temporarily resided at Fort Walla Walla.
Soderini, it seems, had become so disillusioned with his fellow
Jesuits during the march west that when he reached Fort Hall he
decided to leave the society altogether and become, instead, a
secular priest under the authority of Father Blanchet. De Smet
persuaded Soderini to postpone his final decision and, while he
prayed for guidance, to accompany him to Saint Michael's Mission, the new Kalispel reduction.

Although mid-October is a time of changing seasons in the
Pacific Northwest, warm weather blessed De Smet and his entourage all along the well-worn Colville Road that stretched several hundred miles almost due north from Fort Walla Walla. Just
short of Fort Colville, De Smet's entourage encountered a pack
train of seventeen horses going to the Pend Oreille River by way
of the pass near Calispel Mountain, so he released his guides and
attached himself to the newcomers. Meanwhile, Father Hoecken
learned of De Smet's approach from other travelers, so he went
to the eastern slope of Calispel Mountain and escorted his fellow Jesuits the rest of the way to Saint Michael's Mission, near
present-day Albeni Falls, Idaho.

De Smet's appearance at the main camp of Kalispels occa-
sioned a great celebration as the natives fired guns and sounded
trumpets. Flustered as much as flattered by the welcome, De
Smet promised to pass a few days with the Indians; Father Mengarini and the mechanic Biledot, meantime, continued on to
Saint Mary's with the bulk of the mission's supplies. Father Soderini, at De Smet's insistence, agreed to remain at Saint Michael's to assist Father Hoecken.

De Smet so enjoyed his brief rest at Saint Michael's Mission
that he permitted himself yet another diversion when three Coeur d'Alene emissaries implored him to come with them to see
their new mission named for Saint Joseph. Not wishing to reject
such a sincere request, and deciding that the Coeur d'Alenes
could use the cattle in his possession, De Smet agreed to go even
though the season for winter storms fast approached. A visit to
the Coeur d'Alenes, De Smet decided, would also afford him an

opportunity to confer privately with Father Point, who had returned to the Coeur d'Alenes after the Flatheads' fall hunt.

Before long De Smet regretted his decision to test fate by hurrying to the Coeur d'Alene mission. He was barely out of sight of the Kalispel mission when ominous reddish clouds drenched him with rain. The temperature suddenly dipped, snow followed, and the trail iced over. On the third day out, just as De Smet reached the summit of a mountain, a blizzard struck, and for the rest of the way to the mission "the snow that fell off the branches inconvenienced us greatly, and our horses slid and stumbled at almost every step on the narrow winding path."

If trouble had divided Stellam and Father Point at Saint Joseph's Mission in 1843, no enmity existed when De Smet arrived in November 1844. The mission seemed so harmonious, so religiously rigorous, that De Smet could only congratulate Father Point on his accomplishments. Point had, for example, prepared a large number of children and adults to receive their first communion, a ceremony in which De Smet enthusiastically took part. In fact, about the only aspect of the mission De Smet wished to change was to rededicate it back to the Sacred Heart, a desire no doubt prompted by the oil painting of the Sacred Heart of Jesus he brought all the way from Europe to present to the tribe.

In addition to instructing children and adults in Christian doctrine, De Smet set aside time to discuss personal matters with Father Point. Actually, Point seized the opportunity first by stating his grievance against De Vos and, to a lesser degree, Mengarini. De Smet already knew the story—he heard it from De Vos—so what Point said did not particularly disturb him. What did upset him was Point's shocking revelation that he no longer believed in, nor would he defend, the reduction system as a suitable model for the Rocky Mountain Mission.

The Flatheads and Coeur d'Alenes, and probably even the Kalispels, Point declared, already exhibited too much dependence on white men—especially the chief factors at Forts Walla Walla and Colville—to ever become authentic reductions. In addition, the food cycle for interior Northwest tribes revolved with the seasons of the year; thus, the Indians seemed to be away from the mission as often as living in it. As a veteran of several Flathead buffalo hunts, Point knew from firsthand experience that when a tribe left the mission and returned to the forest or plains, it placed its Catholic beliefs at risk. At such times the tribesmen returned to their primitive, pagan life-style. A true reduction, in Point's judgment, might be possible for only one Rocky Mountain tribe, the Blackfeet. Their warlike nature had thus far kept whites at arm's length, and they were, therefore, the least corrupted of all the Pacific Northwest tribes.

De Smet recalled Point's previous recommendations, in 1842, regarding a reduction for the Blackfeet. His arguments made sense, and if not for the constraints of frontier travel and his commitments to other tribes, he would have followed up on them long ago. Point's defection from the reduction concept disturbed De Smet. From De Smet's perspective, the reductions provided the single unifying theme for the twenty-one Jesuits now in the Oregon country. Father General Roothaan personally supported his efforts to further that system among the Flatheads and other tribes. De Smet knew Point's penchant for writing letters directly to the father general, and he certainly did not want him calling attention to any internal problems in the Rocky Mountain Mission. The less said about Father Point, the better, De Smet decided, so, after their conversation, he simply suppressed the contents of De Vos's dossier on Point. It never surfaced again.

Turning to other, more pleasant, matters, De Smet completed several maps he was preparing on the inland Northwest river system. Not surprisingly, De Smet tended to name rivers according to the church's calendar of saints, with a special preference toward Jesuit martyrs. He called the two streams at the bottom of Lake Coeur d'Alene the Saint Ignatius and the Saint Joseph. "They in turn are formed by a great number of branches, the four principal of which are known today by the names of the four Evangelists; and the various mountain streams which form these last bear the names of all the Catholic hierarchy of the United States. I have moreover counted forty-eight little lakes, lying at

the base of the mountains, which are named after venerables of
the Society of Jesus." Similarly, De Smet named the rivers around
Saint Mary's Mission for Saint Francis Xavier, Saint Francis Bor-
gia, Saint Aloysius, and, of course, Saint Ignatius. For European
editions of his maps only, De Smet also included the names of
contemporary Jesuits such as Hoecken, Point, Joset, Claessens,
and Specht. In French editions of his books he liked to name
lakes after family members: Gustave, Sylvie, Elmire, Rosalie, Clem-
ence, and so on. Benefactors to the missions might likewise be
honored, as in Lake De Nef and Lake De Boey. Interestingly,
in spite of the pride with which he labeled watercourses, few of
De Smet's place-names survived his lifetime as a missionary, and
his unpublished maps, with only a few exceptions, seldom reached
the hands of non-Jesuits.

De Smet and four guides left the Coeur d'Alene mission bound
for Saint Mary's on November 19, 1844, in the midst of a persistent winter storm that had not yet blown itself out in spite of four
days of constant rain and snow. Proceeding up the slushy Saint
Joe River on slippery trails took considerably more time than
usual. Imagine then De Smet's anguish when, just as he and his
party reached the imposing mountains at the end of the valley,
two Nez Percés emerged from the snow-white forest. They provided "a most terrifying description of the state of the trail," De
Smet noted in his journal; "In view, therefore, of the unremitting
snowfall, we concluded that the passage was at present impracticable and impossible; moreover, the waters were now coming
down from the mountains so fast and in such volume, that we
thought of nothing but returning in haste."

But reversing direction held dangers, too. Little brooks the day
before suddenly became swollen torrents; the Saint Joe River had
already risen an estimated ten feet above normal. Time and again
the priest and his guides swam across the river, dodging free-
floating stumps and logs as they went. "Once I found myself
under water," De Smet writes of a brush with death, "but I held
fast to my beast, which dragged me to the farther shore." That
night the river continued to rise until, about midnight, one of
the Indians awoke the camp with warning shouts. Horses and

mules instinctively bolted up the mountainside, but De Smet reacted slower than they and barely had time to locate his shoes and cassock before knee-high water breached his tent and threatened to suck him down the valley. "But here, as in a hundred other places," De Smet informed his family, "Providence had furnished us a means of escape; there were two infirm little canoes of bark at the precise spot where we had encamped, and by their means we were enabled to take refuge, with arms and baggage, though all soaked, upon an eminence two miles away." Later, when the immediate danger subsided, one of the Coeur d'Alenes raced to Sacred Heart Mission for help; even so, it took two days before five canoes returned to rescue Black Robe. The Indians, De Smet said, "seemed to rejoice in the mishaps that had brought me to them again, and manifested the same cordiality and gladness with which they had received me the first time."

But De Smet had no intention of tarrying at Sacred Heart. Saint Mary's Mission remained his goal, and to that end he resumed his journey on December 4. He planned to retrace his steps from Sacred Heart back to the Kalispel camp, and from there take the Clark Fork River to the Bitterroot Valley. The route would be longer but easier than scaling mountains in the dead of winter. Regrettably, his plan failed. After he had traveled only four days up the Clark Fork River with a team of Kalispel paddlers, the river became choked with ice. Looking mournfully at the thin bark construction of his canoe, De Smet conceded defeat: "Thus I found myself stopped for the second time, my pilots declared that to advance was to expose ourselves to imminent danger." A Kalispel volunteered to take a message to Father Mengarini at Saint Mary's by snowshoeing across the mountains. De Smet, however, had no option but to return to the Kalispel camp at Albeni Falls and pass the winter at Saint Michael's Mission.

The village at the falls of the Pend Oreille River proved to be an ideal place for wintering, De Smet deeming it "well chosen, picturesque, agreeable and convenient." Thousands of deer came down from the mountains, providing easy prey for the hunters, while "a dense and interminable forest protected us from the north winds, and a countless number of dead trees standing on all sides furnished us with abundant fuel for our fires during the inclement season." In other ways, too, the next several months formed one of De Smet's most memorable experiences as a missionary. Despite cold weather, Indians completed building Saint Michael's Mission chapel in time for a spectacular Midnight Mass celebration on Christmas Day, 1844. A choir of three hundred voices opened the service by singing Christian hymns in their native language; a solemn High Mass, concelebrated by Fathers De Smet, Hoecken, and Soderini, followed. Long lines of Indian adults received baptism for the first time on that sacred day, and De Smet could not help reflect with a great deal of pride that the same rite took place at both Saint Mary's Mission and the Coeur d'Alene Mission of the Sacred Heart. "Here, indeed," De Smet concluded, " the Indian missionary enjoys his courage, his zeal to labor to bring men to the knowledge of the true God, in spite of the poverty, the privations of every description, and the dangers with which he has to contend."

At the beginning of February 1845, De Smet, now joined by Father Hoecken, renewed his attempt to reach Saint Mary's Mission. Upwards of five feet of snow clogged parts of the trail, but even that did not deter him. And when he finally arrived at Saint Mary's, the enthusiastic welcome by the Flatheads made all the travails of sixteen days on the trail seem worthwhile. But he did not mean for this visit to be an extended one. As soon as the Easter holidays passed, De Smet announced his intention to return to the Kalispel village so that he could assist in the relocation of Saint Michael's Mission. The site chosen by Father De Vos near Albeni Falls had its attributes, De Smet did not deny that; still, he preferred an even more isolated site farther up the Pend Oreille River, one where white pioneers would not be so quick to come in contact with the natives.

De Smet chose as the new site of the Kalispel reduction an indentation in the Pend Oreille River appropriately called the Bay of the Kalispels. Wide, lush prairies adjacent to the river seemed ideal for agriculture and settlement, while close-by cedar and pine forests would provide numerous logs for mission buildings. A modest waterfall on the river suggested to De Smet the location of a future sawmill. By chance, De Smet also discovered a small cave in the hillside bordering the prairie, and it inspired him to thoughts of the cavern in Manresa, Spain, where the young Ignatius Loyola once lived for a year. This cinched De Smet's decision; the Bay of the Kalispels would be the site of his newest reduction, and it should commemorate Saint Ignatius Loyola.

After ceremoniously felling the first tree, De Smet embarked on a quick round-trip to Fort Vancouver to buy supplies. He returned to Saint Ignatius Mission in July 1845 leading a string of eleven pack animals laden with plows, spades, pickaxes, scythes, and carpenter's tools. Meanwhile, Hoecken had supervised the erection of fourteen log houses plus a large barn to shelter thirty head of cattle. He also built a fence to surround three hundred acres planted in grain. All of this greatly cheered De Smet, and he resolved to stay even longer at the developing reduction. In the course of his time with the Kalispels, De Smet took several excursions by horse and canoe, stopping whenever he came in contact with an Indian village. As a consequence, De Smet established two new missions, his fourth and fifth in the Oregon country: Saint Francis Regis, below Fort Colville, and Saint Paul, on the bluff overlooking the post.

Now that the interior reductions seemed to be taking shape so nicely, De Smet decided to satisfy a yearning that had been sitting in the recesses of his memory for three long years. As far back as July 1842, Father Point had urged De Smet to let him make contact with the Blackfeet Indians, claiming that their aversion to white men made them an excellent subject for a Paraguayan-style reduction. More importantly, the warlike Blackfeet dominated nearly all of the docile tribes within several hundred miles of their secluded Rocky Mountain homeland, so true conversion of the interior tribes would likely never be achieved until the Blackfeet themselves accepted Christianity. De Smet never denied Point's logic, but in 1842 he had not had the manpower to spare for a Blackfeet mission, even a tentative one. The longer Point's ideas remained in De Smet's mind, the more they intrigued him. He decided to act now.

The chief factor at Fort Colville disagreed with De Smet and attempted to dissuade him from going to see the Blackfeet. So did both Fathers Michael Accolti and John Nobili. Father Nobili, who had come to the Oregon country on the *Infatigable*, knew the disposition of many tribes and thought De Smet's plan foolish. He said so, too, in a hastily written warning to Father General Roothaan. The Blackfeet, Nobili contended, would resent De Smet's intrusion because they believed the Jesuits strengthened the resolve of their enemies by introducing to them a powerful new Master of Life. He had even heard that tribal leaders vowed to kill the first priest they met. De Smet answered, "I am not unaware that my life there will be much in danger," and then he advanced a contrary argument. The Blackfeet would not harm him but cherish him because through him they, too, could learn about the Master of Life. He would go, he said, because he could not contain his "irresistible desire to visit those poor unfortunate savages, plunged as they are in the deepest Indian superstitions."

In the end, Father De Smet, not Father Nobili, correctly gauged the Blackfeet situation. What neither of them foresaw, however, was that the Flatheads would react with anger and disappointment when De Smet, their Black Robe, extended to their traditional foes the spiritual power they believed belonged to them and them alone. For the Jesuits to do such a thing, in their estimation, amounted to a betrayal, the moral equivalent of an arms merchant supplying both sides in a war.

Having made his decision to meet the Blackfeet in their own territory, De Smet wasted little time hurrying northward to the Canadian Rockies. En route up the Clark Fork River on the first leg of his journey, he happened one afternoon upon three men dressed in the tattered garb and slouched hats of beaver hunters. One of the men called across the river to De Smet by name. Curious to know who hailed him, De Smet crossed to the other side, where he found his friend Peter Skene Ogden and two Hudson's Bay Company officers. De Smet and Ogden had not seen each

other since their barge trip on the Columbia River in 1842, and
the meeting elated the priest. "It would be necessary for you to
traverse the desert, to feel yourself insulated, remote from brethren, friends, to conceive the consolation and joy of such an encounter," he explained to his friend Archbishop John Hughes.

The most eagerly awaited news of the day for Hudson's Bay
Company operatives, Ogden reported, concerned the settling
of the Oregon country boundary between Great Britain and
the United States. The United States advocated a division of the
jointly occupied territory at the forty-ninth parallel, but England
refused, in part, Ogden assumed, because the Hudson's Bay Company did not wish to lose Fort Vancouver. In truth, the British
Foreign Office agreed to draw the boundary along the forty-
ninth parallel boundary, but only from the Rocky Mountains to
the Columbia River and from there down that stream to the
ocean, because in doing so they reserved for themselves Puget
Sound, the best commercial harbor north of San Francisco. De
Smet listened attentively, then told Ogden that with his own eyes
he saw vast numbers of Americans arriving daily in the Oregon
country. Most of them, he said, located on lands south of the
Columbia, in the Willamette Valley, but others followed the
Cowlitz River north to Fort Nisqually at the bottom of Puget
Sound. Certainly their numbers would influence the negotiations. Both men wondered aloud if the boundary issue would be
settled peacefully.

And how, De Smet asked, would the Indians fare in these
international negotiations? "The poor Indians of Oregon, who
alone have a right to the country, are not consulted. Their future
destiny will be, undoubtedly, like that of so many other unfortunate tribes who, after having lived peaceably by hunting and
fishing for centuries, will finally disappear, victims of vice and
malady, under the rapacious influence of modern civilization."
Increasingly, De Smet drew closer to the conclusion that only on
reservations could Indians find a safe haven, both in the Pacific
Northwest and elsewhere. He did not yet have a firm structure
for his philosophy, but more and more the plight of the Indians
in political affairs occupied his thoughts.

Wishing that the news they shared could have been less foreboding, but nonetheless pleased at their chance meeting, Ogden
and De Smet parted company the next day. Resuming his route
to the Blackfeet homelands, De Smet's path took him directly
across the rugged Selkirk Mountains of present-day northern
Idaho. Under even the best of conditions Indian trails could be
intimidating, but traveling through this mountainous country
required special qualities of endurance—and trust in one's mount.

> We sometimes traversed undulatory woods of pine and cedar, from
> which the light of day is partially excluded. We next entered somber
> forests, where, axe in hand, we were forced to cut our way and wind
> about to avoid hosts of trees that had been leveled by the autumnal
> blasts and storms. Some of these forests are so dense that at the
> distance of twelve feet, I could not distinguish my guide. The most
> certain way of extricating one's self from these labyrinths is to trust to
> the horse's sagacity, which, if left unguided, will follow the track of
> other animals. This expedient has saved me a hundred times.

Latching onto the Kootenai River, De Smet followed it dutifully, having learned from the Indians that at its bend it flowed
north, in the direction of the Blackfeet. Beyond the forty-ninth
parallel, De Smet entered territory entirely new to him. Finally,
on the fourth of September, approximately forty miles north of
the forty-ninth parallel, De Smet veered away from the Kootenai
and approached Lake Columbia, the recognized source of the
Columbia River. From this reedy lake the Columbia River flows
northward two hundred miles, turns sharply at the "big bend,"
and begins its mighty rush one thousand miles southward to the
Pacific Ocean.

Reaching the source of the Columbia invigorated De Smet.
He had, on several previous occasions, camped at the source of
the Missouri River, and he could not help but wonder how many
men in all of North America, nay in all of the world, could say
that they had touched the fountainhead of both these mighty
streams. At such moments De Smet liked to unsheathe his pen
and jot down his feelings so that he could later share them with
his family. Ordinarily he would send a letter to his brother
Francis in Belgium, who, in turn, made copies for distribution

throughout the family. De Smet paid the Hudson's Bay Company to deliver his mail to Europe, buying the postage out of an annual income he derived from a savings account managed by Francis, essentially an accumulation of interest on money left to him by his father's estate.

Sometimes his letters illuminated the cultural traits of Indians he met along the way. At other times De Smet emphasized the physical beauty of the mountains, rivers, or plains. On this particular excursion into present-day British Columbia, De Smet concentrated on food. Thus he described a meal he and his Indian guides took with a fur trader at Lake Columbia: "The first dish he presented me contained two paws of a bear. A roast porcupine next made its appearance, accompanied by a moose's muzzle, which had been boiling all night. The latter I found delicious. Finally the great kettle, containing a sort of hotch-potch or salmagundi, was placed in the midst of the guests, and each one helped himself according to his taste; there was the choice back-fat of the buffalo-cow, venison, cutlets, beavers' tails, quail, rabbits, dumplings and a substantial broth."

Continuing on, De Smet and his Indian companions drifted away from the Columbia River on September 9, looking to cross the Rocky Mountains by White Man Pass. Beyond that summit the trail went straight to the Bow River, and there, De Smet's guides indicated, he would find the Blackfeet. Unfortunately, their projection proved to be too optimistic. Indeed, the scouts did locate signs of Indian camps, but not of the Blackfeet. At least the camps left tracks for the scouts to follow, so for several days that is what they did until, eventually, two of them made contact with a tribe. "One of them returned the same evening, with the news that he had found a small camp of Assiniboins of the Forest; that they had been well received; that a disease reigned in the camp, of which two had lately died, and that they expressed great desire to see the black-robe."

Although Assiniboins were not the Blackfeet, De Smet could not reject them, so he hurried forward. "The Assiniboins are filthy beyond conception," he soon learned from bitter experience; "they surpass all their neighbors in this unenvied qualification." Even the dogs are rascals, De Smet noted, nominating them as the most "adroit and incorrigible rogues to be found in the forest." If he failed to barricade himself in his tent at night, the dogs would enter and snatch away all of his leather clothes. As a matter of fact, one evening he neglected to install the blockade, and he awoke in the morning without shoes and minus one leg to his pants.

For the amusement of his brother, De Smet described a second menu from a feast in the forest:

> I beheld the Indians carve the meat on their leathern shirts, highly polished with grease—filthy, and swarming with vermin; they had disrobed themselves, for the purpose of providing a tablecloth! They dried their hands in their hair—this is their only towel—and as the porcupine has naturally a strong and offensive odor, one can hardly endure the fragrance of those who feast upon its flesh and besmear themselves with its oil.
>
> A good old woman, whose face was anointed with blood of the porcupine, presented me with a wooden platter filled with soup; the horn spoon destined for my use was dirty and covered with grease; she had the complaisance to apply it to the broad side of her tongue before putting it into my unsavory broth. If a bit of dried meat, or any other provision is in need of being cleansed, the dainty cook fills her mouth with water and spurts it with her whole force upon the fated object.
>
> A certain dish, which is considered a prime delicacy among the Indians, is prepared in a most singular manner, and they are entitled to a patent for the happy faculty of invention. The whole process belongs exclusively to the female department. They commence by rubbing their hands with grease, and collecting in them the blood of the animal, which they boil with water; finally, they fill the kettle with fat and hashed meat. But—hashed with the teeth! Often half a dozen old women are occupied in this mincing operation for hours; mouthful after mouthful is masticated, and thus passes from the mouth into the cauldron, to compose the choice ragout of the Rocky Mountains. Add to this, by way of exquisite dessert, an immense dish of crusts, composed of pulverized ants, grasshoppers and locusts, that had been dried in the sun, and you may then be able to form some idea of Assiniboin luxury.

After nearly a week of traveling with the Assiniboins, De Smet concluded that in their company he would get no closer to the

Blackfeet. He decided to push on in another direction. Reentering the forest, De Smet penned some advice to novices who wished to join him on the trail: "One should render himself as slender, as short and as contracted as possible. I mean to say, he should know how to balance himself—cling to the saddle in every form, to avoid the numerous branches that intercept his passage, ever ready to tear him into pieces, and flay his face and hands. Notwithstanding these precautions, it is rare to escape without paying tribute in some manner to the ungracious forest."

On the other side of these woods De Smet and his companions encountered a vast plain—an ocean of prairies, De Smet called it—stretching as far eastward as the eye could see. For nineteen days De Smet had pursued the Blackfeet through the mountains, would he now find them on the plains? In the map in his mind, De Smet calculated that Rocky Mountain House of the Hudson's Bay Company could not be far away. He estimated correctly this time.

The Hudson's Bay Company had established Rocky Mountain House on the Saskatchewan River in 1805, and even forty years later it remained an important location in the fur trade. The chief factor, J. E. Harriote, welcomed De Smet to his house with such politeness and fraternal cordiality that De Smet thought the man must be a Catholic, though he was not. Learning the objectives of De Smet's mission, Harriote informed the priest that he expected the Blackfeet at the fort any day now for their prewinter buying binge. He promised to use his influence to obtain a friendly reception for Black Robe, though, as a man of experience in these matters, he cautioned De Smet about the dangers inherent in traveling to the Blackfeet camps. As before, De Smet dismissed the warning.

On the twenty-fifth of October, thirteen Blackfeet Indians sauntered into Rocky Mountain House ready to trade furs with Harriote. After making his bargain, the chief factor informed the Indians that a visitor waited for them—Black Robe. Curious, they agreed to a meeting. At the appointed time they came so cautiously, said De Smet, it was as if they stalked an enemy. Since De Smet did not wish to deceive warriors with such a fierce reputation, he told them straight away why he had come so far to see them: he sought peace between the Flatheads and the Blackfeet and he wished to teach them the words of the Great Spirit of the whites. At this disclosure a chief stepped forward to shake De Smet's hand. Then he embraced the priest, rubbing Black Robe's cheeks with his nose. Next, the head man invited De Smet to return with him to his village so that he could speak the words of the Master of Life to all of his tribesmen.

Such spontaneous affection puzzled De Smet. Could this man be a Blackfeet warrior? Indeed he was. The past year had been a difficult one for the Blackfeet, and tribal leaders sought ways to change their fortune. In recent months the Blackfeet had clashed in battle with the Flatheads, Crows, and other tribes three times, losing dozens of warriors and hundreds of horses to their enemies. Then a new strain of smallpox infected several bands of the tribe, taking a terrible toll of lives. Perhaps the Black Robe could intervene on their behalf with his Master of Life and make their lives better—thus the invitation to visit them in their village. But the invitation came so suddenly that De Smet could not leave Rocky Mountain House as quickly as they wished. He proposed, therefore, that the Blackfeet warriors return to the village and prepare the people for his arrival; he would follow in a few days, guided by his own scout and interpreter.

Because he knew no Indian languages, De Smet constantly relied upon an interpreter for an honest translation of what transpired at his Indian conferences. Previously, that had not been a problem. But at Rocky Mountain House the chief factor, who earlier acted as De Smet's go-between, could not leave his post, and the only other interpreter available suffered a low reputation as a dangerous, untrustworthy man. Still, De Smet had to hire him or forsake the opportunity to meet with the Blackfeet. So, laying his life before God, De Smet left Rocky Mountain House on the last day of October in company with the unnamed interpreter-guide and a single horse wrangler, a mixed-blood Cree. In this he again rejected Harriote's advice.

Trouble brewed from the start. "Notwithstanding his good resolutions," De Smet sadly reported, "my interpreter did not long leave me in doubt of his true character." For ten days the man led Black Robe aimlessly across the plains, seemingly as lost as the priest. Finally, one night he simply disappeared. "Although my situation was extremely precarious in this dangerous desert, without interpreter, without guide, yet I could not but feel relieved of a heavy burden by the departure of this sullen and gloomy fellow," noted De Smet in a reference to his fear that he might have been murdered by the man. During the next eight days De Smet and his solitary horse wrangler wandered in vain across rolling hills, seeing neither Indians nor whites. A four-day snowfall finally ended all hope of ever finding the Blackfeet. It also scuttled De Smet's plan to return to Saint Ignatius Mission on the Pend Oreille for the winter. Realizing defeat, De Smet resigned himself to spend the winter of 1845–46 at Fort Augustus, by his recollection the nearest Hudson's Bay Company fort. Connecting with the Blackfeet would have to wait for another day.

Fort Augustus, near present-day Edmonton, Alberta, enjoyed many advantages as a winter hideout. Chief trader John Rowand generously provided De Smet with accommodations at his glass-windowed Big House, and food would certainly not be a problem. "On my arrival at the fort," De Smet explained, "the ice-house contained 30,000 white-fish, each weighing four pounds, and 500 buffaloes, the ordinary amount of the winter provisions. Such is the quantity of aquatic birds in the season, that sportsmen often send to the fort carts full of fowls. Eggs are picked up by thousands in the straw and reeds of the marshes." And so De Smet spent the winter eating, relaxing, and ministering to the Catholic population at the fort.

By March of 1846 the bleakness of winter gave way to the cheering dawn of spring. De Smet had his schedule already made out; his "pulse beat to approach nearer the mountain, there to await a favorable opportunity to cross it, so that I might arrive as early as possible at the mission of Saint Ignatius." On the twelfth of the month De Smet said his good-byes to the Rowand family and, accompanied by three half-bloods, started toward the mountains with three sledges drawn by dogs, two for baggage and one for the priest. Mushing straight down frozen riverbeds, they reached Fort Assiniboine on the Athabasca River in only six days. From there, local intelligence informed De Smet, the river flowed directly to Fort Jasper in the Rocky Mountains, a distance of approximately three hundred miles.

It required nine days of hard travel to reach Fort Jasper. Once there, however, De Smet marked time while he waited for snow to melt in the mountains. Colin Fraser, superintendent of this Hudson's Bay Company outpost, saw to the comfort of his guest, who agreed to stay at least through Easter Sunday. The bounty of the Oregon country never failed to amaze De Smet as he once again summarized for his family the content of the post's larder:

> A little note of the game killed by our hunters during the twenty-six days of our abode at this place will perhaps afford you some interest; at least it will make you acquainted with the animals of the country, and prove that the mountaineers of Athabasca are blessed with good appetites. Animals killed—twelve moose deer, two reindeer, thirty large mountain sheep or bighorn, two porcupines, 210 hares, one beaver, two muskrats, twenty-four bustards, 115 ducks, twenty-one pheasants, one snipe, one eagle, one owl; add to this from thirty to fifty fine white-fish every day and twenty trout, and then judge whether or not our people had reason to complain; yet we heard them constantly saying: "How hard living is here? The country is miserably poor—we are obliged to fast."

On April 25, believing that the path through the mountains must now be open, De Smet returned to the trail. Indians at the fort pledged to travel with him all the way to the other side of the mountains, but as the miles wore on they dropped away in ones and twos until, finally, says De Smet, he stood virtually alone looking at the Whirlpool River "in one of those wild ravines where nothing meets the eye but ranges of gloomy mountains rising on all sides, like so many impassable barriers." But De Smet knew these mountains could be crossed, because a Hudson's Bay Company brigade did so annually.

Beginning in the mid-1830s most of the furs collected by the Hudson's Bay Company in the Columbia Department found a place on ships bound for London by way of Hawaii and China.

A special express service, however, rushed company documents and vital papers to Quebec once each year. Traditionally, the brigade left Fort Vancouver in the spring, ascended the Columbia in barges as far as Boat Encampment, the northernmost point of the river, and transferred to canoes on the Great Portage River. Once at the base of the Rocky Mountains, the company men hiked across Athabasca Pass, a depression of less than six thousand feet amidst towering peaks twice as high. De Smet intended to wait for the voyageurs, letting them clear the path over the pass; then he would retrace their steps to Boat Encampment on the Columbia River and float down to Fort Colville.

Toward the evening of May 6 the first two trailbreakers from the Columbia brigade reached De Smet's camp. From them De Smet learned that the route across Athabasca Pass was usable and that the main party would soon crest the summit at the Committee's Punchbowl, the traditional spot to drink a toast to officers of the Honourable Company. Grateful for their good news, De Smet and his companions set out the next morning to begin their own ascent of the pass. Using snowshoes, they made good time across drifts sixteen feet deep, meeting the main group of eighteen Hudson's Bay Company gentlemen after traveling only eight miles. In a reunion of sorts, De Smet shook hands with Frank Ermantinger, a brief acquaintance from his visit to Fort Hall in 1841, and the two company commissioners with whom he and Peter Skene Ogden had chatted the previous autumn. There followed a hurried exchange of incidental news, for both parties were anxious to reach their destinations. Before the two groups separated, company officers gave De Smet permission to hitch a ride on the barges at Boat Encampment as far as he wished to go on the Columbia.

According to Ogden's calculations, De Smet would have to make at least thirty miles a day for two and one-half days in order to reach Boat Encampment before the barges left for Fort Colville. Accepting the deadline as a second challenge—chief factors Rowand and Harriote both told De Smet earlier in the winter that it would be impossible for one as corpulent as he to cross the pass—De Smet increased his pace.

We went in single file—alternately ascending and descending—
sometimes across plains piled with avalanches—sometimes over lakes
and rapids buried deeply under the snow—now on the side of a deep
mountain—then across a forest of cypress trees, of which we could
only see the tops. I cannot tell you the number of my summersets. I
continually found myself embarrassed by my snow-shoes, or entangled in some branch of a tree. When falling, I spread my arms
before me, as one naturally would do, to break the violence of the
fall; and upon deep snow the danger is not great—though I was often
half-buried.

The next morning De Smet crested Athabasca Pass—there was
no time to celebrate the moment—and he immediately began
the treacherous descent of the Great Western Slope on Le Grande
Côte heading for Pacific Creek. At the foot of the mountains yet
another obstacle presented itself, this time in the form of an icy,
swollen stream that flowed into the Wood River. For a day and
one-half De Smet struggled along the floor of the valley, compelled to cross the stream not less than forty times. " We marched
in our wet clothes during the rest of our sad route," he wrote;
"The long soaking, joined to my great fatigue, swelled my limbs.
All the nails of my feet came off, and the blood stained my moccasins or Indian shoes."

At last, on the tenth of May, De Smet and his beleaguered
companions reached Boat Encampment on the Columbia River.
Fortunately, the Hudson's Bay Company barge remained moored
to the shore, though the captain announced his intention to
shove off that very day. The barge needed to get as far down the
river as possible before the melting snow swelled the river any
more. In order for a pilot to properly maneuver the barge, his
paddlers had to maintain a speed in excess of the current, otherwise the river controlled the boat. Understanding the urgency of
the situation, De Smet quickly repackaged his gear and stowed it
in the barge. He was ready to go.

Guided by an expert Iroquois pilot and powered by ten paddlers, the Columbia brigade's barge darted across Martin Rapids,
Great Rapids, and Dalles of the Dead before sunset of the first
day. On succeeding days the men pulled on their oars from dawn
to dusk, going as fast as the current would take them. Only once

did De Smet fear for his life. Just above Fort Colville, at Little Dalles, the aura of danger in the boiling rapids dead ahead re-kindled for him the memory of the Okanogan Dalles disaster in 1842, so De Smet asked for permission to walk around the rapids. The rest of the boatmen, however, chose to run the rapids rather than line the vessel through with a rope, a painstaking, muscle-straining process. When they shoved off from shore, for the second time in his western experiences, De Smet watched as "a whirlpool suddenly arrested their course and threatened to bury them beneath its angry waters. Their redoubled efforts proved ineffectual—I saw them borne on with an irresistible force to the engulfing centre—the bow of the vessel descended into the abyss and filled." Falling to his knees, De Smet buried his face in his hands, averting his eyes from the swirling foam. Miraculously, at least to De Smet, "the whirlpool filled, and threw them from its bosom, as if reluctantly yielding up the prey which it had so tenaciously held."

After his roller coaster ride on the Columbia, Fort Colville presented a peaceful sight to De Smet. He discovered that Father Nobili had also recently arrived, making the occasion even more pleasurable. If De Smet had spellbinding tales to tell of his recent adventures, Nobili certainly had no reason to be reticent when the two missionaries exchanged stories. During the past year Father Nobili had traveled widely in the Okanogan country north of the forty-ninth parallel. He, too, walked great distances, en-countered secluded villages, and endured hardships, eating dogs and wolves along the way. In the process, Nobili's health broke, and he now sought medical attention at Fort Vancouver. The two Jesuits traveled the rest of the way together.

The progress of the priests and sisters in the Willamette Valley both astonished and gratified De Smet. Clearly, Bishop Blanchet had things well in hand for the Catholics of the region. Seeing no reason to remain in the vicinity, De Smet merely gathered some supplies and prepared to return to the interior missions as quickly as possible. Anyway, he much preferred to be in the field than behind the superior's desk at Saint Francis Xavier.

Before he left Saint Francis Xavier a powder horn accidentally exploded near De Smet's face, seriously scorching his nose, cheeks, and lips. It did not threaten his life, but it did delay him long enough to miss the Hudson's Bay Company barge returning to Fort Colville. Now he would have to make his own travel arrangements to Fort Walla Walla. But at least doing so allowed him to stop as often as he liked at the new towns and villages that sprouted up in all directions on the shores of the Columbia River.

The Dalles justifiably earned its reputation as the most dynamic town on the middle Columbia River. Here the powerful Columbia compressed itself into a terrifying series of chutes, rapids, falls, and narrows. Barges stopped to portage their cargoes around the cataracts, so businesses blossomed and people congregated there. What better illustration, thought De Smet, of how the presence of white pioneers corrupted the Indians. For centuries The Dalles had been the site of a great Indian fishing fair, a wondrous location where tribes came from near and far to net the salmon and to trade with each other products from their own territories. Now, he lamented, the site existed merely as an exchange point for the Indians and the Oregon Trail immigrants. The natives provided food, horses, canoes, and guides, and they received in return outrageous wardrobes of tattered clothes. Indians paraded through town masquerading in the dress of wagoneers, sailors, lawyers, Germans, Frenchmen, and Spaniards, convinced that in so doing they embellished their reputations. "One wore a pair of trousers turned inside out, another a coat much too short, with a torn pair of skin-tight trousers which betrayed the absence of a shirt; a lace head-dress was the crowning touch to this bizarre costume."

In a long discourse, De Smet described the miseries of the Indians, noting especially their continuing reliance on superstitious idolatry in spite of religious instruction that had begun when the Methodists opened a mission in The Dalles a decade before. The deterioration of their villages, especially as the numbers of white men encroached on their lands, similarly repelled the priest. "Imagine their dwellings, a few poor huts, constructed of rush, bark, bushes, or of pine branches, sometimes covered with skins or rags—around these miserable habitations lie scattered in profusion the bones of animals, the offal of fishes of every tribe, amidst accumulated filth of every description." In De Smet's estimation the arrival of the whites and the degeneration of the Indians provided a clear cause-and-effect relationship. Moreover, he suspected that the flash point of conflict between the Indians and the pioneers drew closer with the arrival of each new wagon train. Who could make it different, who could reverse the process? he asked himself. Missionaries could. They would be a second part of his emerging philosophy on Indian affairs, after reservations. Then and there De Smet resolved to return to "the states," where he could locate more missionaries for the reductions under his jurisdiction.

De Smet found much to think about as he resumed his journey to Saint Mary's Mission in the Bitterroots. In addition to changing conditions for the Indians of the Oregon country, there were personnel matters to reconsider. Father Soderini's name appeared first on his list. After a full exposition of feelings, Soderini still wished to quit the Society of Jesus, so De Smet, exercising his special authority as a superior, gave that permission. Next, he needed to consult with Father Point.

Point wished to transfer to another Indian mission, preferably one administered by the Jesuits of France, not Missouri. He advised De Smet that he already had written such a request to Father General Roothaan in Rome; De Smet need not endorse it, merely deposit it in the mail at Saint Louis. De Smet approved and even agreed to carry a second letter, the contents of which Point this time did not divulge. Both of these letters eventually reached the father general in February 1847. Roothaan had no difficulty arranging Point's request for reassignment as outlined in the first letter. The second letter deserved more deliberation, for it presented in detail Point's growing disaffection with De Smet's plan for a series of Paraguayan-style reductions. This letter subsequently became the source of much friction between De Smet and the father general.

De Smet could hardly believe his eyes when he reached the gates of Saint Mary's Mission in August of 1846. That the mission flourished under the influence of Euro-American civilization was clearly evident. Buildings, fields, fences, and livestock all bore silent witness to the partnership of progress between the missionaries and the Indians. Forty head of cattle, the nucleus of a great herd, suggested in De Smet's view that soon it would no longer be necessary for the Indians to leave the mission to hunt buffalo, deer, and elk. Sawmills and a flour mill likewise foretold the coming of a new life for the natives. Regrettably, De Smet did not recognize that such progress came at a price, namely, the erosion of the natives' own traditions and culture. He would have found such a consideration as foreign to him as the language the natives spoke.

In spite of the many comforting advances at Saint Mary's, Father Point informed De Smet of a growing problem. During his recent absence the Flatheads had become increasingly aggressive toward other tribes. Convinced that the powers of De Smet's Master of Life protected them in battle, the Flatheads taunted neighbors and enemies alike. Just before De Smet's arrival at Saint Mary's, for example, a large number of Flatheads left on a buffalo hunt with the clear intention of invading the lands of their allies, the Crows. It did not matter to them that in doing so they would upset the delicate territorial balance of power existing among the Crows, Flatheads, Nez Percés, and Blackfeet. One of De Smet's primary goals for the Indians of the Pacific Northwest had always been to end the incessant intertribal warfare that divided and crippled the nations. Now it seemed his religious instruction actually contributed to tribal divisiveness. Worried by what he heard, De Smet decided that before he left for Saint Louis he would make one more attempt to unite the interior Northwest tribes in peace. A prolonged Indian war would, after all, destroy his precious reductions.

Hoping to avert disaster, De Smet hurried after the Flathead hunting party, taking Father Point with him. A small group of Flatheads at Saint Mary's furnished a protective escort. Alas, they arrived at Three Forks too late to recall the hunters. Undaunted, De Smet, Point, and several guides pushed on to the east, across Bozeman Pass. When they reached the Yellowstone River, they found signs of the Flathead hunting party. Incredibly, it appeared that the Flatheads had been joined by several dozen lodges of Nez Percés and even a few Blackfeet tepees. Anxious to intercept the combined camp, De Smet nevertheless proceeded with caution. "In traveling through these wilds," De Smet explained to his provincial, "great care is to be had in order to avoid the sudden attack of some of those straggling war-parties that infest this neighborhood purposely to search for scalps, plunder and the fame of some daring exploit."

When he sensed that the combined Flathead camp drew farther and farther away from him, in desperation De Smet ordered his trusted interpreters Gabriel and Charles to ride forward while he and Point followed at their own pace. A day and one-half of nearly continuous riding allowed the two advance scouts to make up a fourteen-day head start by the slow-moving combined camp, but they arrived too late, just in time to see the Flatheads and the Crows face each other with drawn battle lines. The Crows, once the allies of the Flatheads, believed they had much to fear from an alliance of Flatheads, Nez Percés, and Blackfeet, especially one that now invaded their territory. Alarmed at the impending battle, Gabriel and Charles overlooked their personal exhaustion, mounted fresh horses, and hurried back to report the dreadful news to De Smet.

Try as he might, De Smet still failed to reach the scene of the battle until after the Crows had launched three attacks on the Flatheads. Remarkably, the Flatheads acquitted themselves extremely well, repelling all of the advances. Then, when the Crow horses showed signs of fatigue, Victor, the grand chief of the Flatheads, ordered his warriors to advance, a bold maneuver that panicked the Crows, who fled in disarray across the sagebrush landscape. Arriving at the scene of battle, De Smet found the Flatheads smugly readying themselves for a counterattack that would never come.

As soon as he entered the combined camp, De Smet confronted, disarmed, and admonished the Flatheads. Then he dispatched a messenger to the Crows, conveying his desire to effect a reconciliation. But the messenger returned to camp at nightfall reporting that the Crows had completely deserted the battlefield. De Smet considered going after the Crows himself, but Charles advised against it. Let the Crows lick their wounds in solitude. Failure to mend the tribal relationship between the Flatheads and the Crows greatly disappointed Father De Smet. Still, the events of the recent two-day war presented him with an equally significant, if unanticipated, opportunity.

Thirteen lodges of Blackfeet traveled with the combined camp, and after witnessing the battle between the Flatheads and Crows many of the Blackfeet came to the conclusion that the turn of victory resulted from some magical power possessed by the Flatheads. They saw with their own eyes how the Flathead warriors prayed on bent knee before and during the battle, and to this they attributed the fact that not a single Flathead died in combat. One Nez Percé warrior did die, but, they surmised, he fell because he failed to use the proper words taught by the Jesuits at Saint Mary's Mission. The Crows, meantime, carried away nine dead warriors because, presumably, they did not pray to the Black Robe's Master of Life at all. The Blackfeet further believed that the Crows suffered a loss of courage because they believed themselves overpowered by the Flathead's unseen spiritual force. Indeed, once during the summer of 1845 the Blackfeet had themselves engaged the Flatheads in battle, and they likewise felt intimidated by the magic prayers and ceremony. Impressed by what they considered the great medicine of the Black Robe, a cadre of Blackfeet chiefs in the combined camp dispatched Nicholas, the first Blackfeet to be converted at Saint Mary's, to ask De Smet how his tribe could receive the words of the Great Manitou. Through me, De Smet responded. And to Father Point he commented with satisfaction, "Having failed to obtain the desired interview with the Crows, our attention will be now turned toward the Blackfeet."

The Blackfeet chiefs in the combined camp wanted De Smet to go with them to the main band of their tribe. De Smet did not hesitate to reply in the affirmative. These were, after all, the same tribesmen he had failed to locate the previous summer and fall. The Blackfeet, now joined by De Smet and Point and escorted by most of the remaining Flatheads and Nez Percés, a parade of more than four hundred persons in all, headed north toward Fort Benton. Along the way De Smet and Point enjoyed unparalleled success evangelizing the Blackfeet, mainly because the recent victory of the Flatheads over the Crows had mightily impressed Big Lake, chief of the Blackfeet. If De Smet spoke to the Great Spirit, then Big Lake would listen to De Smet. If the sign of the cross could make the Flatheads better warriors, why not the Blackfeet, too?

In a glorious grand council on a wide island in the Missouri River adjacent to Fort Benton, Fathers De Smet and Point mediated a formal peace between the Flatheads and Blackfeet. The two tribes forgot old disputes and forgave feuds as they and their various allies pledged a lasting truce. In an effort to guarantee the peace, De Smet and Point privately decided that Point should remain with the Blackfeet as their designated missionary. Ironically, Point had gotten his wish to live with the Blackfeet just as the father general processed his reassignment to eastern Canada. De Smet, meantime, would descend the Missouri River to Saint Louis "to inform our superiors of the state of the missions and the necessity of increasing the number of missionaries."

Three days after the peace council concluded, on September 28, 1846, amid the shouts of a thousand Indians and the discharge of a hundred guns, Father De Smet shook Father Point's hand for a final time and boarded a skiff for the journey to Saint Louis. Proud of his accomplishments among the Indians of the Pacific Northwest, De Smet sped downstream a satisfied man. Seeing new country energized him even more. In spite of his extensive travels across the Oregon country, De Smet had never before floated the Missouri between Forts Benton and Union. Accordingly, he took copious notes about this stretch of the river, recording exact distances between tributaries and all notable landmarks.

Tirelessly De Smet's two paddlers hurried the boat downstream, pausing to stop only twice a day. Fortunately, game came close to the waterline, and in five days the travelers killed seven does, one buck, four buffalo cows, five wild turkeys, "a wolverine for fun, as his flesh is of no value; and a grizzly bear out of pure

104 FATHER PETER JOHN DE SMET

malice." De Smet noted that the bear "tried to be even with us; after being shot twice he made a furious leap from a height of twenty feet, meaning to fall upon our skiff and rend us in return." Luckily the bear missed the boat, though he surfaced in the river and attacked the skiff at water level. When he came within arms length an Indian killed him.

On October 11, after 525 miles floating free on the river, De Smet and his canoemen beached their frail craft in front of Fort Union. For a single day De Smet allowed himself some rest, accepting with pleasure the polite hospitality offered by the gentlemen of the fort. Then as he resumed his journey on the thirteenth, tempestuous winds appeared out of dark clouds, churning the river into waves and once even upsetting the skiff. While drying his clothes on shore, De Smet conceived the idea of stitching together some garments to form sails, and indeed, the very next day his canoe made nearly seventy miles on the water.

Downstream from Fort Berthold—a post erected since the last time De Smet traveled this way in 1842—Indian villages increasingly lined the banks. Indians frequently motioned for De Smet to come ashore, and he usually obeyed. "You seldom have cause to repent of this small condescension," he noted; "You accept the calumet; you furnish something to fill it with; you smoke one or two rounds with them in their manner; both sides exchange little items of news; if they see that you are without provisions, they hasten to give you the choice pieces from their hunt; then you embrace and part friends." To decline an invitation, on the other hand, he said, "would irritate them and expose you to great danger."

Near the Knife River, De Smet nearly realized his fears when a band of armed Indians surprised him in camp. De Smet braced himself for trouble, but "fortunately the chief recognized my cross and black robe by the firelight; he ran to me, threw away his hatchet, embraced and hugged me." This act greatly relieved De Smet, for in the firelight he recognized these warriors to be Arikaras, "a meeting with whom in the desert is always dreaded by the white men for they are thieves and murderers." It took De Smet a few moments to compose himself and invite his guests to enjoy roasted buffalo hump and a cup of sugar-sweetened coffee, a request no Indian could refuse. The Arikaras repaid their host by entertaining him the rest of the night with songs and dances.

As the traveling season now stretched thin, De Smet and his crew paddled four days and nights straight through to reach Fort Pierre by the last day of October. Thus far De Smet had spent a little more than a month on the water, yet he still had a thousand miles to go. After a stay of three days at the American Fur Company post, De Smet pushed on. From Fort Pierre to Saint Louis new fur trading posts sprouted up on the shoreline nearly as often as old Indian villages, or so it seemed to De Smet. When possible he stopped at the posts to baptize half-blood children or simply to introduce himself to the various bands of Indians. More than once tribal elders and chiefs asked De Smet to remain with them, requests to which he could only respond that he would plead the Indians' case to the great chiefs of his order.

Below Fort Vermilion the fall weather deteriorated rapidly and game grew scarce. At Council Bluffs, De Smet walked ashore with mixed feelings of relief and sorrow. The Potawatomi mission had floundered after De Smet left it in 1840, and eventually the Jesuits had moved themselves and many of the Potawatomis to Sugar Creek in Kansas Territory. In 1846, Council Bluffs existed pretty much as "a temporary establishment of the Mormons, driven out from their city of Nauvoo on the Mississippi; there are more than 10,000 of them here." At the request of Brigham Young, De Smet described in close detail the topography of the western lands beyond the Rocky Mountains, answering "a thousand questions about the regions I had explored." The Saints subsequently chose the Salt Lake Valley for their new Zion, and historical legend attributes the choice to De Smet's advice. "My accounts of the villages in Utah pleased them greatly," De Smet later explained, but he did not mention that, in fact, he had never crossed the Uinta Mountains or even visited the Great Basin—he had only heard descriptions of it from fur trappers at the Green River rendezvous in 1840 and from Thomas Fitzpatrick a year later. "Did this determine them to select Salt Lake? I cannot say," De Smet pondered. Probably not, say the biographers of Brigham Young.

When he reached Westport, Missouri, De Smet bought a ticket on the last steamboat of the season going to Saint Louis; he arrived at his destination on the first of December. Never again would De Smet weave together such an extensive and diverse series of journeys as he completed between 1843 and 1846. Logging not less than forty-four thousand miles, he crossed two oceans and the Columbia River bar; floated downstream on both the Columbia River and the Missouri River; and, in an effort to establish new reductions and make peace between the Flatheads and Blackfeet, rode across bleak desert landscapes and snow-shoed over steep mountain summits. And lest it be forgotten, De Smet also begged money on two continents, maintained a world-wide correspondence, and converted hundreds of Indians to Christianity. Only in the manner in which he handled personnel matters did De Smet fail in his extensive tour of the Rocky Mountain Mission. Unfortunately, it did not take long for that defect to be noticed by the father general in Rome.

CHAPTER 4

New Challenges, 1847–1851

WHEN he reached Saint Louis on December 1, 1846, De Smet felt weary, and rightfully so. During the calendar year he had journeyed more than sixty-five hundred miles, principally on foot. Yet within a few days of his arrival in Saint Louis, De Smet boarded a steamboat bound for New Orleans to seek out Father James Van de Velde, S.J., who had succeeded Father Verhaegen as superior of the Missouri Vice-Province. De Smet did not intend for this to be a social visit. Van de Velde had business in Louisiana, and De Smet had business with him.

The only topic on De Smet's agenda involved a letter dated in Rome on August 6, 1845, which he had received upon his return to Saint Louis. In the letter Father General Roothaan relieved De Smet of his responsibility for the Rocky Mountain Mission and named as his successor thirty-five-year-old Father Joseph Joset, S.J. Roothaan concluded his letter to De Smet with this terse statement: "Your post, will be in Saint Louis. From there you will be in a position to serve your dear Indians from afar." Numb with humiliation, De Smet hoped Van de Velde would use his influence with the father general to reverse the decision. Van de Velde, however, dashed that prospect when De Smet caught up with him. First of all, he possessed no authority to reverse the father general's order; second, he actually appreciated the reassignment of De Smet to Saint Louis and designated him the treasurer of the university.

Why had Roothaan replaced De Smet? What had De Smet done to deserve such an abrupt dismissal? A series of letters from Roothaan to Fathers De Smet, De Vos, and Joset provides some insights to those questions. To begin, the Nicolas Point affair had blemished De Smet's reputation with the father general. When De Smet pocketed De Vos's dossier of complaints about

Father Point at The Dalles in August 1844, De Vos complained to Rome and thereby exposed De Smet's management of the entire Rocky Mountain Mission to the father general's scrutiny. Roothaan bristled at De Smet's arbitrary action, though he also reprimanded De Vos for releasing the notes and accounts in the first place. The father general had his suspicions about Father Point and would have liked to have seen any "evidence" against him. De Smet had interfered and, worse, had refused to divulge the contents of the file to even the father general. None of this pleased Roothaan.

Roothaan also challenged De Smet with two other indictments made by De Vos: that he practiced hit-and-miss Christianity among the Indians, starting missions but never remaining in them long enough to lay a secure foundation, and that his itinerant travels wasted time and money. "How can the neophytes of the Rocky Mountains be abandoned?" Roothaan asked De Smet rhetorically, "How can one just baptize here and there—and then run off?" Roothaan further scolded De Smet that the society could not "assume charge of all the countries" to which he had a taste to travel. De Smet's "unnecessary" journeying, a wanderlust that fostered an expansionist program of missions beyond the resources of men and money available to the Jesuits, said Roothaan, obscured the basic goals of the Rocky Mountain Mission.

Another factor in Roothaan's decision involved the grandiose, borderline romantic statements De Smet regularly made regarding the Christian disposition of the Rocky Mountain tribes. Roothaan blamed De Smet for enticing the society into opening a new mission field among the Flatheads by exaggerating the opportunities for conversion in the letters and reports he wrote in 1840 and 1841. Indeed, De Smet shamelessly promoted the Flatheads within his order, even calling them a "knight-errantry of the Mountains." Later Jesuits who left Europe to labor in this presumably productive Christian environment complained to Roothaan that the Indians acted far from docile and that their commitment to the faith was tenuous at times. It was not like they expected it to be at all. Yes, the Flatheads, Coeur d'Alenes,

Kalispels, and affiliated tribes of the Oregon country welcomed missionaries. True, they did not curse or lie, and they knew their prayers. But their faults in the areas of gambling, polygamy, and violence raised serious questions regarding their genuine acceptance of Christianity. Moreover, their ardor for Catholicism, and even the Jesuits, seemed to cool after only a few years. The inland Pacific Northwest missions were not as De Smet advertised them to be.

Roothaan tended to accept criticism of De Smet as if it were fact instead of opinion. He did not consider that Bishop Blanchet promoted the ecclesiastical potential of the Oregon country as much as or more than De Smet did. How else to explain the fact that in 1846, his holiness the pope made the Oregon country an archdiocese, the second one in all of America after Baltimore, yet it contained but a smattering of actual Catholics and only a few priests? Similarly, when certain priests let it be known in Rome that De Smet wore the cloak of worldliness too well for their taste, Roothaan singled out De Smet as a Jesuit who did not pray devoutly, one who did not keep his religious commitment. "Try, dear Fathers, to keep the religious spirit," Roothaan admonished the other Jesuits in the Rocky Mountain Mission in a pointed, and embarrassing, reference to De Smet, "that is the essential point: religious before all else, even before missionary and apostle because no true missionary or apostle ceases to be a religious."

Oddly, Roothaan did not challenge De Smet for resurrecting the Paraguayan reduction concept and installing it in the Oregon country. If ever he had a justifiable complaint, that was it. The reductions required huge outlays of men and money, yet they worked only insofar as the natives remained isolated from white men. By the time De Smet established his first reduction at Saint Mary's in 1841, maritime explorers, fur traders, and Protestant missionaries already knew the Oregon country well. Gold miners and farmers could not be far behind. Congress entertained no fewer than three bills calling for the annexation of the Oregon country in the 1820s, and by the 1830s the federal government had authorized two substantial surveys of the land with an eye to future settlement. De Smet's seventeenth-century concept never had a realistic chance of success by the 1840s.

In addition to finding fault with De Smet's modus operandi as a missionary, Roothaan expressed his displeasure at what he called problems in the "Willamette, etc." Specifically, the father general regarded the location of Saint Francis Xavier Mission, De Smet's "motherhouse" in the Willamette Valley, a bad investment. It may have been conveniently close to the Catholic enclaves nurtured by Bishop Blanchet, but it was too remote from the interior missions and therefore probably unnecessary. Roothaan would have preferred a site on the Columbia River, if any at all. In addition, the novitiate at Saint Francis Xavier laid out an extensive farm, but no one stayed to farm it because all available priests and brothers lived at the interior Indian missions. Roothaan blamed De Smet for this fiasco.

Roothaan did not need to elaborate on his reasons for dismissing De Smet; he simply announced the change in leadership for the Rocky Mountain Mission, and that closed the matter. Although De Smet disapproved, his Jesuit vow of obedience required him to accept the decision. Still, De Smet recoiled from the accusations and felt personally offended, even to the point of bitterness. And he had seen it coming. In December 1844, while spending Christmas with the Kalispels, De Smet had received a hint from someone, probably Father Soderini, that certain Saint Louis Jesuits represented him to Father General Roothaan not as a dedicated missionary but, in De Smet's words, "as one who loves to travel and who had very little else in his head." Some of those Jesuits residing in Saint Louis, De Smet fumed at the time, did not even know what it took to teach the Indians; they only wished to completely divorce themselves from the Rocky Mountain Mission. "I invite them to come and make a trail of it," sniffed De Smet, "provided they have a good stock of zeal and fervor for the conversion of the Indians."

Humiliated by his removal from the Rocky Mountain Mission, De Smet sulked for a time, and then he rebounded. Ultimately De Smet realized that if he could not go to the Indians in the Rocky Mountains, neither could he turn his back on them. And there was something he could do for the Rocky Mountain Mission, even if it be "from afar," using Roothaan's phrase. He could raise money and buy supplies for the Rocky Mountain Mission, acting in an unofficial capacity as their procurator. Missions required huge amounts of operating capital, and De Smet volunteered to supply it. For example, it cost roughly thirty-five hundred dollars to send a unit of four missionaries from Saint Louis to the Oregon country. Each Jesuit at a mission required approximately two hundred dollars annually just for personal maintenance; supplies for the Indians added additional expenses. To build new mission buildings, or to service old ones, took even greater amounts of money. Indeed, De Smet could help the Rocky Mountain Mission by exercising his God-given talents as a beggar.

Financially speaking, the Rocky Mountain Mission began a downward spiral into red ink as early as 1844. In that year Father General Roothaan separated the Oregon country installations from the Missouri Vice-Province in all matters affecting money. On the surface the directive did not appear to be unreasonable, for it merely authorized the Oregon country missionaries to develop their own line of credit with the Hudson's Bay Company in London. The Missouri Jesuits, who previously had served as middlemen, now dropped out of the financial loop. But Roothaan's idea did not take into account that although provinces and vice-provinces assigned fiscal agents to monitor their financial condition, the Rocky Mountain Mission had none. The Rocky Mountain Mission needed a fiscal agent, a procurator, in the parlance of the Society of Jesus—a person who raised funds, bought supplies, and shipped them to the missions. De Smet decided that he would assume that role, unofficially, for the Oregon country. Van de Velde agreed that he could, as long as his doing so did not interfere with his responsibilities at the university.

Ever mindful that public recognition is a necessary first step to soliciting funds, De Smet decided to publish more of his letters about the western Indian missions. At the request of several American Catholic magazines he submitted fifteen epistles originally written to Archbishop John Hughes of New York. Then in

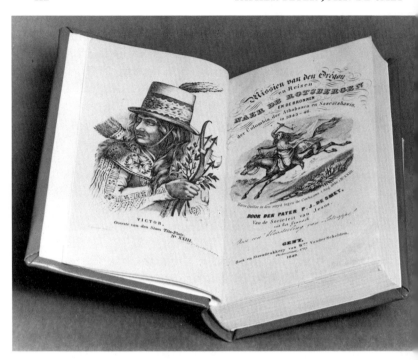

De Smet published two different French translations of *Oregon Missions and Tra* *over the Rocky Mountains in 1845–46,* New York, in 1848, and this Flemish edition 1849. The illustrations are by Father Nicolas Point, S.J. Courtesy of Oregon Provi Archives of the Society of Jesus, Gonzaga University.

April 1847, he reformatted them into the nucleus of his second book, *Oregon Missions and Travels over the Rocky Mountains in 1845–46.* Later that year, when he went to Europe, De Smet arranged for a French-language edition.

Oregon Missions became an instant favorite with the American reading public. The notoriety substantially benefited De Smet, the vice-province, and, especially, the Rocky Mountain Mission. Benefactors opened wide their doors, and consequently their purses, to the globe-trotting Belgian missionary whose books they read. Who would not be flattered by a visit from such a famous priest? De Smet clearly understood the direct correlation between his personal notoriety and the amounts of money he could raise for the missions; consequently, he encouraged the growth of his reputation. In view of the fact that the father general recently reprimanded De Smet for making fictitious or unwarranted statements in his letters, it is interesting that De Smet further risked his good standing in the Society of Jesus by promoting himself—and that the society let him do it.

The French edition of *Oregon Missions* filled more than four hundred pages, contained several lithographs from Father Point's original drawings, and included De Smet's own map of the lake and river system of the Pacific Northwest. First-person accounts by explorers were exceedingly popular in Europe at that time, frequently generating spirited conversations in posh drawing rooms. The publication of artist George Catlin's book *Letters and Notes on the Manners, Customs and Conditions of the North American Indian* in 1841, followed by his exhibition of western paintings in Paris in 1845, added a new dimension to the continental curiosity about the American frontier.

De Smet's books enjoyed a special place in the lexicon of travel narratives that northern Europeans read so avidly at that time. Ordinary persons found De Smet's books fresh and invigorating, with original material about the mysterious lands and inhabitants of the Great Plains, the Pacific Northwest, and the Rocky Mountains. He had a natural bent for storytelling and a witty, picturesque way of translating American idioms into French. One noticed this particularly in his descriptions of Indian life-styles, their camps, and the wondrous natural environment in which they lived. Best of all, because De Smet wrote his letters mostly to friends and family, in reading them the public felt that they, too, shared the campfire with Black Robe. Finally, De Smet possessed a viewpoint regarding the Indians that no other explorer of his time could share—a Christian dimension that made his pious observations appear to be the gospel truth.

In the spring of 1847, De Smet, now nearly fully recovered from the hurt associated with his reassignment to Saint Louis, accompanied his friend Father John Elet to Europe. After seeing to the foreign publication of *Oregon Missions,* De Smet spent some time with his family in Belgium and then proceeded on to Paris. In subsequent weeks he begged money from Paris to Rome. At the Eternal City, De Smet met directly with Roothaan. Nowhere in the writings of either party is there an indication of what they discussed.

Despite the warm reception he received everywhere from benefactors during his European sojourn, De Smet persuaded no priests or seminarians to relocate to the Oregon country, much as he tried. The negative response by the clergy did not really surprise De Smet, because in 1848 Europe seethed with an uneasy, resurgent revolutionary spirit that made all men, not just clerics, fearful of the future. Unnerved by the political atmosphere, De Smet decided to leave for New York as soon as he finished the rest of his business. He departed France in April 1848 with no regrets and about fifty-five hundred dollars in cash donations.

Shortly after returning to Saint Louis University, Father Elet assumed the duties of vice-provincial for the Missouri Jesuits, an appointment that indirectly favored De Smet. Elet liked De Smet and understood his desire to protect and even expand the society's western Indian missions. De Smet, in turn, trusted Elet as a kindred spirit and therefore did not hesitate to prevail upon him with a request to establish a new mission on the upper Missouri—he thought for either the Sioux or the Blackfeet. Roothaan had specifically prohibited De Smet from returning to the Rocky Mountain Mission, but with Elet's indulgence perhaps De Smet could make an impact somewhere else on the vast American frontier. Elet pondered De Smet's request and decided that although he could not commit the vice-province to a new mission on the upper Missouri, he at least could allow De Smet to mingle with the Sioux. It could do no harm.

Father De Smet's concept of which tribes might be "the Sioux" in 1848 consisted only of a vague notion about seven tribes that once dominated the Great Lakes region before migrating to the upper Missouri country in the mid-seventeenth century. The four eastern tribes of the "Seven Council Fires" called themselves Dakotas; pioneers referred to them collectively as the Santees of the Minnesota River. Yankton and Yanktonai tribes straddled the middle Missouri River near the Vermilion River. The Lakotas ruled the High Plains west of the Missouri River. One day soon the U.S. Army would refer to these tribes as Tetons, though individually they consisted of Oglalas, Brulés, Miniconjous, Sans Arcs, Two Kettles, Hunkpapas, and Blackfeet, the last not to be confused with the Blackfeet of the Rocky Mountains. Most whites, including De Smet, simply bound this confusing array of tribes together as Sioux, a French corruption of an Ojibwa word.

When De Smet had first visited the Yankton Sioux in 1839, he had viewed them mainly as adversaries to his mission at Council Bluffs, and he did not make any judgments regarding their suitability for future mission endeavors. On subsequent visits to various Sioux bands, in 1840 and 1842, however, the seriousness of the tribe impressed De Smet, and he even thought them anxious to receive the benefits of Christian religion. But then in 1846, on his way down the Missouri River from the Oregon country, De Smet acquainted himself with several of the Lakota tribes. In comparison with the Flatheads they failed miserably. De Smet pronounced the Lakotas unworthy prospects for future missions because they were "generally more cruel than those [tribes] sojourning west of the Rocky Mountains. Probably this arises from their almost incessant wars, which inflame them with a love of plunder and a thirst for vengeance." But he also believed that "a few missionaries would find a great deal of work here and would gather a fine harvest" under the right circumstances. It would not hurt to reevaluate the Sioux one more time.

De Smet hurriedly boarded the last steamboat of the season heading up the Missouri in 1848, remaining on board as far as Bellevue, a village not very far from Council Bluffs. Anxious to move inland, away from the river and its mercantile influences, De Smet joined a party of fifteen men freighting supplies for the American Fur Company. De Smet did not know exactly where to find the Sioux Indians, he would be the first to admit, but these gentlemen convinced him they did. De Smet also knew that he needed their assistance, because on the unforgiving Great Plains an injury to a lone man or his horse could be fatal. Besides, with someone to lead the way and help with camp duties, he would have more time to write letters. If someday Elet decided to locate a mission for the Sioux, a great deal of money would be required, and in De Smet's mind he linked future funding with present publicity. Thus, De Smet pledged to write a series of letters on this journey that could become, someday, his third book.

For ten days the travelers followed a northerly route that paralleled the Missouri River, a tedious, uncomfortable journey across a sterile landscape. At midday, when the sun beat down from directly overhead, temperatures regularly exceeded the century mark. Dancing mirages teased the travelers with illusions of water and shade. Pestering gadflies, mosquitoes, and gnats made long days in the saddle seem interminable. But De Smet did not mind any of this; it felt good just to be out of Saint Louis and back on the frontier. Not until they reached the mouth of the Niobrara River did the wary travelers meet their first Indians, a band of Poncas.

The Poncas, like the Sioux, spent the summer months prowling the plains in search of buffalo. They also liked to posture for strangers, so when the little band of fur traders approached within four miles of their camp, several hundred warriors rushed forward to demonstrate their strength. But, in a scenario that greatly renewed De Smet's confidence in himself, as the Indians reached the end of their long charge, several of them recognized Black Robe at the head of the column and immediately slowed their horses to a nonthreatening walk. The horsemen dismounted, De Smet shook their hands, tobacco appeared from the pockets of the traders, and everyone sat down to talk. None of the Poncas had met Black Robe before, but they had heard about him from other tribes. De Smet thought this quite incredible, and that evening he stayed the night with the Indians in their village. In the morning he decreed the Poncas to be "the Flat-Heads of the Plains."

When the fur traders reached Fort Pierre, they decided to stay for a while. If the priest still wished to contact the Sioux, he would have to do it with someone else. So De Smet hired Colin Campbell as an interpreter-guide and set out anew. With Camp-

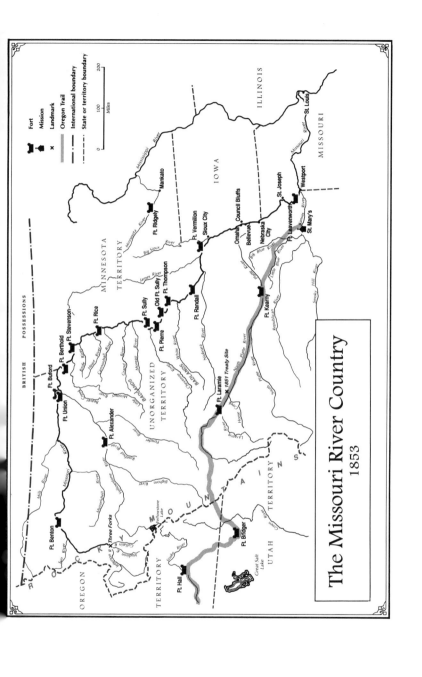

The Missouri River Country
1853

Fort
Mission   ✗
Landmark
Oregon Trail
International boundary
State or territory boundary

0   100   200
Miles

BRITISH POSSESSIONS

MINNESOTA TERRITORY

MINNESOTA River

ILLINOIS

Mankato

Ft. Ridgely

IOWA

Ft. Vermilion
Sioux City

Omaha   Council Bluffs
Bellevue
Nebraska City
St. Joseph
Westport
St. Louis

MISSOURI

Ft. Leavenworth
St. Mary's

Ft. Buford
Ft. Berthold
Ft. Stevenson

Ft. Rice

Ft. Sully
Old Ft. Sully
Ft. Thompson

Ft. Pierre

Ft. Randall

Ft. Union

Ft. Alexander

BADLANDS

UNORGANIZED TERRITORY

BADLANDS

Ft. Laramie
✗ 1851 Treaty Site

Ft. Kearny

Ft. Benton

Three Forks

Yellowstone Lake

R O C K Y   M O U N T A I N S

Ft. Bridger

Great Salt Lake

UTAH TERRITORY

OREGON TERRITORY

Ft. Hall

Snake River

bell's assistance De Smet traveled west to the uplands of the
Niobrara and White Rivers, in the direction of the Black Hills,
on a trail that paralleled the South Fork of the Cheyenne River.
Although he still did not see any Sioux, for the moment De Smet
felt satisfied just being an explorer, investigating for the first time
the Mauvaises Terres, or Badlands, in western South Dakota. The
sights he saw he thought were "the most extraordinary of any I
have met in my journeys through the wilderness . . . a theater of
the most singular scenery."

At last, on his twenty-fifth day out of Bellevue, De Smet approached a camp of Brulé and Oglala hunters. Almost certainly
they had heard of De Smet's message of Christian prayer and
compassion from other tribes on the plains, yet they did not
attempt to hide from him a tribal celebration then in progress
that saluted the successful return of a war party. As De Smet
explained it, the Indians engaged in a howling, stomping scalp
dance punctuated by discordant yells and fearful gestures under "the lugubrious tone of a large drum." Their prize trophies
consisted of "thirty-two human scalps torn from defenseless old
men, and from women and children." As a guest, De Smet decided it would be inappropriate for him to condemn the ceremony, even though he considered it pagan, so he endured it in
silence for the sake of future good relations.

But for the better part of the next month De Smet did speak of
Christian values as he instructed the Indians in the fundamental
doctrines of Catholicism. De Smet genuinely enjoyed his time
among the Sioux, in part because these days reminded him of a
time, not so long ago, when he first ministered to the Flatheads
of the Rocky Mountains. Once again De Smet was a missionary,
doing missionary things. Exhilarated by the experience, De Smet
reversed his earlier opinion about the Sioux. He still believed the
tribe to be unnecessarily fierce and wild, and he especially despaired at their partiality for superstition, but he also thought
they could be successfully converted to Christianity.

Toward the end of October brooding clouds loosed heavy
rains and occasional flakes of snow on the Great Plains. De
Smet knew he must soon bid farewell to the Brulés. But before

leaving he promised them that someday they would have a mission and missionary of their own. Almost certainly De Smet intended for his comments to bolster the faith of the tribesmen, for it is unlikely that he could envision such an event taking place in the near future. In fact, it would be more than a decade before even De Smet himself would follow up with another visit to the Sioux.

Returning to the Missouri River, De Smet took a small canoe back to Saint Louis. During the first leg of the journey, as far as Council Bluffs, De Smet and his hired paddler enjoyed good weather and abundant food. After that, an early winter storm overtook them, and for two days thick clouds enveloped the river in a colorless, freezing mist. A cutting, cold wind forced De Smet and his guide to seek refuge in a dense forest, and there they subsisted for several days on a diet of wild honey. When the storm finally blew itself out, the two men returned to the canoe, but the cold snap chased them down the river, and they could manage only ten days more before the Missouri became so irreversibly clogged with chunks of ice that prudence forced them to leave the water and take to the trail. It took two grueling days on foot just to reach Saint Joseph, Missouri. There, De Smet released his guide, bought a horse, and galloped overland to cut off the last steamer of the season, knowing full well that the requirements of fuel would force it to stop frequently along the river. He overtook the boat the next day and stayed with it the rest of the way to Saint Louis. Ironically, wrote De Smet, "Scarcely was I subjected to the heat of the stove in the cabin in the steamboat than I was seized with a violent sore throat—it being my first indisposition through the whole of my long journey."

Like most Saint Louisians, De Smet considered the "Indian summer" days of October a time to enjoy a moment of sunshine and colorful foliage before the damp days of winter settled into the Mississippi Valley. But this year the kinks in his muscles seemed harder to massage away and the soreness in his knees seemed to penetrate just a little deeper, so he spent most of the fall months of 1848 indoors. He occupied himself clearing away a huge backlog of unanswered letters.

Although he was the author of hundreds of letters and four books, De Smet struggled with grammar in both the English and French languages. He could speak at least five languages well, yet when writing English his sentences tended to be overly long and tangled. He chose verb tenses by how he felt and punctuated inconsistently, mostly at whim. De Smet also tended to overuse certain words, several of his favorites being "impetuosity," "labyrinth," and "astonish." Oddly, at the very same time that De Smet struggled to perfect his skills in the English language, his proficiency in French atrophied. When it came time for him to prepare his letters for publication in Belgium, for example, De Smet required the assistance of an editor every bit as much as he did for his English-language material. A Jesuit grammarian who probably also served as a censor read most of his official reports to the federal government. Thus, extracts from these documents in religious magazines do not accurately reflect De Smet's deepest concerns about federal Indian policy.

In that regard, De Smet often voiced his opinions to government officials about the attitude of the undisciplined white pioneers who hunted and homesteaded on the Great Plains. Knowingly or unknowingly, they significantly altered intertribal relations from the Missouri River all the way to the Rocky Mountains. American Fur Company documents available to De Smet proved conclusively that the number of wild animals, especially buffalo, killed by white men increased yearly. Tribes depended on buffalo and other game animals for food, and when they lost these resources on their own lands they either coerced other tribes into altering their own hunting patterns or, worse, violated traditional boundaries. Either case could precipitate general intertribal warfare on the plains. Already powerful nations such as the Sioux absorbed the territory of small and peaceful tribes along the Missouri River, De Smet explained, leaving the weaker tribes to face starvation and extermination in this chain reaction of survival of the fittest.

Describing the desperate situation of the smaller tribes, De Smet wrote to the directors of the Association for the Propagation of the Faith: "Such is their misery, they are forced to scour the country in every direction, and in little bands, are most happy if they escape the ambush of an enemy more powerful than themselves, and who frequently massacre the old, the women, and the children. Each year shows an increase of these revolting scenes—melancholy forerunners of an approaching and tragical issue." In letters to federal government officials De Smet proposed a remedy for the deplorable consequences he foresaw on the Great Plains. Like an echo, he restated some of his earlier arguments that whites be totally and absolutely removed from lands exclusively reserved for the Indians. Only missionaries should be allowed to contact the natives. Meanwhile, federal authorities needed to impose an effective embargo on ardent spirits, "that deadly scourge of the Indian." If Bureau of Indian Affairs officials responded, their letters have not survived. Perhaps they chose to ignore De Smet's recommendation as biased and self-serving.

Early in 1849, Father Elet appointed Father De Smet the assistant vice-provincial and procurator of the Missouri Vice-Province of the Society of Jesus, an administrative unit that included about two hundred Jesuits spread unequally among the novitiate at Florissant, nineteen residences, Saint Louis University, and other colleges at Bardstown, Kentucky, and Cincinnati, Ohio. As the assistant, or *socius*, De Smet answered official correspondence, carried out direct administrative orders of the vice-provincial, and traveled between stations as necessary. The duties of an assistant vice-provincial, then, were exactly the kind of repetitive, time-consuming, regimented tasks that De Smet had neither a taste for nor a desire to accomplish. This new assignment did not, by the way, affect De Smet's unofficial status as procurator for his order's western Indian missions.

Father Elet assigned De Smet to the procurator's office in the hope that he could work the same financial miracle for the vice-province that he had for both Saint Louis University and the Rocky Mountain Mission. During his brief tenure as the treasurer of the university, De Smet had completely repaid a $23,000 loan and closed the year 1848 with a surplus. He kept university funds separate from provincial accounts. When De Smet took over as procurator for the vice-province, he assumed responsibility for an annual operating deficit of $2,200, plus a $40,000 debt. Confidently, quietly, De Smet refinanced several small loans, restructured the accounting system for the vice-province, and exploited several new sources of income. If old Josse De Smet once felt disappointment that his son became a Jesuit rather than a businessman, the way Peter John now took control of vice-province accounts would have pleased him very much. In fact, it took De Smet no longer than November 1, 1850, to build for the vice-province an endowment fund balance of $48,900, which, at 5 percent interest, yielded an amount almost equal to the annual operating deficit.

Managing finances for the Rocky Mountain Mission continued to require a little more dexterity. In 1844, Father General Roothaan released the Saint Louis Jesuits from any financial responsibility for the Oregon country missions. After that, the father general paid for the missions' basic supplies with an annual draft of 40,000 francs (about eight thousand dollars), which he placed with the Jesuit province in London. They, in turn, paid the credit account owed by the Rocky Mountain Mission to the Hudson's Bay Company at their headquarters office. De Smet used the money he raised only to buy "extras" for the Oregon country missionaries. But in time Roothaan's yearly gift diminished in size, first dropping to 32,500 francs and then dwindling to 20,000 francs. This put the pressure on De Smet to raise additional funds.

The Association for the Propagation of the Faith, a French advocacy group for Catholic missions that began in 1822, became one of De Smet's most important, and regular, sources of money. He used his personal list of philanthropic benefactors to supplement the association's annual gift. But conflicts arose. By the late 1840s European bishops demanded that De Smet raise money for all the world's missions, not just his own in America. Should he not channel the donations he received into the treasury of the Association for the Propagation of the Faith from which he drew so deeply? Jesuits, to the contrary, considered De Smet an independent fundraiser for their own order, though of course they also wished to receive their share of the association's allotment to all missions. Charitable gifts by the association fairly dried up during the turbulent year of 1848.

This complicated matters, especially since the Hudson's Bay Company, which previously had sold supplies to Catholic missionaries at a reduction, now refused to provide any discount. Dr. McLoughlin retired, and apparently his replacement in the Hudson's Bay Company bore a grudge against De Smet because the Jesuit had broken the company's monopoly on Columbia River commerce when he had chartered the *Infatigable* to take him and his entourage of clergy to Fort Vancouver. The captain of the *Infatigable* had carried other passengers and additional cargo, and in doing so he had encouraged other non–Hudson's Bay Company vessels to enter the lucrative Columbia River trade. As a result, the Oregon missions' accounts at Fort Vancouver grew higher just as the annual subsidies from both Roothaan and the Association for the Propagation of the Faith diminished. Because it took nearly two years to send a letter from Rome to Fort Vancouver, the superior of the Rocky Mountain Mission did not know until it was too late that his charges at the fort exceeded the society's deposit with the London office of the Hudson's Bay Company by roughly six thousand dollars. In the meantime, the 1849 California Gold Rush greatly inflated the price of all goods along the entire West Coast. When De Smet realized the effect of these changes, he must have grimaced. At any rate, he considered it a solvable problem if he could expand his list of philanthropic benefactors in both America and Europe.

Being intimate with Rocky Mountain Mission affairs both soothed De Smet and frustrated him. "I am like a soldier," he confessed to his family; "Upon receiving an order I obey instantly and go where I am sent, but, like the soldier, I too have my preferences, and need I say they are for the land of the Indians?" His vow of obedience to the Society of Jesus confined De Smet to a desk piled high with papers, but in his heart, he said, "I long for the plains, the deserts, the wild life of the Indians, with its dangers, privations, and fatigues, which were, in truth, treats compared to the monotony of my present existence."

If De Smet hoped to return to the frontier anytime soon, that ambition suffered a damaging blow when he received a letter from Rome dated February 17, 1849. In a tersely worded communiqué, Father General Roothaan reprimanded De Smet for "deplorable" judgments regarding the dispensing of province funds in the Oregon country between 1840 and 1846 while he acted as superior of the Rocky Mountain Mission. He further accused De Smet of offending against his vow of poverty during the same period. Derogatory letters about De Smet to that effect had, apparently, been sitting on Roothaan's desk for some time, but the father general had said nothing until he learned that Elet appointed De Smet procurator of the Missouri Vice-Province. Then he wrote to both Elet and De Smet expressing his disapproval.

Elet, De Smet's friend, saw no need to unnecessarily embarrass a sensitive man, so he refrained from revoking De Smet's appointment as vice-province procurator in spite of the father general's bluster. He could not, however, minimize his fellow Belgian's personal mortification over the affair. But De Smet asked for no sympathy and set out to clear himself "of the false charge." In a long, detailed reply to Roothaan on April 3, De Smet explained that his financial accounts with the Oregon missions had been several times submitted to, and approved by, both Fathers Van de Velde and Elet. If the Rocky Mountain Mission experienced debt, it might be because no one followed his recommendations. Of the serious charge that he violated his vow of poverty, De Smet professed incredulity and defended his expenses: "In what concerns my personal expenditures, apart from the modest sum paid my guide, I made three journeys from the Rocky Mountains to Saint Louis without spending a dollar. Last year when I visited the Indians [1848], I traversed three thousand miles of territory, was absent four months, and the entire expense of my journey amounted to $50. . . . When in Paris [in 1847], finding myself at a distance from the Jesuit house, I more than once dined on two or three pennies' worth of chestnuts."

It is worthy of notice here that the Society of Jesus did not pay for most of the travel taken by De Smet. In a complicated arrangement of the kind manipulated by lawyers of the very rich,

Father De Smet enjoyed the luxury of an annuity established by two of his brothers and a sister in 1835. After De Smet had re-signed from the Society of Jesus and therefore had become a diocesan priest, no vow of poverty bound him to decline the money. The interest amounted to less than three hundred dollars a year, but it served a useful purpose. When De Smet returned to the society in 1837, he resumed his vow of poverty, but his pro-vincial allowed the account to remain independent of province funds as long as De Smet used the proceeds for good works. This money, for example, helped pay for his first trip to the Rocky Mountains. In 1848, De Smet's family favored him a second time with an interest-bearing account, this time specifically designat-ing the funds for "excursions in the Upper Country," meaning the upper Missouri River. Accordingly, De Smet drew upon those funds when he visited the Sioux later that year. It is to be regretted that Father General Roothaan nagged De Smet about violating his vow of poverty when in fact De Smet had done nothing of the sort, for his superiors knew, and approved, of all his family arrangements.

De Smet also thought it unfair that only a few months earlier, in the spring of 1848, Father Roothaan had told Father Elet to assure De Smet that he enjoyed the father general's full confidence. Why this sudden reversal? The truth of the matter is that Roothaan lashed out because of the demise of the Rocky Mountain Mission. Of late Father De Smet's chain of reductions, once the subject of glowing reports, now seemed on the verge of extinction. Roo-thaan blamed De Smet, citing the grand manner in which he extolled the virtues of the Flatheads and predicted their future greatness under the reduction system. Roothaan did not consider that some of the reasons behind the faltering Rocky Mountain Mission could be laid at his door. It was he, after all, who dissolved the financial ties between the Rocky Mountain Mission and the Missouri Vice-Province. Whatever the case, after receiving De Smet's carefully worded rebuttal, Roothaan absolved De Smet of the charges made against him. There were many things about the Oregon missions that still remained inexplicable to Roothaan, but for now he retreated from his accusations.

Returning to his administrative and bookkeeping duties, De Smet followed a busy schedule that made up for time lost during the recent unpleasantness. He even found enjoyment by rewriting a series of five letters he originally penned during his 1848 excursion to the Great Plains and sending them to the publishing arm of the Association for the Propagation of the Faith. Although other Jesuit missionaries searched out souls for Christ on the American frontier as tirelessly as De Smet—Fathers Hoecken and Nobili come immediately to mind—Black Robe distinguished himself from all others by his ability to play up missionary work in a variety of Catholic newspapers, magazines, and books. Moreover, the intuitive way in which he satisfied the public's curiosity, plus his natural ability to tell anecdotes, made De Smet the most recognized Catholic missionary in the nineteenth century.

During the winter of 1849–50 De Smet suffered from an annoying, reoccurring case of rheumatism that settled in his limbs and joints. Preferring to think of his malady as nothing more than old age, he playfully asked his niece Sylvie to describe him to her children as "a man of medium height, with gray hair rapidly turning white. A nose, of which neither Greek nor Roman could complain, occupies the center of a large face. A near neighbor to the nose is a mouth of ordinary size which only opens to laugh and make others merry. A peculiarity of his is to inculcate others the love of God. The rest proclaims a man of fifty years of age, weighing 210 pounds." But, at the same time, De Smet characterized himself to Father General Roothaan as a man "quite capable of again facing and enduring the privations inseparable from long journeys." Then, as if to plant a suggestion, he added, "At a word from your Paternity, I will immediately start for the Western plains." But the offer fell on infertile ground, for the only trips De Smet took during 1850 involved vice-province business. As he lamented to the interpreter at Fort Pierre, "I have so much business on my hands here, with nobody to take my place, that my superiors have put off my departure to the Indian Country to some other time; when I cannot say."

All of that changed, however, when De Smet received a letter from David D. Mitchell, superintendent of Indian affairs at Saint Louis. On April 19, 1851, Colonel Mitchell asked De Smet if he would attend, in the capacity of a government envoy, a general council to be held at Fort Laramie. Two weeks earlier Congress had appropriated money to sponsor a general council with the Indian tribes living south of the Missouri River and north of Texas. "The objects of the Government are just and humane," Mitchell explained to De Smet, "and intended entirely for the benefit and future welfare of the Indians." The status and effect of the Oregon, Mormon, and California Trails, twin-rutted ribbons that sliced across traditional Indian hunting lands on the Great Plains, needed to be clarified in discussions with the tribes.

Success at Fort Laramie depended upon full participation by the tribes, so Mitchell asked interested parties, such as De Smet, to "unite and use your best exertions to aid in assembling the Indians at Fort Laramie, on the first of September, 1851." Specifically, De Smet would proceed up the Missouri River as far as Fort Union, preaching to the Indians about Catholicism as he normally would, but also distributing a circular announcing the conference. "Should your other engagements permit," Mitchell informed De Smet, he could also escort a representative body of chiefs from the Northern Plains tribes to the council site. The government, of course, would pay for any travel expenses involved. In an aside, Mitchell asked De Smet to make sketches and maps of the plains and mountains. Or he could provide "any information with regard to the habits, history or other interesting matters appertaining to the Indians."

De Smet, naturally, wished to accept Mitchell's invitation. He considered it a twofold opportunity. First of all, he could "announce the consoling word of God to the poor benighted savages of these distant regions." Second, he could assist government agents to understand the Indian side of the complex issues surrounding the western overland trails. It was as simple as that. At no time did De Smet intimate that he would promote U.S. government viewpoints to the Indians, though in later years certain parties would accuse him of exactly that—betraying, as it were, the Indians' confidence in him.

Father Elet approved De Smet's request to join the government commission. Ordinary rules of the society required Jesuit missionaries to work with partners, so Elet assigned Father Christian Hoecken, S.J., a veteran of fifteen years in the American Indian missions and a brother of Father Adrian Hoecken at the Kalispel Indian mission, to accompany De Smet. Unfortunately, just as De Smet prepared to depart, Father General Roothaan lashed out at De Smet in another letter. He only recently had received word that Saint Mary's Mission in the Bitterroots had been closed and sold. After 1850 the buildings at Saint Mary's belonged to Major John Owen.

This distressing news triggered in Roothaan a remembrance of past complaints about De Smet, and he struck out angrily. The father general resurrected an earlier charge against De Smet, berating him for writing letters that contained excessively encouraging, even misleading, statements about the Rocky Mountain Mission, thereby leading to discomfort and disappointment by the missionaries who subsequently volunteered for assignments to the Oregon country. "More than one person assures me," Roothaan wrote to De Smet, "that your relations [letters], published with so much *éclat*, are products of imagination and poetry." In his opinion De Smet also compromised the future of the missions when he made promises to the Indians that he could not possibly keep. Roothaan believed that Saint Mary's Mission failed because sincere missionaries and pious Indians alike believed De Smet's overblown description of the Rocky Mountain Mission. In his judgment De Smet did not deserve to meddle in Indian affairs ever again and should remain in Saint Louis at his assigned administrative post.

As before, De Smet dashed off a convincing defense in a letter to Roothaan. "Again I am being criticized," he confided to his friend Father Van de Velde, "and am completely crushed by the disapproval that comes from the highest authorities, for not only are the accusations false, but the consequences of this will be the abandonment of a large number of the Indians, for whom I would gladly sacrifice the remainder of my life." Roothaan called his letters overblown fabrications, yet the father general himself, countered De Smet, "imposed it upon me as a duty to write very fully and to enter into minute details upon everything." He included in his rebuttal several declarations by Fathers Accolti, Ravalli, Mengarini, and Joset, each of whom testified to the faithfulness of the Flatheads and others—until 1849, that is, when the reverberations of gold fever could be felt even in the Bitterroot Valley.

De Smet quoted from other personal letters in his possession, citing in particular one from Father Accolti in June 1847 that stated: "I can assure you that when conditions are viewed without prejudice, the reality [of the Rocky Mountain Mission] surpasses all reports that have been hitherto recorded. I state facts, and exaggerate nothing." A letter of Father Ravalli, written about the same time, made its point even more explicitly:

> I can say in all sincerity that in the midst of the Flatheads I find myself in a terrestrial paradise. In Father De Smet's letters which I read in Rome, and in the different reports he wrote while I was in Willamette, I feared his statements were exaggerated, and that his rhetorical flights were intended to charm the reader; but since Providence has granted my desire in sending me to the mountains, I know now that if any criticism could be made of those letters it would be that Father De Smet had minimized the good dispositions of these Indians.

As to the second charge against him, that he made too many promises to the Indians, De Smet pointed to corroborating statements by other missionaries in the field. He showed that it was not necessary for missionaries in the Oregon country to make "rash promises" to the Indians about the value of Christianity, for the Indians already had quite enough preconceived notions about what the white man's religion should do for them. The ritualistic ceremony of the Catholic Church mesmerized the Indians. Tribesmen convinced themselves that the prayers of the Black Robe, the crucifix they wore on their breast or painted on their shield, and so on, provided protection for them from the weapons of their enemies. In addition, they fully believed that where the missionaries trod, independent traders and fur company posts, rich with machine-made clothing and metal goods, would soon follow. If the Indians felt deceived by Christianity, they deceived themselves, De Smet reasoned.

Father Elet needed to make a decision. If he held De Smet in Saint Louis until Roothaan replied to the priest's defense, De Smet would miss the opportunity to provide a religious presence at the Fort Laramie Indian council. De Smet's appearance could be an immeasurable advantage to the Indians at the council, to say nothing of the future benefit to other Jesuit missionaries. Therefore, using the discretionary authority incumbent in his position as vice-provincial, Elet allowed De Smet and Hoecken to proceed to Fort Laramie.

Happy to leave his troubles behind, on June 7, 1851, De Smet joined Hoecken on board the steamboat, *St. Ange.* At least eighty other men, most of them engaged in American Fur Company business, squeezed aboard. "They went in quest of earthly wealth, Father Hoecken and I in search of heavenly treasures," remarked De Smet. An unusually heavy snowfall on the northern Great Plains during the winter of 1850–51, coupled with a sudden spring thaw, created a heavier than normal current on the Missouri, which took on a lakelike appearance in the many places it flooded beyond its regular banks. "In ordinary times," De Smet wrote, "the sawyers and sand-banks are the principal obstacles to navigation in the western waters; they had now entirely disappeared, and gave the pilot no anxiety. But other dangers had taken their place." Small boats, houses, barns, and fences, all torn away by the irresistible current, littered the banks and filled the riverbed, making it a virtual floating lumberyard. There were greater dangers yet to come.

Four days out of Saint Louis a passenger succumbed to cholera, and after that victims fell in twos and threes until the steamboat resembled a floating hospital. Father De Smet himself suffered a "bilious attack" that confined him to his bed for nearly ten days. Hoecken, meanwhile, ministered to the sick by himself, visiting and praying, rubbing victims with camphor, and, when needed, burying them on shore. De Smet warned Hoecken of the danger he exposed himself to, but he spoke too late. Early on the morning of June 19, Hoecken became delirious with a fever, and with little more than a farewell to his brother Jesuit, he passed away later that day. De Smet conducted the burial service on shore, but only after first extracting from Captain Joseph La Barge a promise that on the return trip of the *St. Ange* the ship's crew would exhume the coffin and transport it to the Jesuit cemetery at Florissant.

Devastated by Hoecken's death, De Smet nevertheless knew he must press on. He had come too far—more than five hundred miles—to turn away from the Fort Laramie council. Increasing traffic on the Oregon Trail irritated an already combustible situation, and if he could help find a solution he must do it, traveling on alone if necessary. Moreover, he should do all in his power to remain current and knowledgeable regarding Indian affairs and intertribal relations. Someday, he believed, the Great Plains would "form several great and flourishing states," but then what would become of the Indians? How would the federal government compensate the Plains tribes for the destruction of game and timber they suffered? "This is indeed a thorny question," he confessed. Like many others in his time, De Smet continued to see in reservations for the Indians "an asylum, a permanent abode that will be incorporated with all the rights of citizens of the Union." It might be their best chance for survival, for "if they are again repelled and banished farther inland, they will perish infallibly," a reference to his earlier position that the bison and other animals upon which the Plains tribesmen depended for food were already vanishing.

Only after the *St. Ange* reached the fresh air of the High Plains near the Platte River did the shipboard epidemic subside. By then it had claimed more than twenty lives. Once beyond Fort Pierre, De Smet began to take daily horseback trips to visit inland Lakota, Arikara, and Mandan villages, spreading the word as he went about the impending conference at Fort Laramie. At last, on July 14, nearly five weeks out of Saint Louis, De Smet sighted the familiar log stockade enclosing Fort Union.

It took fifteen days for De Smet to organize an overland expedition to Fort Laramie. First, he coaxed several chiefs from the Assiniboins, Minnetarees, Arikaras, Mandans, and Crows to travel

with him to the treaty grounds. Next, he persuaded Alexander
Culbertson, superintendent of American Fur Company opera-
tions on the Upper Missouri, to go along, too. Finally, the priest
hired an assortment of Creole, Canadian, and mixed-blood
wagon masters to assist with the two four-wheeled wagons and
four small carts he had brought with him all the way from Saint
Louis on the *St. Ange*. The entire party consisted of about thirty-
five persons, all of them men.

Since no established trail existed between Forts Union and
Laramie, a distance estimated to be about eight hundred miles,
De Smet decided to blaze his own path. Moving in a south-
westerly direction beyond Fort Union on Saint Ignatius Day 1851
(July 31), the caravan set its daily course by dead reckoning.
Riding the trail revitalized De Smet's spirit. "The mind becomes
clearer, the faculties are more alive, and ideas spring forth spon-
taneously," he wrote. Clearly, De Smet still liked to see what lay
beyond the rise of the next hill. His once hearty appetite, stifled
in Saint Louis by a boring existence, returned, too. "Travelers in
these upper regions enjoy an excellent appetite," noted De Smet;
"One and even two buffalo tongues, a side of venison or other
meat, and some additional trifles, are not considered a large portion for one meal." Each evening before he crawled beneath his
buffalo robe cover, De Smet made notes by the flickering light of
the evening campfire about the sights he had seen during the
day. He did this partially to satisfy Superintendent Mitchell's
request, but mostly for his own amusement. Groves of stunted
trees, heaps of white clay, and piles of stones became make believe "forts with their turrets and bastions, towers, domes, walls
in decay, castles and edifices" under De Smet's facile pen.

Unfortunately, De Smet's scouts overestimated their expertise, and the whole party spent a good deal of time either lost or
backtracking. De Smet named one such mistake "the valley of a
thousand miseries," saying it accurately reflected his experience
during most of the trip. Still, everyone reached the Oregon Trail
at a spot near present-day Casper, Wyoming, minus only one
disabled cart. The tribesmen "were filled with admiration on
seeing this noble highway, which is as smooth as a barn floor

swept by the winds, and not a blade of grass can shoot on it on account of the continual passing." The Oregon Trail is the "broadest, longest and most beautiful road in the whole world," De Smet told his Indian companions as he tried to explain about the thousands of emigrants who passed this way each year. But, he said, "their countenances testified evident incredulity" until they examined in detail some of the forsaken campsites along the trail. Picking up discarded eating utensils, cooking articles, axes, and dinnerware, they swarmed around De Smet asking for explanations. "How wonderful will be the accounts given of the Great Medicine Road by our unsophisticated Indians," De Smet chuckled, "when they go back to their villages and sit in the midst of an admiring circle of relatives!"

As the party moved east on the Oregon Trail, long since empty after an early spring rush to cross the mountains, the eight-day journey to Fort Laramie passed quickly. The council site, however, lay yet another thirty-five miles farther on, at the mouth of Horse Creek in present-day Nebraska. Superintendent Mitchell moved the "Big Smoke" there on August 17 after thousands of Arapahoes, Cheyennes, Crows, Arikaras, Assiniboins, Mandans, Gros Ventres, and other tribesmen exhausted the supplies at the fort, an outpost normally provisioned to sustain no more than two hundred residents. William Sublette established Fort Laramie in 1834 partly because of its abundant natural resources, but he never calculated the effect of twenty thousand horses grazing in the vicinity or the waste from ten thousand lodges.

Convening on September 7, 1851, the Fort Laramie council lasted for ten days. De Smet approved of the proceedings, inasmuch as Thomas Fitzpatrick, a friend of long standing, acted as an official commissioner and the chief interpreter. Indian Bureau superintendent David Mitchell sat in the council as the second commissioner. Jim Bridger also made an appearance; De Smet knew him because his children attended Catholic boarding school in Saint Louis. Additional attendees included Robert Campbell; A. B. Chambers, editor of the *Daily Missouri Republican;* and reporter B. Gratz Brown, all Saint Louisians and all well known to De Smet. The priest's role, like that of Bridger, was limited to that of a geographer and an informant who could explain to Superintendent Mitchell the lay of the land he proposed to divide among the tribes. In fact, it would be De Smet who, after his return to Saint Louis, actually drew the map of the boundaries assigned to the Crows, Sioux, Assiniboins, and other tribes.

The assembled tribes, De Smet reported happily, exhibited a truly admirable harmony at Horse Creek, in spite of the fact that the Shoshones bore a longtime grudge against both the Cheyennes and the Sioux. "Implacable hatreds, hereditary enemies, cruel and bloody encounters" were all forgotten as chiefs smoked the calumet, tribesmen opened their lodges to strangers, and everyone partook of the numerous feasts, dances, and ceremonies. De Smet used this feeling of camaraderie to reconfirm the faith of several tribes and to introduce Christianity to others. Daily he offered religious instructions, converting 1,856 Indians by his own count. The reporter for the *Daily Missouri Republican* summarized De Smet's relationship with the Indians: "Father De Smet is highly esteemed by all the Interpreters, Traders, Half-Breeds, and the Indians, and is the medium of great benefit to them. He is peculiarly mild and amiable in his manner. He wins all men by the kindness of his disposition and the respect and esteem of all by the purity and uprightness of his life. The Indians regard him as a Great Medicine man, and always treat him with marked respect and kindness."

In the absence of buffalo the Indians ate dogs—all except the Shoshones, who took exception to the practice. For his part, De Smet found dog meat to be "really delicate, and I can vouch that it is preferable to suckling-pig, which it nearly resembles in taste." De Smet also liked another dish, this one a stewlike substance made up of sun-dried plums mixed with meat. "I must own that I found it quite palatable," confessed De Smet; "but hear what I learned subsequently, as to their manner of preparing it. When an Indian woman wishes to preserve the plums, which grow in profusion here, she collects a great quantity, and then invites her neighbors to her lodge to pass an agreeable afternoon. Their whole occupation then consists in chatting and sucking the stones from the plums, for they keep only the skins, which, after being sun-dried, are kept for grand occasions." De Smet took his education in European schools and therefore came to America an idealist. In the beginning he viewed Native Americans as "noble savages," princes of a primeval forest. That stopped, of course, after the Potawatomi experience, and with the passing of each year he recognized that Indians, like whites, can have as many revolting qualities as natural attributes. Their cruelty toward captives, preference for multiple wives, and sinful laziness shocked him. Uncleanness, especially in the preparation of food, annoyed De Smet, but he considered this, at least, a defect he could overlook.

When a government caravan of twenty-seven wagons arrived at Horse Creek on September 20, federal agents distributed fifty thousand dollars' worth of food, supplies, and presents for the Indians. After that the social atmosphere in the camp reached new heights. Chiefs came forward to receive suits of clothes and were, "for the first time in their lives, pantalooned; each was arrayed in a general's uniform, a gilt sword hanging at his side. Their long, coarse hair floated above the military costume, and the whole was crowned by the burlesque solemnity of their painted faces." Predictably, the great council ended in disarray and confusion. One morning scouts reported that buffalo herds could be seen on the South Fork of the Platte, three days distant, so the Indians broke camp and departed.

Although he had not been closely involved with the formation of specific treaty articles, De Smet sincerely hoped that the council would be the "commencement of a new era for the Indians— an era of peace." According to the terms of the agreement, the commissioner of Indian affairs recognized certain lands for each of the tribes who signed the agreement, and he promised that the Indians' land would be theirs forever. He further guaranteed the tribesmen protection against white encroachment and agreed to provide fifty thousand dollars' worth of supplies and provisions to be divided among the tribes each year for the next half-century. The Indians, in return, promised to make peace with each other and to recognize the "right of the United States

Government to establish roads, military and other posts" within their domain.

As an experienced frontiersman, De Smet must have known that the Indians' promises would be next to impossible to enforce. Indian tribal structure did not permit one man, even a chief, to commit his tribe in such matters as the delimiting of tribal lands; much less could he permit roads to cross or posts to be built on tribal hunting grounds. Nor could mere words on a piece of paper erase generations-old bad feelings among tribes for whom the ultimate test of manhood took place in combat. But ever the publicist, De Smet knew he could not acknowledge such realities to readers of his letters, so he grandly predicted that "in the future, peaceable citizens may cross the desert unmolested, and the Indian will have little to dread from the bad white men, for justice will be rendered to him."

Just as surely, De Smet probably believed that the federal government would live up to its side of the bargain. Not that doing so would be in the best interest of the Indian. Disillusioned, De Smet wrote: "Since the discovery of America the system of removing and of exiling the Indians farther inland, has been assiduously exercised by the whites. In the early times, they went by slow degrees, but . . . the system has been pushed with more vigor. At present this policy marches with gigantic steps; resistance on the part of the natives could but hasten their ruin. The drama of spoilation has reached its last act, both east and west of the Rocky Mountains. The curtain will soon fall upon the poor and unhappy remnants of the Indian tribes."

Late on the afternoon of September 23, Father De Smet shook hands for the final time with the Northern Plains Indian chiefs with whom he had traveled from Fort Union and set off in the direction of Saint Louis with a group of federal officials and a dozen or so Indian "deputies" chosen to visit the Great Father in Washington, D.C. In both 1840 and 1841, De Smet had traveled west on the Oregon Trail; now he would make the trip east for the first time. At Fort Kearny, Superintendent Mitchell and his cadre of commissioners broke away toward Nebraska City on the Missouri River; De Smet, Fitzpatrick, and the Indian delegation remained on the Oregon Trail as far as Fort Leavenworth. There Fitzpatrick persuaded De Smet that it might be beneficial for their Indian guests to witness the progress in agriculture and mechanical arts achieved by the Potawatomis at the Jesuit mission on Sugar Creek. De Smet agreed, so the delegation detoured slightly from their original plan, which had been to go directly to Saint Louis.

When they arrived at the Sugar Creek mission, the Potawatomis set the table with heaping bowls of potatoes, carrots, turnips, squashes, parsnips, melons, apples, and peaches. In doing so they achieved the desired result for Fitzpatrick and De Smet. "We see here a happy people, well fed and well clothed," chief Eagle Head of the Arapahoes informed De Smet; "We hope that the great Father will take pity on us and on our children. We wish to have Black gowns with us, and we will cheerfully attend to their words." The two men thus viewed the diversion to the mission so worthwhile that they reconfigured the schedule to permit yet another stop, this one at Saint Louis University. Meanwhile, other adjustments were taking place in Washington, D.C. In a move that shocked some, but was anticipated by others, the U.S. Senate revised backward the annuity provision in the Fort Laramie treaty from fifty years to fifteen years.

Three days after leaving Saint Mary's Mission, De Smet and his charges boarded a Missouri River steamboat at Westport for the trip to Saint Louis. The steam-belching, bell-ringing "fire canoe" terrified the Indians as it approached the dock, but once on board they clambered to the promenade deck like unrestrained children, set up camp, and occupied their time by hailing each passing village with shouts and songs. When the boat docked in Saint Louis on October 22, De Smet showed the Indians the sights of his adopted city, and he even arranged for a grand banquet to be held at the university—partial repayment, he hoped, for the countless dinners the Indians provided him at the grand council. By his calculations, De Smet traveled 5,457 miles on this journey.

CHAPTER 5

Chaplain and Peacemaker, 1852–1859

FOLLOWING his return to Saint Louis University in the fall of 1851, Father De Smet resumed his career as a reader of financial ledgers and a writer of vice-provincial correspondence for the Missouri Jesuits. Neither of these tasks kept his interest. Writing did. Each evening he spent long hours composing and recomposing chapters, six of them in all, that recounted in lurid detail the struggles and triumphs of his recent expedition across the Great American Desert from Fort Union to Fort Laramie. By February of 1852 the manuscript stood well enough on its own for De Smet to ask Father Peter Verhaegen to cleanse the text of "Anglicisms and Flandricisms," little witticisms or colloquial phrases De Smet relied upon when he wrote in his usual conversational tone.

A month later De Smet submitted the material to Father Edward Terwecoren, editor of a new Catholic magazine in France called *Précis Historiques*. Father Terwecoren's journal suited De Smet's literary ambitions ideally. Begun for the express purpose of encouraging vocations to the priesthood, the journal particularly included "edifying letters," or anecdotal, inspirational stories by the men of God in distant lands. Ever conscious of the advantages of well-placed publicity, De Smet responded to Father Terwecoren's initial call for material.

De Smet also made copies of the manuscripts he sent to *Précis Historiques* for Father General Roothaan, mostly out of respect, but also as a subtle reminder that the accusations made against him during the previous spring—charges that his lofty and deceptive statements about the Flathead mission caused both the Jesuits and the Indians to expect too much from each other and consequently led to a decline of faith in the Rocky Mountain

Mission—had not yet been resolved. Although De Smet answered Roothaan's charges before he departed for Fort Laramie, the father general so far had not replied.

Within a month of reopening correspondence with Roothaan, De Smet received a response. On April 15, 1852, the father general directed a letter to De Smet informing him that he acquitted him of the charges made a year earlier. Still, Roothaan restated for the record the deficiencies that he believed led to the failure of De Smet's Rocky Mountain Mission. This time Roothaan recognized the inadequacy of the reduction system:

> It seems that the idea of renewing the miracles of Paraguay amid those mountains was a Utopia. In the first place, we could not hope for the means which our Fathers received from the Crowns of Spain and Portugal. Then, it was impossible to keep the whites at a distance; then, too, the nature of the land is quite different and one cannot hope to wean the bulk of the savages from their nomadic life during a great part of the year when they are on the hunt and scattered and disbanded, some to the right and some to the left. Impossible for the missionary to follow them—their savagery is renewed—perpetuated.

Finally, Roothaan correctly assessed the reasons for the failure of the Rocky Mountain Mission. De Smet disagreed. In his mind the Paraguayan concept would have worked if only he had been given more time. As far as he could see, the only flaw in the reduction system was that he had been removed from the Oregon country missions—and the father general himself did that. De Smet expressed a personal opinion; Roothaan spoke the truth.

There were other factors contributing to the decline of piety among the Columbia Plateau tribes. When De Smet left the Oregon country in 1846, the Rocky Mountain Mission comprised six relatively stable missions. But within a year the relationship between the missionaries and the tribes changed dramatically. Once open and welcoming of priests, the young men from the Flatheads and other tribes returned from the winter hunt in 1846–47 aloof and indifferent to De Smet's successors. Almost immediately Father Joset, De Smet's replacement as superior of the Rocky Mountain Mission, reported that the Flatheads gave themselves up "to their old war dances, to savage obscenity and to shameless excesses of the flesh. . . . We knew that we were not to blame for such a change and we bewailed it all the more when we saw that they went on constantly getting worse." The fact that De Smet and Point had exported Catholicism to the Blackfeet, providing the Flatheads' ancient enemies with a commodity previously controlled by them, certainly had a lot to do with the changing relationship. But De Smet never accepted that reality, either.

The murder of fourteen people, including Dr. Marcus Whitman and his wife, Narcissa, at Waiilatpu on November 27, 1847, also negatively affected the Jesuits and their Rocky Mountain Mission. Outraged by the actions of a few Cayuse dissidents, Reverend Henry Spalding publicly vilified the Jesuits by telling all who would listen that the Jesuits used the Indians as pawns in a Catholic plot to destroy Protestantism in the Oregon country. He charged them with masterminding not only the Indian attack but also the Cayuse War that followed. Nor can one discount the effect of the discovery of gold in California on the Rocky Mountain Mission. Prices on the Pacific Coast skyrocketed after 1849, significantly driving up the cost of administering the missions. Father Michael Accolti replaced Joset in 1849 as superior of the missions, and he became so strapped for funds that he advocated relocating some of his Jesuit confreres on the Willamette River of Oregon to the American River of California, letting them dig gold, sell it at a profit, and return the proceeds to the Pacific Northwest. Roothaan disapproved of these plans when he learned of them, but by then Accolti had already gone to California.

Accolti's impertinence so riled Roothaan that on October 30, 1851, the father general completely divorced the Rocky Mountain Mission from the Missouri Vice-Province and placed it directly under his authority. What De Smet thought of this decision we do not know. Perhaps receiving a pardon from the father general satisfied him enough. In any case he declined to comment.

During the summer of 1851, while De Smet counseled at Fort Laramie, Father John Anthony Elet, De Smet's friend and superior, passed away. Father William Stack Murphy, S.J., took over as the new provincial of the Missouri Vice-Province, and he asked De Smet to remain in the same administrative offices De Smet had filled for Elet before leaving for Forts Union and Laramie— that is, unless Murphy reassigned De Smet to Holland or Belgium.

Before he passed away, Elet confided to Roothaan that De Smet might be more useful to the Missouri Vice-Province, and the Oregon Indian missions, if he resided in Europe and raised money full-time. The physical growth of the Missouri Vice-Province and the growing need for a general overhaul of the Indian missions, both in Kansas Territory and the Oregon country, suggested an even greater dependence on the charity of wealthy Europeans in the future. De Smet, though not wishing to separate from his beloved Indians, nevertheless agreed to accept Elet's idea out of obedience to his superiors. Writing to the provincial in Holland, he stated: "To be able to live the life of a religious in the practice of obedience, and when occasion presents, to still be useful to America, if such be the will of my Superiors, is, before God, my earnest desire." Father Murphy, however, chose not to activate Elet's plan and retained De Smet in Saint Louis. From that point forward until his death, De Smet remained the procurator and *socius* of the Missouri Vice-Province.

If De Smet could not live in Europe for the benefit of the Missouri Vice-Province, he could still raise money there on occasion. Accordingly, in April of 1853, De Smet took leave of his duties in Saint Louis and accompanied his friend Bishop John Miége, S.J., the vicar apostolic of the Indian Territory, to Europe on society business. Roothaan passed away on May 8, and the society needed to elect a new father general. The two priests reached the continent in eleven days on the fast-moving steamer *Fulton,* arriving on May 20. Bishop Miége made his way to Rome; De Smet stopped in Paris to deliver a lecture about his work among the Indians to a meeting of the Society for the Propagation of the Faith. After that, De Smet made the rounds of known and potential benefactors to the American Indian missions.

By 1853, Father De Smet enjoyed a deserved reputation in Europe as a great traveler and missionary. His name glimmered in

Europe as the author of two exciting books and numerous magazine articles about the far western frontier of America. Personally, De Smet did not crave the spotlight of acclaim, though it is
easy to see how his public personality led his critics to think
otherwise. In truth, De Smet fancied himself a writer or his-
torian, a detached observer and recorder of human deeds and
events, not a public personality. He did not particularly enjoy, for
instance, speaking in public. He only did it as a means to an
end—specifically, to fatten the purse of the Indian missions. One
person who heard De Smet speak to an audience at a Belgian
seminary characterized the dynamic priest's demeanor at the
podium as calm almost to the point of being cold. Another young
man remarked that De Smet "speaks French badly," though he
hastened to explain that "even this carelessness of speech is agreeable," meaning interesting.

On the other hand, Father De Smet nearly always yielded to
the requests of children, even large, fidgeting audiences of them,
to explain the customs of North American Indians. In schools at
Brussels, Ghent, Antwerp, Namur, and the Sorbonne, De Smet
dressed in Indian paraphernalia, sang campfire songs, costumed
audience volunteers, and told death-defying tales about haz-
ardous encounters with bears, steep mountain passes, and the
peculiarities of Mother Nature. At the conclusion of these per-
formances he asked the children to list their names on a scroll,
telling them that he kept a stockpile of Christian names that he
used when baptizing Indian children. De Smet could also be
persuaded to appear before student audiences at colleges, boarding schools, convents, and seminaries, because from them he recruited men and women for the New World missions. De Smet is
credited with having brought more than eighty priests, brothers,
and nuns to America during his lifetime.

But children and students do not give money, parents do, so
De Smet learned to advertise himself to adult audiences, too. He
ordinarily announced his forthcoming appearances in a city by
calling the nineteenth-century equivalent of a press conference.
Sometimes he even furnished written press releases containing
such immodest quotes as: "Since my last visit to Belgium I have

traversed districts devoid of missions, and where probably no European has ever set foot." Having thus heralded his arrival, De Smet made himself available for newspaper interviews and lectures. After that he contacted the families of current Jesuit missionaries, traditional benefactors of the society, plus members of religious organizations, all of whom jumped at the chance to entertain a celebrity. Whenever possible, De Smet distributed Indian souvenirs.

Clearly, De Smet demonstrated the instincts of an expert fund raiser. It is estimated that his total accumulation from begging reached nearly a quarter of a million dollars, an amount that would easily translate into four times that amount today. In some ways it bothered De Smet that he seemed always to be handling money, either raising it in Europe or disbursing it in Saint Louis. On the other hand, he looked upon fund raising as an Ignatian principle solidly grounded in the constitution of the Society of Jesus. Ignatius Loyola believed that all good deeds eventually shine through to the world. A witness to a good act, for example, may be inspired to do something similar. To enlarge the circle of observers, Ignatius advocated the writing of letters and the publishing of books as legitimate means by which one could let his light shine before all men. Moreover, even as they should preach in public, bury the dead, and offer the Mass, Jesuits should also raise money for the continuation of their good works. In fact, between 1547 and 1556, Ignatius laid down five principles of fund raising for members of the Society of Jesus. De Smet never felt shy about raising money, because he considered it an integral part of his Jesuit vocation.

Happy thoughts occupied De Smet on his journey back to the United States. For one thing, when he rendezvoused with Bishop Miége in Paris in mid-November of 1853, he owned a full purse. He also escorted eight new candidates for the Missouri Vice-Province. The bishop led an additional five recruits, another pleasant surprise. Moreover, Miége brought good news from Rome; the new father general of the Society of Jesus, Father Peter Beckx, S.J., pledged himself to maintain the society's traditional emphasis in education and the missions.

Financial matters occupied large blocks of De Smet's time after his return from Europe in December 1853. "I am now in Ohio, now in Kentucky, now . . . in Missouri," he wrote to one correspondent: "Our colleges, residences, and missions are far apart, and I have to go with the Father-Provincial in all his visits. One thing . . . gives me anxiety from time to time. I hold the general or common purse and have to supply all needs; and this purse is never full; the greater part of the time it is flat." De Smet also kept the accounts for the Rocky Mountain Mission, and after 1854 he received some relief in that area. In that year Father General Beckx renamed the Rocky Mountain Mission the Oregon Mission, combined it administratively with California, and placed all of the Pacific Northwest Indian installations under the financial control of the Turin Province of Jesuits in Italy. In a major move, Father General Beckx turned to older and more established provinces, like Turin, to provide money and missionaries for less well developed missions throughout the world.

With the Turin Province now bearing some of the financial burden for the Oregon Mission, De Smet briefly entertained the notion that he might be able to return to the missions himself:

> My heart, I admit, is ever with the Indians. They frequently send me pressing invitations to return. I am happy to be of use to them here, at least in temporal affairs, and to be able to send our missionaries the means to continue the evangelization of the tribes. The scarcity of our Fathers in St. Louis makes it impossible for me to be relieved of my duties at present, but I have not given up hope, and I beg God unceasingly, if such be His will, to allow me to pass my remaining years in the Far West.

Alas, a return to the missions was not part of De Smet's immediate future. For the time being he would have to satisfy himself by vicariously returning to the western frontier. As usual, De Smet found that release by writing essays for the *Précis Historiques*. Between 1854 and 1856 he readied twenty-seven essays for publication despite the fact that his eyesight began to fail and he could no longer write under artificial light. Sending souvenirs to his family also gave De Smet great pleasure. Porcupine quill–embroidered moccasins, tanned buffalo robes, and long-stemmed clay pipes were particularly prized in Europe and therefore made wonderful gifts. Also eliciting much appreciation were personally annotated maps such as the grand map of frontier America De Smet sent to his brother Charles in April 1855 with the accompanying instructions: "Hang this map in a conspicuous place in your house, and now and then glance at it. You will be able to trace the countries through which I have traveled in my journeys from New Orleans to Halifax, and from Nova Scotia to the Athabasca glaciers north of the Rocky Mountains. Quietly seated in your chair, you can follow me through the seas, prairies, and mountains I have traversed, beset with innumerable dangers; in steamboats, bark canoes, on horseback, and on foot."

As the calendar turned to 1854, De Smet's desire to return to the West as a missionary took on a new, unexpected twist. He just wanted to get out of Saint Louis. Confiding his fears to his brother Francis on September 8, De Smet wrote: "The times are becoming terrible for Catholics in these unhappy States. Nowhere in the world do honest men enjoy less liberty." He referred to the growing anti-Catholic attitude then being tolerated, if not fostered, in Saint Louis. By the middle of the nineteenth century nearly one hundred thousand persons resided in Saint Louis, a significant number of them Catholic immigrants recently arrived from Europe. Saint Louis Catholics already supported a large cathedral, a seminary for priests, several boarding schools, a hospital, and Saint Louis University with their charity; now the church added eleven new parishes. But the immigrants to Saint Louis also included numerous radicals and demagogues who brought with them from Europe a hatred for and distrust of the Jesuits, secular priests, and Catholics in general. As a result, beginning in 1852, Saint Louis detached itself from its frontier earthiness and became a fertile breeding ground for a violent anti-immigration, anti-Catholic political party called the Know-Nothings. In them De Smet found much to fear.

Assuming the role of a spoiler in state and national politics from roughly 1852 to 1856, the Know-Nothings made a name for themselves by harassing immigrants and, by association, the Catholic religion of Irish, German, and Polish refugees. As procurator for his province, De Smet frequently traveled between Saint Louis and other Jesuit installations at Louisville, Cincinnati, Chicago, and Milwaukee, and he came to know firsthand the organized discrimination inherent in this anti-Catholic movement. Sadly, De Smet commented, "The right to defame and exile is the order of the day in this great Republic, it is now the rendezvous of the demagogues and outlaws of every country." To his nephew Paul, he confided: "Our situation is far from pleasant. We live in constant apprehension, yet not in fear. In any case, it is well to be prepared and pray much."

The Jesuits at Saint Louis cherished all the support they could get during this stressful period, and, fortunately, not the least of their continuing, and public, champions included Senator Thomas Hart Benton, Missouri's most prominent politician. In March 1852, Benton's twenty-two-year-old son Randolph, an active Protestant like the rest of his family, neared death after a severe illness. The senator sought theological comfort from his old friend Father De Smet, who hastened to Randolph's bedside just hours before he died. The distraught senator deeply appreciated the priest's devotion and henceforth became, for both De Smet and the society, a trusted and valuable ally in the political arena of Washington, D.C.

For the next several years De Smet intentionally kept a low public profile lest he antagonize the Know-Nothings. A meeting with General William S. Harney in May 1858, however, broke his concentration. The general forthrightly asked De Smet to join a military expedition he was assembling to invade Utah Territory. The previous autumn a force of some three thousand soldiers had attempted to escort a new governor to Utah Territory, but Brigham Young, the leader of the Church of Jesus Christ of Latter-day Saints, or Mormons, succeeded in halting the federal column by cutting them off from their supplies while they were still a good distance from Salt Lake City. Young, apparently, saw in the escort a hidden agenda to impose U.S. territorial authority over his independent State of Deseret. General Harney had orders to form a new army, rescue the first battalion, protect the governor, and restore order in the territory.

De Smet knew General Harney only by his reputation as a foul-mouthed Indian campaigner whom the *New York Times* once described as a "vulgar, ungentlemanly personage, who treats men with familiar brutality." In 1855, Harney achieved notoriety when he made the first-ever U.S. Army expedition to the upper Missouri country and landed a devastating blow on the Brulé Sioux. The Lakotas called him "Mad Bear," one leader remarking that "the Big Chief of the soldiers is an awful man, when he speaks to us he makes us tremble." Now Harney intended to direct his considerable organizational talents against the members of the Church of Jesus Christ of Latter-day Saints, and he offered De Smet the position of chaplain of the U.S. Army. Why? Primarily because Harney worried that certain western tribes might join with the Mormons and attack his command; under those circumstances De Smet could intercede with the Indians.

General Harney also knew that in the autumn of 1846, De Smet had met Brigham Young at Winter Quarters, a temporary city established by the Mormons not far from Council Bluffs. Young and about ten thousand Mormons had fled Nauvoo, Illinois, after a pitched battle with non-Mormons had left Joseph Smith, the sect's founder, dead. Young sought a refuge in the far West and believed De Smet could help him choose the most distant and remote hideaway. At the time, De Smet pitied the sect for their persecution and considered Young a "kind and polite gentleman." A decade later De Smet held a different opinion.

After he came to know more about their practices and beliefs, De Smet characterized the Latter-day Saints as an "abomination of abominations" composed of "polygamous fanatics." Joseph Smith, the founder, exhibited "no moral character" and only pretended to have a revelation from God. De Smet likened the Book of Mormon to a novel, calling it a composition of adroit phrases connected by "a tissue of contradictory plagiarisms and absurd inventions." Furthermore, De Smet wrote an article about the Mormons, criticizing them for destroying the fragile nature of the Salt Lake valley by denuding the hillsides of trees and redirecting the valley's scarce water supply into irrigation ditches.

Harney was not the first government official to request De Smet's presence on an overland expedition, nor would he be the last. The newly appointed governor of Washington Territory, Isaac I. Stevens, for example, had urged De Smet to join him when he set out for the Pacific Northwest in 1853, knowing that the missionary's experience with the Blackfeet could be especially valuable to his expedition. De Smet had declined that invitation. But Harney's offer intrigued him. Yes, he would go along on Harney's expedition; it would be a pleasure to see the Mormons "mastered and expelled," preferably to Mexico. All of these judgments, by the way, were from a priest who not so long before had complained about the religious persecution of Catholics by the Know-Nothings. It is doubtful that De Smet's attitude toward the Mormons, if he knew it at all, would have distressed Harney; the general himself is reputed to have said, off the record, that he would "hang Brigham first and try him afterward."

As if De Smet needed additional reasons to accept Harney's offer, the general informed De Smet that approximately three-fourths of his army unit of two thousand men professed an allegiance to Catholicism. As chaplain, De Smet would be present to renew the faith of the men while they marched under arms. De Smet harbored yet a final motive for joining Harney's expedition. As he explained to the vice-provincial: "It is probable that I shall proceed from Utah to the Flathead Mission to confer with the Fathers about a new establishment among the Blackfeet."

Father Murphy could hardly restrain the eager De Smet from immediately abandoning his desk piled high with province business. After all, De Smet's reasons for going did make sense. In Murphy's view, Roothaan's prohibition that De Smet should establish no more missions had died with the father general. Moreover, did not De Smet deserve a chance to revisit the Rocky Mountain missions that he had nurtured these many years? Murphy therefore approved De Smet's request to accept the appointment as chaplain of the U.S. Army and envoy extraordinary.

The Utah Expedition left Fort Leavenworth on June 15, 1858,

but it never reached Salt Lake City. Approximately five hundred miles out of Fort Leavenworth, near the ford of the South Platte River, on July 8, General Harney received word that the Mormons had submitted to federal authority and he could return to his post. This news punctured De Smet's plans to visit the Pacific Northwest. De Smet took the news philosophically, though, for he had already seen enough changes in the burgeoning Great Plains and did not need to proceed any farther. "The face of the country is entirely changed," De Smet noted in his journal, referring to the numerous white settlements and "extensive and beautiful farms that have been established in all directions" since he first crossed the Southern Plains in 1840.

Theoretically De Smet favored progress and settlement of the plains. Seeing it up close again, after an absence of several years, however, was something of a shock. In 1851, De Smet had viewed the Oregon Trail with a band of Indian chiefs en route to the Fort Laramie council, and at that time the litter he and his companions saw made them giddy with curiosity. The continued deterioration of the Great Medicine Road no longer amused De Smet, it disgusted him, littered as it was with

> the wrecks of wagons and the skeletons of oxen, but especially the remains of the wardrobe of the traveler: legs of pantaloons and drawers, a short-bosom, the back or arm of a flannel vest, stockings out at toe and heel, crownless hats, and shoes worn through in the soles or uppers. These deserted camps are also marked by packs of cards strewed round among broken jars and bottles; here you see a grid-iron, a coffee-pot or a tin bowl; there a cooking-stove and the fragments of a shaving-dish, all worn out and cast aside.

Rubble repelled De Smet, but even worse, how could the Indians not regard such rags and refuse as "the harbingers of the approach of a dismal future for themselves"?

The uniqueness of the Great Plains and its potential uses for mankind raised many questions for De Smet. He loved the plains and showered it with praise in many exuberant letters to friends and family. At one point he compared the plains on the middle section of the Platte River to the groomed estates of European noblemen, citing in particular "the undulations of the river, the waving of the verdure, the alternations of light and shade, and the purity of the atmosphere." Such a description may have been accurate when De Smet first encountered the virgin plains, but the dynamic five-year period after 1846, when the United States first felt the bellicose strains of Manifest Destiny and the Mexican War, changed all of that. After the midcentury mark the westward movement took on an urgency that threatened to destroy the gardenlike west that De Smet knew as a young man.

Equally disturbing, while America fought the Mexican War, over in Europe a series of modest revolutions rocked France, Austria, Italy, and Prussia, pushing more and more immigrants across the Atlantic Ocean to the American frontier. By a quirk of fate, De Smet himself fed Europe's appetite for information about the Missouri River country through his publications, particularly his two books. Caught up in the spirit of Manifest Destiny, De Smet invited husbandmen from Europe and America to furrow the plains and receive in return an ample reward. "Europe's thousands of poor, who cry for bread and wander without shelter or hope, often occur to my thoughts," De Smet wrote in one publication, "'Unhappy poor,' I often cry, 'why are ye not here? Your industry and toil would end your sorrows. Here you might rear a smiling home, and reap in plenty the fruit of your toil.'" He predicted confidently that someday "the sound of the axe and hammer will echo in this wilderness; broad farms, with orchard and vineyard, alive with domestic animals and poultry, will cover these desert plains to provide for thick-coming cities, which will rise as if by enchantment with dome and tower, church and college, school and house."

This left De Smet with several dilemmas. On one hand he wanted the West to remain as he had first viewed it, a pristine frontier ruled by proud native tribes. On the other hand he also felt the spirit of Manifest Destiny and wanted Americans and Europeans to use the land as God intended, for cultivation. He did not wish to see the Indian unfairly treated, yet he hoped that the plains, "naturally so rich and verdant," could be used to their potential. But if white pioneers occupied the land, what then would become of the Indians? How could the natives not feel

anger, or even revenge, he wondered, when they saw the homeland of their fathers "about to pass into the hands of the rapacious white man: and they, poor mortals, accustomed to roam
at large and over a vast space, free like the birds of the air, will
be enclosed in narrow reserves, far from their cherished hunting grounds and fine fisheries, far from their fields of roots and
fruits; or driven back into the mountains or to unknown shores"?
Alas, he did not know the solution to the problem. Some of the
pieces to the solution were already in his mind, but not all.
Perhaps he could devise a complete answer upon his return to
Saint Louis when he resumed his administrative tasks.

"My stay in Saint Louis was short," De Smet wrote happily in
his journal. Although he intended to resign his army commission,
no sooner did De Smet arrive back at Saint Louis University than
General Harney solicited his assistance a second time. While the
Utah Expedition marched back and forth across the Great Plains
the previous summer, the Coeur d'Alene Indian War raged in the
territories of Oregon and Washington. The secretary of war, in
an attempt to isolate this troublesome region, created a new
military department, and he made Harney, the army's most experienced Indian fighter, its commanding general. Harney knew
from personal experience that De Smet was a cooperative campaigner. More importantly, De Smet had once engaged in missionary work with some of the warring tribes. So, for the second
time in a year, Harney asked De Smet to accompany him on an
expedition. The general and his staff planned to leave New York
City by ship on September 20, 1858, and proceed to Fort Vancouver by way of Panama and San Francisco. He hoped De Smet
would accept his invitation to travel with him and use his influence to restore peace.

Once again, Father Murphy exhibited kindly patience with his
socius and gave De Smet permission to join General Harney in the
field. Father General Beckx, unlike Roothaan, admired De Smet
for his energy and resourcefulness, thus making it easier for superiors of the Missouri Vice-Province to release him from his ordinary duties without fear of contradiction. As before, Murphy
justified the leave by citing the potential for religious work.

"I consented to retain my position of army chaplain in the new army," De Smet confirmed; "I hoped to be of some service in that capacity to the men, but above all to the Indian tribes of the mountains." Then he added: "I desired greatly also to be in touch with my missionary brethren in the difficulties which the war would doubtless bring upon them."

Without doubt, De Smet's missionary brethren could use a dose of consolation and assistance. When Father General Beckx had combined the Oregon and California missions, he had placed both units under the authority of a single provincial—not a very wise move, it turned out. Unfortunately, Father Nicholas Congiato, S.J., who made Santa Clara his headquarters, better understood the conditions in California than in Oregon, and eventually he lost touch with the major influences affecting the inland northwest Indian missions. Four years too late, on March 1, 1858, Beckx realized his mistake and separated the California and Oregon missions from each other, though both regions remained financially dependent upon the Turin Province. By then the damage had already been done in the Pacific Northwest.

The relationship between the Jesuits and the Indians in the Oregon Mission, never the same after De Smet left in 1846, suffered a new tremor when Isaac Stevens, governor of Washington Territory and superintendent of territorial Indian affairs, began to pester the interior tribes into accepting reservations. Reluctantly, in 1855 the Indians ceded large parcels of their land in a series of controversial treaties. Whenever possible at these conferences the governor invited the local Jesuit missionaries. During the course of the council, Stevens frequently directed his remarks specifically to the priests, thus making it appear to the Indians that the Jesuits leaned agreeably to the side of the federal government. That impression continued when the Jesuits encouraged the tribes to heed the governor's plan. They did so not because of Stevens's superior wisdom, but because the missionaries knew, better than the Indians, what fate held for those tribes who did not subordinate their interests to the government's. Finally, when the Jesuits spoke to the governor about the needs of the Indians, pleading for schools, trade shops, mills, hospitals, and orphanages on the reservations, the Indians erroneously thought that the Jesuits were assuming responsibility for these projects. In short, the Indian relationship with the Jesuits in the Pacific Northwest exhibited a great deal more dynamism than it did in the simple, halcyon days of De Smet's first mission to the Flatheads.

In spite of Stevens's treaties and reservations, white men did not stay away from the Indians' lands, especially after the discovery of gold near Colville in Washington Territory. Like a catalyst, the gold rushers stimulated an already volatile situation. Meanwhile, the Jesuits found it increasingly difficult to hold the tribes in peace at overburdened and underfunded missions. Matters passed a point of no return in May 1858, when the Indians defeated Colonel Edward Steptoe in a direct confrontation and a full-scale war followed.

On October 16, while they refreshed themselves in San Francisco, General Harney and Father De Smet received the news that the Indian war in Washington Territory had ended. Newspapers confirmed that Colonel George Wright had settled the outcome of the Coeur d'Alene War when he defeated several hundred Spokanes and Coeur d'Alenes in two brutal battles during August and September. The full military report included these developments: Colonel Wright twice chastised the Indians, then dictated mandatory peace treaties for both the Coeur d'Alenes and the Spokanes and summarily hanged eleven Indians. At the moment, he held thirty-three "notorious" natives as hostages at Fort Walla Walla. Continuing on to Fort Vancouver, Harney enjoyed the luxury of a full week to decide what to do next.

The official cessation of hostilities pleased Harney, though he knew from personal experience that peace on the frontier could be delicate and unpredictable. There were, after all, an estimated forty-two thousand native people within the military department for which he took responsibility on October 24, and, as his senior officers reminded him, not all of the tribesmen had been defeated by Colonel Wright. De Smet chipped in that most likely even the conquered Indians would retain their prejudices against

De Smet sat for this photograph in October 1858, when he stopped in San Francisco on his way to Fort Vancouver. Courtesy of Oregon Province Archives of the Society of Jesus, Gonzaga University.

the whites in spite of pledging peace. Moreover, "there were false reports to be rectified. Otherwise the war might break out afresh."

Inasmuch as both De Smet and Harney wished to avoid further bloodshed, one thinking more of the Indians and the other more of his soldiers, they decided on October 28 to send directly to the Indian camps an envoy who would meet privately with the chiefs and reinforce for them the benefits of peace and the foolishness of war. De Smet volunteered; Harney agreed. Such a service was, after all, the exact reason why the government had transported De Smet from one end of the continent to the other. Harney professed great confidence in De Smet's ability to influence the interior tribes to make peace, but he also cautioned the priest to tell the Indians that if they turned a deaf ear to this message, in the spring his troops would "most assuredly be placed upon their trail." Harney's orders from the secretary of war required as much.

Leaving Fort Vancouver on October 29, 1858, with only a single companion to serve as guide and interpreter, De Smet hastened to Fort Walla Walla to see the Coeur d'Alene and Spokane hostages. They were still there, and so, too, was Colonel Wright— and even Father Congiato, late of Santa Clara. Indians throughout the region grew restless, Congiato reported to De Smet, mainly because of the hostages. They must be released if the government seriously hoped to maintain peace. De Smet offered to relieve Wright of the responsibility for the hostages. He would take them with him "into their own country, if it were only to pass the winter." Wright refused. De Smet shot back that such an action was consistent with the spirit of Harney's written orders that all post commanders should provide De Smet with guides, escorts, animals, and even express messengers. Surely that list also included hostages by inference.

Wright, an obstinate man who had seen bloodshed in the Indian wars up close, refused to release the hostages, being either unable or unwilling to see that by paroling the prisoners to De Smet the priest gained immediate credibility with the tribes and therefore greatly increased the chance of success for his peace mission. At this point the post commander, who understood better than Wright that De Smet acted with the complete approval of General Harney, interceded and released the prisoners to the priest. The captives, said De Smet, "were greatly surprised at my arrival, after an absence of eleven years," especially "in view of the unhappy situation in which they found themselves."

It did not take long, just three days, for De Smet and his Indian charges to follow the trail from Fort Walla Walla to the foot of Lake Coeur d'Alene. De Smet strode down the trail purposefully, anxious to see his brother priests at Sacred Heart Mission; the Indians followed along, just as intent upon returning to their home villages. "In these long evenings, seated around the camp-fire, the Indians loved to relate to me, with really touching simplicity, the principal things that had happened since I left them, such as the death of their chiefs, etc.," De Smet remembered later; "On my side, I did not lack interesting things to tell them."

Once again De Smet breathed the pure air of the mountains, a treat he had dreamt about many times during his forced absence. "When one has been traveling for some time through monotonous and treeless countries, having to camp every night by some fringe of brush insufficient to maintain a good fire, or on the banks of a little river, brook or stream; and then when one comes to a noble forest, where gigantic trees rise on the border of a vast lake, whose water is clear as crystal, the emotions aroused in one by the contrast are such as cannot be described." Here, too, De Smet found "several Coeur d'Alene families, who received me with the liveliest cordiality. The unexpected return of the prisoners heightened the universal joy still further." That night a heavy snowfall and a steady rain enveloped the camp, making it impossible to leave in the morning. None of that, however, prevented Father Gregory Gazzoli, S.J., from slogging the forty miles from Sacred Heart Mission to greet De Smet. "The good Father gave me a great deal of news," says De Smet, "some consoling and some sad, concerning the country and the Indians."

When at last De Smet arrived at the new Coeur d'Alene Mission of the Sacred Heart of Jesus, Father Louis Vercruysse, S.J.,

and Brother Francis Huybrechts, S.J., provided their own welcome. They also informed De Smet that snow filled all the passes
of the mountains and heavy ice already floated on the rivers and
lakes. De Smet would have to postpone until spring any plans he
might have had about going on to the Flatheads' mission, six
days distant and deep in the mountains. This news, of course,
distressed De Smet, but not greatly. To spend the winter among
the Coeur d'Alenes could be quite agreeable.

The church, a massive structure of frontier-adapted Italian Renaissance design, sat prominently on a knoll above the North
Fork of the Coeur d'Alene River. Sacred Heart Mission boasted
eight log houses for Indians and priests, a barn and stable, a mill
to grind wheat, plus blacksmith, carpenter, and bake shops. Two
cultivated fields yielded "prodigious crops," averaging 80–120
bushels of wheat per acre even when harvested with primitive
equipment. The complete mission of homes, work buildings, and
church, De Smet judged, would be "a credit to any civilized
country." Even more than the physical comforts the mission
provided, De Smet appreciated the religious devotion of the Indians. Saying Midnight Mass for the Coeur d'Alenes on the great
feast of Christmas 1858 provided a moment of intense satisfaction
for the missionary priest. "It reminded me," he said, "of the
reunions of the early Christians, who were of one mind and one
soul."

As usual, De Smet maintained a heavy schedule of correspondence during his trips, so the weather-enforced wait of eighty-
seven days at Sacred Heart helped him to clear away all outstand-
ing obligations. Among the most important letters he penned
that winter was one directed to Major Alfred Pleasonton, General Harney's aide. In it De Smet suggested a conference between the Indian leaders and General Harney at Fort Vancouver.
Based upon his discussion with Indians, De Smet reported, the
tribesmen did not necessarily accept the idea that they had been
bested by a superior military force. Instead, the war came to
a conclusion because the Indians tired of it. Perhaps a face-to-
face conference would truly bring about a lasting conclusion to
the war.

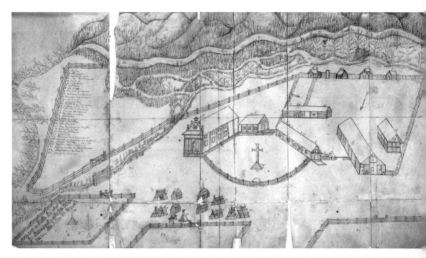

De Smet drew this sepia ink illustration during the winter of 1858–59 when he reside
at the Coeur d'Alene Mission of the Sacred Heart of Jesus. Twenty-three location
including mission buildings, Indian dwellings, and natural features, are numbere
and identified. Courtesy of De Smetiana Collection, Jesuit Missouri Province A
chives, Saint Louis IX-C9-2.

Impetuous in the extreme when it came to travel, even in
winter, De Smet did not wait for Pleasonton's reply. Ignoring the
fact that forty-three days of snow had packed drifts solidly in
the mountain passes, in mid-February 1859, De Smet left Sacred
Heart anyway. His itinerary called for stops at the Kalispel mission on the Pend Oreille River, old Saint Mary's Mission in the
Bitterroot Valley, where many Flatheads still lived, and, finally, a
first-ever visit to the new mission, Saint Ignatius, established just
five years earlier in the Mission Valley. Winds, rain, ice, and snow
all hindered De Smet's progress. It took twenty-two days alone
to cover the first one hundred miles.

Even so, the arduous trip to the three missions provided precious moments for De Smet, as the Kalispels, Kootenais, Flatheads, and Pend Oreilles he met welcomed him "home" with
sincere joy. How could he not feel a flush of success in what he
had accomplished during the 1840s when everywhere the principal chiefs assured him that even still they "continued to assemble

morning and evening for prayers, to ring the angelus at the accustomed hour, and to rest on Sunday." But how could he also not feel sad at the modest Jesuit presence among the interior Indians. "Doubtless, in the absence of the missionaries," De Smet concluded, "the enemy of souls has committed some ravages among them, but by the grace of God the evil is not irreparable."

At the final stop on his journey, the new Saint Ignatius Mission, General Harney's letter caught up with De Smet. The general praised the idea of bringing in some Indian leaders for a council at Fort Vancouver; to further the prospect of goodwill he offered to pay the food and travel expenses for all the chiefs. Suitably encouraged, De Smet made the necessary arrangements for ten chiefs of the Pend Oreilles, Kalispels, Flatheads, Coeur d'Alenes, Yakimas, and Spokanes to travel with him to meet the general. One of the chiefs, De Smet informed Harney, would be Kamiakin, the reputed ringleader of the war and thus an important piece in the puzzle for a permanent peace. When he heard the news, Harney passed the intelligence along to his superior with a prediction that a lasting peace would certainly result from the meeting.

It took a solid month for De Smet and the Indians to make their way out of the mountains: "For ten days we had to clear a way through thick forests, where thousands of trees, thrown down by storms, lay across one another, and were covered, four, six and eight feet with snow; several horses perished in this dangerous passage." He had forgotten, De Smet chided himself, how demanding travel in the Rocky Mountains could be, how strenuous compared with travel on the Great Plains and the upper Missouri River country. "We suffered much and ran many dangers on the route," he wrote in lighthearted fashion, "but aside from some serious bruises and scratches, a hat battered to pieces, a torn pair of trousers, and a black-gown in rags, I came out of it safe and sound."

When the entourage reached Fort Walla Walla on May 13, the Indians paused for a few days; De Smet went ahead to Fort Vancouver. Unfortunately, in De Smet's absence the Flathead agent, John Owen, who accompanied the party on his own responsibility, tried to impose his will on the chiefs, acting as if their "surrender" had been his personal accomplishment. Owen's haughty attitude frightened Kamiakin, and one night he just disappeared into the darkness. Harney, when he found out, exploded in anger, but what could he do? The council with the other chiefs, however, took place as arranged.

During the course of the Indians' three-week stay at Fort Vancouver, Father De Smet and General Harney followed different agendas with the chiefs. De Smet thought it particularly important to impress upon the Indians the progress associated with white man's civilization and therefore showed the Indians "the principal cities and towns of the State of Oregon and Washington Territory, with everything remarkable in the way of industrial establishments, steam engines, forges, manufactories and printing establishments." Consistent with his object lesson of showing the tribesmen not only the benefits of cooperation but also the futility of resistance, De Smet conducted them to other locations as well: "The visit which appeared the most to interest the chiefs, was that which they made to the prison at Portland and its wretched inmates, whom they found chained within its cells."

For Harney the most important event on the Indian schedule took place on May 28, 1859, when he sat down in council. The general's gruff demeanor and sledgehammer personality probably impeded discussion, but in any case the Indians expressed their desire for peace. They promised not to make war again, and they pleaded for protected reservations. Harney reiterated the government promises in the treaties previously concluded by Stevens and Wright and then passed out some official letters proclaiming the chiefs to be "good" men.

Harney shared with many others of his time a belief that the Indian race as a whole, not just the tribes of the Pacific Northwest, were destined to gradually disappear, and he could not prevent that. But Harney, in spite of his fatalistic attitude, showed special interest in a plan suggested to him by Father De Smet. The priest's plan called for the United States to reserve and

As part of the three-week peace council in May and June of 1859 at Fort Vancouver, Washington Territory, the Indian chiefs had their picture taken with De Smet. The original photograph made the Indians look unkempt and inattentive so De Smet, ever conscious of the need to "sell" his Indians to potential donors, had the picture retouched. The final form, shown above, shows the Indians "cleaned-up" and in a pensive mood. The Indians are, *left to right, front row:* Victor, Kalispel; Alexander, Pend Oreille; Adolphe, Flathead; Andrew, Coeur d'Alene; and *back row,* Dennis, Colville; Bonaventure, Coeur d'Alene; De Smet; and Francis Xavier, Flathead. Courtesy of Oregon Province Archives of the Society of Jesus, Gonzaga University.

protect a vast territory bounded by the Rocky Mountains, the Bitterroot Mountains, the Kootenai River, and the forty-ninth parallel for the exclusive use of the tribes in Oregon and Washington Territory for a minimum of twenty years. White men, except for missionaries of all denominations, would be barred from these lands while the Indians dedicated themselves to education and agriculture. By voluntarily removing themselves to a large and diverse reserve, De Smet observed, the Indians would demonstrate their willingness to adopt the economy, habits, and culture of the white man.

De Smet's Fort Vancouver proposal demonstrates his continuing affection for reservations as the solution to the vexatious "Indian Question." Why, De Smet asked, could not the Indian become a white man in twenty years? The idea of a protected reservation particularly absorbed him after he saw firsthand the changes wrought by energetic white pioneers on the Great Plains. His travels in connection with the Fort Laramie council in 1851, and again with the Utah Expedition, reminded him of the potential of the whole western portion of the continent with its perfect valleys, prime forests, and sufficient rivers. Time and again he advertised the advantages of the Great Plains to Europeans, and he could easily do the same for the Pacific Northwest, yet it troubled him that natives who lived in this land of plenty exhibited neither the education nor the agricultural skills to utilize its full potential. Thus they were almost sure to lose it. "The judgment of the savage is not sufficiently ripe to be able to compete with the wisdom of man born in the bosom of civilization," De Smet concluded, but in twenty years that could change.

The results obtained by the Jesuits in Kansas showed De Smet that the Indians could be civilized under the Euro-American model. But the Indians needed time. One must imagine, De Smet wrote to a patron of the missions in 1858, "two races brought into contact, the one keeping its barbarous habits, the other enjoying all the advantages of civilization. How many years must elapse before there is complete fusion between the two? Neither the second nor the third generation will witness that happy result." In the interests of finding that element of time, De Smet normally advised the Indians to submit to government demands. He did so unofficially at Fort Laramie in 1851 and again now at Fort Vancouver. He regretted that he himself had so little faith that the federal government would live up to its promises, laws, and treaties with regard to the Indians. But De Smet trusted General Harney, and he hoped that this time, for the sake of the Indians, things would be different.

Harney endorsed "the wise and humane suggestion of Father De Smet" and forwarded it to the secretary of war. He recommended it, he said, because such a reservation contained three necessary elements for success: the area contained enough natural resources for the self-sufficiency of the Indians, it did not seem to be in immediate demand by whites other than gold seekers, and it included a network of Jesuit missions. He probably did not realize how closely his position paralleled De Smet's arguments for the establishment of a series of Jesuit reductions nearly two decades earlier. Nothing came of Harney's overture to the War Department, however, in large measure because by the time the secretary received it, Governor Isaac Stevens had already persuaded Congress to ratify his own set of Indian treaties with reservations of his own design for the Umatillas, Yakimas, Nez Percés, Coeur d'Alenes, and other tribes.

De Smet now turned his attention to the return journey to Saint Louis. Although Harney invited De Smet to join him and his staff on board a ship, reversing the voyage that had brought them to Fort Vancouver, De Smet declined because he harbored some vague notion about contacting the Comanche Indians, possibly to interview them as candidates for a future Jesuit mission. General Harney approved De Smet's request to return via an overland route, and he even provided the priest with six good horses, a fine tent, and a letter of introduction to all military personnel.

The first leg of De Smet's journey, up the Columbia River, across the Spokane Desert, and along the North Fork of the Coeur d'Alene River to Sacred Heart Mission, passed without incident. The second leg, from Sacred Heart to the Mission Valley, became a succession of perilous passages. De Smet could have taken any of four or more well-marked trails to get where he wanted to go, but even at nearly sixty years of age he insisted on blazing his own trail. Later, when he wrote about the trip, De Smet asked his readers to "imagine thick, untrodden forests, strewn with thousands of trees thrown down by age and storms in every direction, where the path is scarcely visible, and is obstructed by barricades, which the horses are constantly compelled to leap, and which always endanger the riders." A pair of rivers, one of which he crossed thirty-nine times and the other of which he waded thirty-two times, further slowed his progress. One particularly painful climb up a mountain encountered snow drifts up to twelve feet high and took eight hours. Father Congiato, De Smet's only companion on this trek, remembered the descent: "Sometimes we were on the edge of sheer precipices of rock, sometimes on a slope almost perpendicular. The least false step might precipitate us into the abyss. Without guide, without path, in the most profound darkness, separated one from the other, each calling for help without being able either to give or to obtain the least assistance, we fell again and again, we walked, feeling our way with our hands, or crawled on all fours, slipping or sliding down as best we could."

When he reached Saint Ignatius Mission, De Smet dropped his plan to contact the Comanches on the southern Great Plains. The adversity of overland travel he had experienced thus far convinced him that at his age he should sell his horses at Fort Benton and take a steamboat the rest of the way to Saint Louis. Unfortunately, when he arrived at Fort Benton on July 29, 1859, there was no commercial vessel at the dock, and none was expected soon. Undeterred, De Smet bought a skiff and hired three oarsmen and a pilot to take him to Saint Louis.

Moving downstream with the current, De Smet's canoelike craft made anywhere from fifty to eighty miles each day. When he came upon an Indian village, De Smet usually stopped to converse with the natives, but essentially he considered his month-long journey a glorious, extended camping trip.

> During this trip on the river we passed the nights in the open air, or under a little tent, often on sand-banks, to avoid the mosquitoes, or on the skirts of a plain, or in an untrodden thick forest. We often heard the howlings of the wolves; and the grunting of the grizzly bear, the king of animals in these parts, disturbed our sleep, but without alarming us. . . . During the whole route, our wants were constantly supplied; yes, we lived in the midst of the greatest abundance. The rivers furnished us excellent fish, water-fowl, ducks, geese and swans; the forests and plains gave us fruits and roots. We never wanted for game: we found everywhere either immense herds of buffalo, or deer, antelope, mountain sheep or bighorn, pheasants, wild turkeys and partridges.

Not until he reached Omaha on September 9 did De Smet and his tiny crew meet a steamboat running in their direction. Happily abandoning his "little cockleshell," De Smet cashed out his boatmen with a total of $120 in government funds, boarded the steamer, bought a ticket for $18, and completed the final seven hundred miles of his journey in relative comfort. He arrived at Saint Louis on September 23. Shortly after his arrival, as was his practice, De Smet went to the home of Dr. Moses L. Linton and recorded in his friend's ornate album a brief summary of his journey. For 1858 and 1859 combined, De Smet estimated that he had traveled more than fifteen thousand miles.

CHAPTER 6

While the Nation Fought a War, 1860–1865

DURING his brief tenure as chaplain of the U.S. Army, De Smet spent $1,059.22 of government funds, most of which he paid to guides and interpreters. Although he looked proudly upon his government service, as the designated beggar for the Missouri Vice-Province De Smet needed a better paying job. Thus, as soon as the secretary of war accepted his resignation in 1860, De Smet sailed for Europe, his twelfth trip across the Atlantic, to raise funds for both the St. Louis Jesuits and his favorite charity, the Oregon Mission, formerly the Rocky Mountain Mission. The "thank you" notes he penned upon his return to St. Louis in April 1861 indicate a high level of success. He brought with him approximately 66,000 francs (about twelve thousand dollars): 40,368 francs for the Missouri Vice-Province and 25,630 francs specifically dedicated to offset future travel expenses related to promoting Indian missions.

Thoroughly appreciative of his efforts on their behalf, his brother Jesuits in Washington Territory nonetheless refrained from heaping unconditional gratitude on De Smet. In 1861, Fathers Nicholas Congiato, Gregory Gazzoli, and Adrian Hoecken all complained to Father Felix Sopranis, S.J., the father general's visitor for Jesuit houses in America, that De Smet's excursion to Washington Territory during the winter of 1858–59 had hindered their work by distracting the Indians with old memories and new promises. Father Joseph Giorda, S.J., superior of the Oregon Mission, also wrote to Father General Beckx asking why he did not have access to the funds raised by De Smet. Were they De Smet's to dole out as he saw fit? "I should like to know (if I be not too presumptuous)," Father Giorda asked sarcastically, "to what extent we [in the missions] can draw upon the said Father and upon his purse. For I have never been able to find out whether Father De Smet's money belongs to the Missouri Vice-Province, or to Oregon, or to the Father General." By the same token, could De Smet raise money in Europe in the name of the Oregon Mission and then divert the funds to, say, the Comanches or the Sioux?

Father General Beckx brought De Smet's superior, Father Murphy, into the controversy. Murphy responded that criticism of De Smet stemmed from his ruthless attitude when acting in the capacity of the vice-province procurator: "Our people are very hard in their judgment on this good Father; among outsiders he enjoys the greatest reputation and popularity. To the latter he is said to show himself very benevolent and gracious, but to his brethren not so. To explain, as Procurator of the Province he is most exacting in money affairs, and perhaps querulous and out of sorts if any delay or dispute turns up, as happens, and, furthermore, he easily imagines that he is going to incur some loss or risk." Murphy attributed De Smet's irascibility to "the nomadic life he has led ever since youth; he does not easily accommodate himself to the details of common life [with the Jesuits]."

In the end, Father Beckx weighed all the arguments and decided that as long as De Smet raised good sums of money, he would trust him to expend them wisely and without interference. In this single action Beckx lifted from De Smet's shoulders any previous criticism by the curia in Rome, and the veteran missionary accepted it for what it was, a vote of confidence.

Buoyed by Beckx's decision, De Smet turned his attention to the condition of the Oregon Mission. In the waning summer months of 1861 he paid fourteen hundred dollars for plows, tools, cross-cut saws, household utensils, and various other supplies. Mostly he used money he had brought back from Europe, though he did have some personal funds at his disposal. De Smet looked forward to delivering the supplies, probably as far as Fort Benton, but unforeseen events came up, and he reluctantly entrusted all twenty-four bales and forty boxes, a total of seven thousand pounds, to Charles Chouteau, an alumnus of Saint Louis University and a close friend. The Chouteau family operated the American Fur Company, and as a courtesy they allowed the Jesuits free transportation and freight on their Missouri River steamboats. Alas, the precious cargo destined for the Oregon Mission perished in a fire before it reached its destination. Undaunted by this adversity, De Smet vowed to raise more money and buy more supplies. Next time, however, he would personally escort the consignment to Fort Benton.

Part of the money De Smet needed he raised in East Coast cities such as Baltimore, New York, and Washington, D.C. Not long after his arrival in Washington, De Smet witnessed the disorderly retreat of the Union army in the aftermath of the Battle of Bull Run. For months news about the secession of several Southern states and the formation of the Confederate States of America dominated the conversation of citizens and clerics alike, but nothing prepared the priest for the sad scene he saw: "For miles, a straggling line of haggard officers and soldiers of every branch of the service, in tattered uniforms, without arms and knapsacks, pushed their way pell-mell among the carts, ambulances, and vehicles of every description."

Privately, De Smet blamed slavery for the break between the states. President Abraham Lincoln, he believed, acted correctly in calling for an end to its expansion into new territories. But De Smet, always a discrete pragmatist, realized that his recent good work in the service of the federal government granted him a certain preferred status with public officials in the War Department, and he must now be careful not to jeopardize his position by public expressions on current affairs. "I am keeping my mouth shut about politics," he confided to a friend, "and I wish some of our other brethren would do the same."

De Smet worried that even Saint Louis would be "sacked and burned in case the secessionists get the upper hand." When Lincoln called up volunteers to restrain the Confederacy, Missouri became a "border state," retaining both slavery and its position in the Union. Holding a strategic position on the Mississippi River and benefiting from longstanding commercial ties in both the North and the South, Saint Louis felt pushed and pulled in two directions. "Only a few months ago," De Smet wrote to Charles Van Mossevelde, "business flourished and the population was increasing. Since then forty thousand people have left St. Louis and thousands of houses and stores are vacant."

As young men went off to soldier and families scurried for safety in the outskirts of Saint Louis, the enrollment at Saint Louis University plunged. Consequently, financial resources for the Missouri Vice-Province dipped, and the society's Indian missions suffered accordingly. De Smet thus found it necessary to return to Washington, D.C., in January 1862 to press a claim against the federal government. The Bureau of Indian Affairs owed the Missouri Jesuits fifteen thousand dollars for maintaining and educating four hundred Indian children at the Potawatomi and Kickapoo mission schools in Kansas, and De Smet intended to collect. At the beginning of the Civil War, Father Murphy made a cogent observation to Father General Beckx when he stated that De Smet "spread abroad the name of the Society" by his writings, but it was "by his reputation and influence with bishops and prominent people" that he brought other, less obvious, benefits to the Jesuits. And those benefits would never be more appreciated than during the Civil War.

The commissioner of Indian affairs had many more pressing problems during the first months of the Civil War than to update his account book for services rendered at an Indian school. Besides, he had no money to spend; all federal funds went to the war effort. When politely rebuffed, De Smet forced the issue by suggesting that if the mission schools in Kansas closed, the Indians might lend a favorable ear to the secessionists. The commissioner could only suggest that De Smet contact other "influential persons," beginning with President Lincoln. That is exactly what De Smet did.

President Lincoln customarily set aside certain hours so that ordinary citizens could directly appeal to his generous nature. Thus, De Smet had only to schedule an appointment. For an hour the priest and the president conversed about the present, pitiful condition of the western Indians and the effect of the war

on the missions. De Smet must have made his point about col-
lecting past-due debts from the government, because the president personally arranged further interviews with the secretaries
of interior and treasury, plus the attorney general. After complet-
ing his merry-go-round of meetings, De Smet notified his superiors that he had "succeeded in obtaining a sum of over $11,000
with the promise that the balance due the missions should be
forwarded at an early date."

De Smet also used his position as an author and sometime
government commissioner to join the social whirl of wartime
Washington, D.C. The Belgian ambassador to the United States,
Mr. Blondeel Van Cuelenbroeck, for example, took a personal
interest in his countryman-turned-American and several times
feted him at formal banquets. "These kinds of dinners," De Smet
explained to the father general, "make a great contrast with the
Indian feasts in which I have so often taken part; where they offer you with their hands a chunk of roast dog or bear or a stew
of meat hashed with their teeth." He added that "I did the best I
could among these great personages; but I remain of the opinion
that I shall always be more at ease sitting on the grass and surrounded with savages, each one making his jokes and at the same
time eating with good appetite a fair rib or roasting a piece of
buffalo or fat dog." Although he feigned great discomfort at the
adulation accorded him, De Smet accepted it in good humor, for
he knew that the contacts he made among the socially prominent
and well-to-do would pay off when he asked them for donations
to the missions.

In good time De Smet would return to begging, but in the
spring of 1862 his main thoughts were of the Sioux and the possibility of establishing a permanent mission for them on the upper
Missouri. This had been a goal of his since 1848—one temporarily shelved, however, as a consequence of Father General Roothaan's interference. For more than a decade after the flare-up
with Roothaan, De Smet's opinions about the sixty thousand or
more Indians who lived on the northern Great Plains received a
wider hearing in the parlor rooms of Washington, D.C., than
they did in either Rome or his own province of Missouri. For-

tunately, Father Beckx changed all of that on December 14, 1861, when he personally endorsed a proposal by De Smet to visit the Sioux again, this time with an eye toward establishing a permanent mission. De Smet now had both the money—the twenty-five thousand francs he had raised in 1860 from benefactors in Europe who specified that it be used for the Indian missions—and the official authorization to proceed.

Invigorated by the prospect before him, De Smet prepared for a three-month journey with an intensity born of moral righteousness. First he would take a steamboat to Fort Benton to deliver supplies and renew friendships with the Oregon Mission priests. Then, on his return trip down the Missouri River, he would look for a suitable location to establish a permanent mission for the Sioux. Looking for a way to ease the burden of travel, De Smet suggested to his friend, Missouri Congressman Frank P. Blair, that "if I could go in some official capacity from the government (I ask for no emoluments) my object might be strengthened by it and be more efficacious." De Smet considered his previous status as a government agent, be it as a peace commissioner or an army chaplain, an advantage as long as it did not compromise his credibility with the Indians. Official status as a government agent got him favorable prices at military posts, for example, and it sometimes influenced guides and interpreters to accept his offers of employment. There is no record of a positive answer by Congressman Blair, but in light of the fact that De Smet reported to government authorities at the conclusion of his tour, it is possible that he enjoyed some sort of official, and possibly monetary, relationship.

Captain Charles Chouteau provided De Smet with a private cabin and baggage space gratis on the *Spread Eagle* when it left Saint Louis in May 1862 bound for Fort Benton. Among the many passengers on board, two were notable: Samuel Latta, an Indian agent, and the noted anthropologist Lewis Henry Morgan. De Smet spent many long hours with Latta and the professor, though not entirely in erudite discussions of Native American tribal practices, as one might have expected. Actually, their conversation mostly centered on the ramifications of the Trent

De Smet used the *Florence* and similar steamboats to travel up and down the Misso
River between Saint Louis and Fort Benton, Montana Territory. Courtesy of Oreg
Province Archives of the Society of Jesus, Gonzaga University.

affair, a diplomatic dilemma with Great Britain. In the meantime, Captain Chouteau's pilot, Edwin Bailey, provided all the
additional excitement necessary to make De Smet's voyage a
memorable occasion.

Above Fort Berthold, Captain Joseph La Barge's steamboat,
the *Emile,* caught the *Spread Eagle* and challenged it for control
of the main channel in the river. Bailey, however, refused to back
off, even when the *Emile* pulled ahead and the river began to
narrow. With the two vessels scarcely fifty feet apart and going at
top speed, Bailey swung his rudder to port, deliberately plunging
the bow of the *Spread Eagle* into the side of the *Emile,* shearing
off railings and coming dangerously close to piercing the boilers.
La Barge, fearing for the life of his passengers and the safety of
his vessel, called out loudly for Bailey to stop his engines or he
would put a bullet through him, a threat underscored by several
alarmed passengers on the *Emile* who scrambled to grab their
guns. Wisely, and to De Smet's great relief, the *Spread Eagle* cut
power and drifted back. Were the Indians more or less wild than
the white men on this river? De Smet asked himself.

When the *Spread Eagle* finally reached Fort Benton in June,

De Smet enjoyed the pleasure of personally delivering to his Jesuit brothers at Saint Peter's Mission seventy boxes, bags, and barrels crammed with "a fine assortment of church ornaments and sacred vessels, victuals for nearly a year, garments and bed coverings, which they sadly needed, agricultural and carpenter's tools, several plows, some picks and shovels, an ambulance and a wagon." Most of all, the Jesuits at Saint Peter's appreciated the gift of cloth underwear. When their traditional black gowns became worn and tattered, they could make do with durable buckskin trousers, but leather underwear chafed these Euro-Americans more than they wished to endure.

De Smet did not have long to spend with his confreres in lands the federal government now designated Montana Territory, for he needed to head downriver as soon as possible if he wished to contact bands of Sioux and look for a suitable mission site. Alas, just as he prepared to leave Fort Benton, De Smet learned that an Indian disturbance near Fort Pierre disrupted the entire countryside. Apparently agent Latta distributed the annual government gifts to about three thousand Lakota tribesmen—Brulés, Hunkpapas, Blackfeet Sioux, Miniconjous, Sans Arcs, and Two Kettles—but this only fueled a growing antipathy between those chiefs who coveted the annuity promised by the Fort Laramie Treaty and those who resented the annual distribution of presents because it increased the dependence of the once self-sufficient Lakotas on whites. The intertribal debate turned into a challenge and ultimately resulted in two murders. Vengeful young men of both persuasions fanned out into the countryside attacking each other after that, though white gold seekers headed for Montana and even heavily fortified steamboats also became targets. This complication, De Smet realized, would make it impossible for him to obtain an interpreter or guide to take him into the vast, trackless interior of the country. Under the circumstances, De Smet had no choice but to reserve passage on a steamboat and return directly to Saint Louis. He would not abandon the decision on a permanent Sioux mission; he merely postponed it.

When he reached Saint Louis on August 18, De Smet learned

about an additional cause of Indian unsettlement along the middle Missouri River. A large force of Santee Sioux had attacked the Lower Indian Agency in southern Minnesota, killing twenty white men and taking a dozen women captive. Chief Little Crow and his men next ambushed a relief force of soldiers from Fort Ridgely, and yet another twenty-four men died. From there the Indian uprising spread outward in an ever widening arc in the direction of the Missouri River as the Santees sacked towns, harassed whites, and evaded citizen militia units. De Smet religiously followed the news of the uprising as the months wore on and the Indians wore down. Finally, in late September about four thousand Santees surrendered to the army; hundreds of them received death sentences from a military court assembled for the purpose. Ultimately, President Lincoln pardoned all but thirty-eight of the worst offenders, and the army carried out a "hanging bee" in Mankato, Minnesota, on the day after Christmas 1862. Meanwhile, renegade Santees took up with other Dakotas, the Yanktons, and even some Lakotas. These tribes had nothing to do with the uprising, but their sympathy for the hostiles now somehow implicated all of the tribes known collectively to the whites as "the Sioux."

De Smet's greatest fear, that the superior military force of the U.S. Army would someday exterminate the Plains Indians, seemed eerily close to becoming a reality. In the spring of 1863 the War Department ordered two generals into the field against the Sioux: General H. Sibley's army would march westward from Minnesota and link up with General Alfred Sully's command on the Missouri River, effectively pinching the Indians between them. If he could not halt the armies, De Smet decided he could at least comfort some of the peaceful tribes on the upper Missouri, particularly those who demonstrated an interest in practicing a sedentary, agricultural life.

By coincidence, agent Samuel Latta, who shared De Smet's concerns for the Indians, kept up a correspondence with Father De Smet after their meeting on the *Spread Eagle* the year before. He now followed up on their earlier discussions by formally recommending to the Bureau of Indian Affairs that Father De Smet be allowed to place an Indian mission and school at Fort Berthold for the benefit of the peaceful Arikaras and Mandans. "He proposes to apply $2,000 annually of his own private means for this purpose," reported the agent in making the request, "collecting from the several tribes of Indians such children as they could be induced to give up, to educate and instruct them in agriculture." He further stated, "I am satisfied, from my knowledge of this good man, that he has more influence with the Indians and would accomplish more good than any other man who could be sent into the Indian country."

While federal officialdom mulled over Latta's recommendation, De Smet resumed the duties of Missouri Vice-Province administrator. The most pressing item on his immediate agenda involved the Draft Act of March 3, 1863, a law that conscripted virtually every able-bodied male citizen between the ages of twenty and forty-five into military service. Remarkably, the law included even priests, though they, like others, could exempt themselves by paying a three-hundred-dollar commutation fee. But to do so for the two hundred Jesuits of the Missouri Vice-Province would cost a fortune—to say nothing of the cost to defer all the Jesuits in America. Clearly, the Society of Jesus needed an exemption from the law, and for that special privilege they turned to De Smet, a man known to have friends in high places in Washington, D.C.

De Smet laid the groundwork for his request by first writing to his friend Thurlow Weed, a high-ranking Republican politician, expressing grave concern over the implications of the matter. Taking the moral high ground—a tactic he preferred to protesting the economic implications of the three-hundred-dollar waiver fee—De Smet pointed out that solemn vows taken by consecrated Jesuits strictly forbade them from taking up arms in any cause whatsoever. Content to let the matter simmer for a time, yet willing to play up his role as a peacemaker, De Smet casually informed Weed that "in all probability, I shall leave St. Louis during the first week of May, to make a missionary excursion among the various tribes of the Upper Missouri, including, if I can, the warlike Sioux."

De Smet interpreted Father General Beckx's permission to visit the Sioux in 1862 as a general clearance to make an annual trip to the western Indians, so he therefore set his itinerary for a similar journey in the spring of 1863. He asked for, and received, permission to be temporarily relieved of his assignment as assistant to the provincial so that he could deliver supplies to the Montana Territory missions and then, on the return trip, stop along the way at various Indian villages to bring presents, instruct the natives in Catholicism, and baptize children. Father Joseph Keller, S.J., the new assistant to the superior, took a dim view of De Smet's wandering nature and thought the trip "not so necessary that it cannot be omitted, since its principal object, which is to fetch goods to the missionaries, could be equally attained by putting the goods in charge of the captain of the boat." De Smet sought personal recreation, he added, and by saying so Keller added himself to the small list of Jesuits who looked upon De Smet as a man more concerned with his own interests than those of the society.

What Keller thought of him bothered De Smet, but it did not stop him from leaving Saint Louis for the missions. On this particular trip De Smet not only assembled seventy boxes of supplies, plus a wagon and an ambulance, all of which he took aboard Captain Charles Chouteau's *Nellie Rogers,* but he also escorted two Italian brothers of the society. Ascending the Missouri at this time of the year, De Smet warned the Italians, could be very dangerous. During the winter of 1862–63 a combined force of Santee and Lakota warriors had attacked Fort Berthold, causing much damage to the post. With bad luck, their steamboat could be caught in the middle of an Indian war.

During the course of this particular trip De Smet made friends with Dr. W. T. Martin, a Dublin, Ireland, physician on a round-the-world pleasure tour. At each stop for wood De Smet disembarked to visit the Indians, and on many occasions Dr. Martin joined him: "With true Christian charity, he bestowed all his care and attention on the sick and infirm savages in the camps we came across." In addition to the usual religious medals, holy cards, and fish hooks ("an article very necessary and very much sought after") that De Smet ordinarily distributed to the Indians, he also brought with him on this trip about a thousand baptismal shirts and dresses for infants, the charitable gift of pious ladies in Saint Louis and Philadelphia.

As the steamboat crept up the Missouri River beyond Fort Berthold, the burning rays of the sun drove temperatures to triple digits. Hot winds swooped across the plains with such force that De Smet likened them to an African sirocco. The thin vegetation on shore turned more brownish with each passing day until De Smet said it would not surprise him to see the Missouri River itself completely evaporate. While the river did not completely fade, it did sufficiently dry up to the point that on June 29 a gigantic sandbar at the confluence of the Milk River completely blocked the progress of the *Nellie Rogers*. After several efforts to bypass the obstruction, Captain Chouteau realized the futility of his predicament and landed the passengers and cargo, all two hundred tons of it, on shore. They must wait, he informed them, until a messenger reached Fort Benton, three hundred miles away, and then wagons would come and take the passengers and their baggage the rest of the way.

De Smet and the Italian brothers fared fairly well, all things considered, as they did not lack for experience, manpower, or supplies in this situation. De Smet owned a large tent, a gift from General Harney, which he pitched under some tall cottonwoods. The rest of the eighty or so stranded passengers followed suit with their own equipment, and before nightfall a temporary town sprouted on the banks of the Milk River. In the course of the next several days some bands of Crows and Gros Ventres passed by and looked long enough to satisfy their curiosity, but they always left in peace. The serenity of the moment, however, lasted only until the Fourth of July, because on that holiday, as De Smet recounted the events to his friend Dr. Moses Linton, "we had an alarm, and escaped a great danger as if by a miracle."

Just as the campers lined up for a rifle salute to celebrate Independence Day, forty stern-looking Indian warriors appeared on the outskirts of the makeshift village. The Indians saw white men with weapons in their hands and instinctively opened fire, wounding two persons: "One received two arrows, in the fleshy parts of the arm and thigh, and the other was shot in the body with an arrow that went in up to the feather." In the confusion that followed, the passengers scurried to acquire additional fire-power, and the Indians called up reinforcements, a contingent that, from a distance, appeared to number several hundred warriors. "For my own part," De Smet later recalled, "I had no time to reflect and had nothing to do with fire-arms. I recommended myself to the Lord, and full of confidence in the prayers which I knew were offered for me in many places, I walked, or rather ran, up to the vanguard of the enemy." To his amazement, instead of being trampled by oncoming horsemen, De Smet heard the leader of the band cry out, "It is the Black-gown, who saved my sister." From the dust of reined-in horses emerged the son of Red Fish, a chief of the Oglala Sioux. Black Robe is a friend, the young man told his companions, a priest possessing great power.

De Smet could hardly believe his good fortune. In October 1848, during De Smet's first reconnaissance mission to the Sioux, Red Fish had asked the priest to pray for the safe return of his daughter from her Crow captors. He did, and when she subsequently escaped and rejoined her tribe unharmed, the Oglalas hailed Black Robe as a great hero. Red Fish's son now strode forward with hand upraised, holding back his warriors. As soon as Red Fish's son completed his greeting to Black Robe, De Smet said, the other Indians "looked bewildered, but were kind and shook hands with me." Meanwhile, the white men stood dumb-founded behind a hastily erected stockade, watching the drama unfold; no one moved lest the mood be broken. De Smet talked with the Oglalas for about an hour, at the conclusion of which he gave the Indians "some salutary advice, backed with some coffee, sugar and hard biscuits, and they left us without further molestation." De Smet considered this event "truly providential," a judgment that his disbelieving, but thoroughly relieved, companions readily accepted.

Not until July 30, more than a month after the *Nellie Rogers* had abandoned her passengers, did the wagons from Fort Benton arrive. It took another fifteen days for the single-file caravan of wagons to reach Fort Benton, an experience De Smet likened to an endurance contest for men and animals. All of the inconvenience faded, however, when they reached Fort Benton, a bustling city on the Missouri River. Father Camillus Imoda, S.J., waited at Fort Benton to greet the man the missionaries jokingly referred to as Saint Nicholas.

After a few days of rest—mostly spent treating a poison ivy rash De Smet had developed while waiting at the Milk River camp—Father Imoda escorted De Smet, the Italians, and Dr. Martin seventy-five miles to Saint Peter's Mission on the Sun River. De Smet gloried in his days at Saint Peter's, and not just because of the pleasure he received from bringing much-needed supplies to his fellow Jesuits. Most of all, De Smet enjoyed rekindling that old feeling of being a missionary again, instructing and preaching to the Indians. Ministering to the Blackfeet tribesmen allowed De Smet to forget the violence of the Civil War, the unfairness of the draft laws, and the pressure of constantly begging for money on two continents. He reveled in every moment, and because of that he stayed long beyond the time he had allotted in his original schedule.

Before he knew it, the page on the calendar read "August," and De Smet realized he would soon have to make a decision regarding his return trip to Saint Louis. Unfortunately, for the second year in a row, bands of Sioux warriors made it dangerous to ride anything, even a steamboat, across or through the Great Plains, and that complicated matters. "When I left Saint Louis," De Smet reflected, "I had intended to see a very large number of Indians during the summer and fall, but local conditions and the dangers of the cruel Sioux war, absolutely blocked my plan. . . . The reports that reached us every day, of robberies and massacres committed by the Indians of the plains . . . caused me to take the resolution of returning to St. Louis by the Pacific Ocean."

Assisted by a small group of Indian guides, De Smet and Dr. Martin made their way to Fort Vancouver over trails sometimes familiar and sometimes new to the priest. The first portion of the journey, a ten-day stretch from Saint Peter's Mission to Saint Ignatius Mission, followed sections of the recently contoured

The Military Road, marked with signs that gave the initials "MR," was common
called the Mullan Road by travelers in mistaken honor for its chief engineer. T
pathway was still very primitive when De Smet traveled it in 1863. Courtesy of *H*
per's New Monthly Magazine.

Mullan Road. Along the way De Smet visited Father Joset and
Brother William Claessens at Hell Gate near the present-day site
of Missoula, Montana. They were building a new church for
whites, the first of its kind by any denomination in the region. In
a moment of nostalgic reflection, De Smet paused to admire the
growth of Christianity since 1841, when he became the first clergyman ever to pass between the stone walls of that storied defile.
Now, two decades later, hundreds of whites lived in the vicinity.

A short distance further on, Father De Smet chanced to meet
Father Joseph Giorda, who was traveling from Saint Ignatius to
Saint Peter's Mission, the reverse of De Smet's route. "Our mu-
tual joy was great and profound," De Smet reflected: "We exchanged eagerly all our little budget of news, good and bad—
our hopes and our fears, for the present and the future of our
dear missions and our dear neophytes." Together the two priests
stayed a full day at an Indian camp baptizing infants and distributing medals and other religious items. "It was a pleasant day,

and under the circumstances doubly beautiful, and certainly, to me, one of the most agreeable and consoling of all my long wanderings," De Smet reminisced. These were modern times, indeed, when two Jesuit missionaries could meet each other on the Mullan Road "laid out by the Government engineers."

Meanwhile, back at Saint Louis University, the Jesuits waited anxiously for word of De Smet's whereabouts. Sketchy reports filtered downriver that summer that the *Nellie Rogers* had made it only to the Milk River and had there disembarked its passengers. Then followed news that the Indian war had resumed on the upper Missouri. When De Smet did not return to Saint Louis in a reasonable amount of time, the Jesuits at the university feared the worst. "What increases our anxiety is that the provisions he [De Smet] had with him might have excited the cupidity of the Indians," one Missouri Jesuit wrote to another: "Moreover, the crucifix by which the Indians recognize him, which he always wore on his breast, had by mistake been left in Saint Louis."

As it happened, De Smet, even without his crucifix, rested in complete safety at Saint Ignatius Mission in Mission Valley at that very moment. Now nine years old, Saint Ignatius Mission accepted maturity gracefully. Tribesmen from the Flatheads, Kootenais, Kalispels, and Pend Oreilles—legally called the Confederated Tribes after the Hell Gate Treaty of 1855—made the mission their home. Under terms of the treaty, Washington Territory Governor Isaac Stevens promised to provide schools, craft shops, a sawmill, a flour mill, and a complete hospital for the tribesmen, plus annual cash payments. Unfortunately, neither the federal nor territorial governments redeemed any of those promises. The Jesuit missionaries, however, committed themselves to improving the lot of the Indians in spite of government inaction, and on their own they produced most of the promised facilities, if not the cash. It was for missions such as Saint Ignatius that De Smet begged funds in Europe and America, and it was broken contracts such as the Hell Gate Treaty that made it necessary for him to do so. In fact, no government funds for Saint Ignatius Mission would ever be provided during De Smet's lifetime.

As De Smet and Dr. Martin continued on from Saint Ignatius
Mission to the Coeur d'Alene Mission of the Sacred Heart, a fire
added an element of danger to their trek through thick forests of
pine and cedar:

> A forest fire was raging during our passage, and had spread over a
> dozen miles of the mountain side and even to their highest parts. The
> smoke was very thick, and thousands of tree-trunks, fallen one upon
> another in confusion, obstructed the regular road and all the surface
> of the ground. We succeeded at last, axe in hand, and after plenty of
> minor miseries, in getting out of all the obstacles caused by the
> conflagration. In the course of the 17th we crossed the Coeur d'Alene
> river forty-two times. On the 18th [of September] we reached the
> Mission of the Sacred Heart.

After an enjoyable visit with Father Gazzoli and the Coeur
d'Alenes at Sacred Heart Mission, De Smet and Dr. Martin, now
joined by Father Gazzoli, took a canoe to the lower end of Lake
Coeur d'Alene and from there followed a well-marked path to
the farming community of Walla Walla City. Previously De Smet
knew this area only as one totally isolated from civilization, so to
see it now amazed him: "All places adapted to agriculture were
covered with vast farms, for thirty to forty miles around." Walla
Walla City, taking full advantage of its proximity to both the
Columbia River and the gold mines of Idaho and Montana, bus-
tled with commercial activity. "Its movement and commerce are
very great," marveled De Smet, with "arrivals and departures of
travelers and merchandise from morning till night." These days a
stagecoach connected Walla Walla City with Wallula, the former
site of Fort Walla Walla, thirty miles distant, and from there
a steamboat made regular trips to The Dalles on the Columbia
River.

So many things had changed since his last trip on the Columbia River four years earlier that De Smet thought himself in a
foreign environment. The river still cascaded across chutes and
thundered down falls, but now mechanical steam donkeys pulled
cargo around the most turbulent rapids on wooden rails. Passengers either walked or rode to another steamboat waiting on
the downstream side. Thus, it took one day to ride from Walla

Walla to Wallula, a second day to run the Columbia River a hundred miles or so to The Dalles, and a third day to complete the trip to Fort Vancouver.

At Fort Vancouver, De Smet had barely enough time to adequately renew his acquaintance with now Archbishop Blanchet of Oregon, much less to appreciate the splendors of the new city of Portland, before he boarded a steamer to San Francisco on October 13. The ship made a brief stop at Victoria on Vancouver Island to receive mail, and then took to the open sea for San Francisco, where it arrived on the twenty-first of the month. There Dr. Martin bid farewell to De Smet, choosing to return to Ireland by way of Hawaii, the Philippines, China, and Japan rather than New York and London.

"My health is not good," wrote De Smet to his brother Francis shortly after arriving in New York City on Thanksgiving Day 1863, "but that is generally the case after each long journey that I make. The cessation of fatigues uses me up more or less and it takes me some time to get back into my ordinary equilibrium." In lieu of a long letter, De Smet packed and sent to his family a box loaded with "two beautiful buffalo robes of extraordinary fineness, like silk; one painted deer skin, some moccasins or Indian shoes, seashells from Acapulco and Panama, and some photographs of Pierre Jean." In the same carton De Smet placed three copies of *Western Missions and Missionaries,* a translation of some letters first published in *Précis Historiques* and now bound as a book. He also enclosed six copies of *New Indian Sketches,* his fourth and latest book, a compilation of letters about his experiences in the Utah Expedition and the Coeur d'Alene War in 1858 and 1859.

On his way to Saint Louis, De Smet stopped off in Washington, D.C., to engage the secretary of the interior in a dialogue about the condition of the western Indians. At the conclusion of the conference, both the secretary and the commissioner of Indian affairs asked De Smet to visit the Sioux in the spring of 1864; they even offered to pay his traveling expenses. De Smet informed them, "It is going to be very difficult to obtain peace with those terrible savages." Still, he would go. Advising the father general of his intentions immediately, De Smet assured him, "I have not compromised nor engaged myself in any way with those high officials." That business complete, De Smet resumed his journey to Saint Louis, where the Jesuits at Saint Louis University, who had all but given up hope of seeing their wandering colleague again, celebrated his arrival.

De Smet knew from bitter experience that coming home to the work that piles up on one's desk is the worst part of any trip. During his absence the Missouri Jesuits had received full status as a province, so administrative paperwork had increased for De Smet:

> Immediately at my arrival in St. Louis toward the end of the year [1863], I found the ledger and day-book gaping and calling for a closing. In order to appear decently before his Paternal eyes it took me about a month hard labor, cyphering and corresponding all the while, with the brethren scattered far and wide among the Osages and Potawatomies, in Illinois, in Wisconsin, in Ohio, Kentucky and Missouri. Next came my correspondence with Europe which required immediate attention. I wrote a letter of twenty-four pages, on my last journey and mission among the Indians, to Reverend Father-General, according to promise and as requested.

In between, De Smet wrote another letter of twenty-six pages to his family in Belgium and still more articles for Father Terwecoren, tidbits De Smet called "chaff and mixture to feed his *Précis Historiques;* I gave him thirty-two pages."

If the great missionary's spirit rebounded quickly from the workload awaiting him in Saint Louis, his body felt a greater strain from eight months of overland and ocean travel. Each journey sapped his strength just a little more, and each trip required a longer time to recover. Feeling his age, De Smet confided to his brother in February 1864, "Insensibly life seems to ebb away. I am now in my sixty-fourth year, and I have an inward conviction that my end is near." In his next letter he lamented his physical woes again: "After enjoying robust health for so many years and after so many years of travel, I find the change hard to bear." Within a week, he advised his niece that "my health has been wavering for some months past, and begins to be threatening. I am broken down with all sorts of troubles: I suffer particularly with my head; it is seldom that I can leave my room."

Still, De Smet believed he would be able to make another trip up the Missouri in the spring of 1864. Unfortunately, most of the news from the Sioux War continued to be gloomy. During the summer of 1863, while De Smet was reacquainting himself with the Flatheads and other tribes in the Rocky Mountains, General Alfred Sully badgered the Sioux on the Great Plains, killing a reported three hundred warriors and capturing nearly that many women and children. Sully wintered his army on the Missouri River at a new post, Fort Sully, a few miles below Fort Pierre, and in the spring of 1864 he would almost certainly renew his campaign. The Lakotas expressed little concern, De Smet learned from his contacts on the upper Missouri; they, too, stood ready to make war. The secretary of the interior feared as much, so in March he once again prodded Father De Smet to visit the warring Sioux as a government envoy. To his niece, De Smet wrote: "In case my health should permit, I will have to make an effort to take the road again, to undertake a very long and dangerous journey among the Indian tribes. The interests of our missions, the security of the whites in that country and the happiness and tranquillity of the Indians, all seem to require that I should go."

Commissioner of Indian Affairs W. P. Dole reaffirmed the secretary of the interior's invitation. He did not disguise his motives. The government badly needed an emissary with good standing among the tribes, and he told De Smet bluntly, "It is believed that you can safely visit them in their camps and convey to them any message that the Government may wish to send." De Smet responded truthfully, "In all this, my experience among the Indians has been greatly overrated." As a matter of fact, De Smet hardly knew the warring Sioux bands except perhaps, briefly, the Brulés and Oglalas. His experience among the Sioux was mostly with the docile Yanktons, not the bellicose bands of the Lakotas.

Next, Dole asked if he could pay De Smet's travel expenses for 1864, a cost that the commissioner anticipated would not be much if the priest remained with General Sully and the other peace agents. De Smet declined, saying that under such an arrangement, "Surely my black robe would then cease to be a passport for me into the Indian Country." Fortunately De Smet had his own funds—the interest from bank accounts established by his brothers and sister in Belgium for the express purpose of sustaining his travels. As De Smet informed his superior: "I fear I would lose all caste among the Indians. They have hitherto looked upon me as the bearer to them of the word of the Great Spirit. . . . Should I present myself in their midst as the bearer of the word of the Big Chief of the Big Knives in Washington, no longer their Great Father, but now their greatest and bitterest enemy, it would place me in rather an awkward situation. I have written to the commissioner that if I can go, I will go on my own hook, without pay or remuneration."

Commissioner Dole thereafter conceded that he would not require De Smet to remain with the troops, though he did specify that the priest keep in constant contact with General Sully. De Smet resigned himself to these necessary restrictions, though he predicted that "peace is rendered almost impossible by the recent occurrences. . . . I am sent out under auspices of the government, in the capacity of 'messenger of the word of peace.' Still it is impossible to deceive one's self."

Once De Smet committed himself to the government peace effort, he hurried around Saint Louis making preparations. "I am now occupied in buying goods for the upper missions, to the amount of about $3,000," De Smet advised his superior, though he admitted that thus far less than half that amount of money filled his pocket. He also initiated a correspondence with two interpreters on the upper Missouri to "obtain information regarding the present state of the Sioux Country with respect to the war, [and] as to the disposition of the Indians in regard to peace."

All of this, however, put De Smet behind schedule, and he missed the departure of the *Yellowstone* on April 20. At first he thought he could catch the steamboat by taking a train to Saint Joseph, at the western end of Missouri, but several nights under a bright shining full moon allowed the steamboat to proceed up-river more rapidly than usual, and it actually left the state before De Smet could intercept it. Hastily hiring a carriage, De Smet chased the boat upstream on roads parallel to the river, passed it, and finally went on board at Omaha. De Smet wrote, "As on former occasions, Mr. Charles Chouteau received me on board his boat with his habitual kindness and cordiality. He gave me the quietist and most commodious stateroom."

Unfortunately, the fastest days for the *Yellowstone* were behind her. Above Omaha the volume of water in the river dropped suddenly, and large sandbars rose up to block upriver progress. It took twenty days of cautious maneuvering just to reach Yankton, the capital city of Dakota Territory, a distance of only 242 miles. After passing Fort Randall, the *Yellowstone* maintained a regular, if moderate, speed all the way to Fort Sully, where it arrived on the last day of May. Captain Chouteau intended a stop of only a few hours at this location—rumors of roving bands of well-armed Indians waiting in ambush kept the *Yellowstone* in a continual state of uneasiness and alert—but De Smet knew that some peaceful Yanktons and Two Kettles Sioux lived in the vicinity of the fort, and he asked for a little leeway in the schedule in order to visit them.

In several ways the visit to the Indian camps at Fort Sully greatly unsettled De Smet. For one thing, the meeting reminded him of past promises he had made to the tribesmen that someday the Jesuits would establish a mission for them. Would a permanent mission and school on the upper Missouri ever be possible, De Smet wondered, especially considering the condition of his health and the recent deterioration of Indian-white relationships? The Yankton chief Man Who Strikes the Ree begged De Smet to make no more plans and promises but just remain with him in the Indian village.

Man Who Strikes the Ree also warned De Smet that if he attempted to move about in the interior, he would likely be killed by Lakotas, either Hunkpapas, Miniconjous, or Sans Arcs. He should stay with the Yanktons. Peace seemed so elusive, so impossible to achieve, reflected De Smet, especially when both the federal forces and the Lakotas approached war so eagerly. The Lakotas, unfortunately, were even passionate about combat:

> War is to them not only a business or a pastime, but the occupation par excellence of their lives. The tactics followed by these Indians renders the regular system of warfare impotent or almost useless. They are here to-day and somewhere else to-morrow. . . . The Indian has the gift of being everywhere without being anywhere. These savages assemble at the moment of battle, and scatter whenever the fortune of war is contrary to them. The Indian puts his wife and children in shelter in some retired place, far from the scene of hostilities. He has neither towns, forts nor magazines to defend, nor line of retreat to cover. He is embarrassed with neither baggage trains nor pack-horses. He goes into action when a favorable occasion is presented, and never risks himself without having the advantage of numbers and position on his side. The science of strategy is consequently of little use in operating against such a people.

When the *Yellowstone* docked at Fort Berthold on June 9, Frederick Gerard, a respected Indian trader and trusted friend, reiterated cautions De Smet had already heard about the dangers inherent in probing the interior. Undisciplined warriors just might murder him in pure malice. Arguing from hard experience, Gerard persuaded De Smet to send a messenger to the hostile tribes announcing his presence. If the chiefs wished De Smet to come to their camps, they would invite him; if they wished to meet him at Fort Berthold, they would come themselves. De Smet agreed.

While he waited for an answer to his message, De Smet occupied his time at Fort Berthold by preaching to and converting the Arikaras, Gros Ventres, and Mandans, tribesmen whose homes formed a peace-loving village adjacent to the post. The Mandans appreciated Black Robe's personal interest, but they also wished to hear him speak at a grand council in one of their massive earthen lodges. Using Pierre Garreau as his interpreter, De Smet made known to the Indians the motives of his visit in a clearly focused two-hour address. He came first, he said, to bring to them the word of the Great Spirit and to baptize their children. But he also came a great distance to meet with "their enemies the Sioux, and endeavor, in the name of the Great Spirit, to make them relish the words of peace, of which I was the bearer on the part of the President of the United States." When he finished, Chief Soaring Eagle replied for the Mandans "in fitting and well-chosen words, accompanied by a really remarkable oratorical bearing and gestures." His tribe enjoyed peace, Soaring Eagle said, and they resisted the intimidation of the hostile Sioux to take up the warpath. But much more could be gained by his tribe, he predicted, if Black Robe would stay with them. Faced with the same feelings as when he had had a similar conversation with Man Who Strikes the Ree, De Smet asked for patience.

When the council broke up, Indian mothers poured into the council lodge carrying babies for Black Robe to baptize. In the space of a few moments they formed a triple circle around him, and for the next several hours De Smet baptized children one after the other, 204 of them by his recollection. Teasing his confreres in faraway Saint Louis, De Smet admitted that at times solemn occasions lost their sacred luster in Indian villages: "Everything passed off in the best of order, though not altogether without noise. During the ceremonies, we were honored from time to time with a deafening chorus. All that was needed was for a young savage, seized with terror at the approach of the Blackrobe, to exhibit the strength of his young lungs in piercing yells, to set all his comrades going in the same key. It was really enough to split one's ears. The dogs on the outside added to the uproar by reinforcing the cries of the children with their frightful howls and roars."

The constant bending gave De Smet such a crick in his back that for several days afterward he could scarcely move. Nevertheless, two days later, when the Arikaras, not to be outdone by the Mandans, invited Black Robe to their camp for a council, he went anyway. On the appointed afternoon, De Smet opened the council in the same manner as before by reciting his objectives in coming west this season. The head chief, White Parfleche, answered, and then, after the three-hour meeting adjourned, De Smet took his place "in the middle of the lodge, seated on a buffalo-skin, and all the small children, to the number of 103, were presented to me by twos to receive baptism." These were happy days for the peaceful tribes, and none the less pleasant for De Smet. The way the Indians treated him proved they still loved him, and their piety reinforced for him the continuing need for additional permanent missions on the upper Missouri.

As a priest, De Smet reveled in this renaissance of faith by his beloved Indians, but if he needed a signal that his role as a government peacemaker would likely not be as rewarding, it came the following day when a renegade Sioux war party approached the combined Indian villages, killed a Gros Ventre, wounded an Arikara, and stole some horses. The Arikaras informed De Smet that similar episodes of harassment took place weekly as part of a pattern by Lakota warriors to intimidate the neutral tribesmen at Fort Berthold into joining the alliance of Sioux against white men.

During the course of his pastoral duties, De Smet inadvertently elevated his reputation among the Indians with a bit of meteorological good fortune. During the course of his meeting with the Arikaras, the Indians implored De Smet to produce rain for their fields. A drought in 1863 had completely ruined one thousand acres of crops, and if the same thing happened two years in a row, the Indians would face a doubly hungry winter in 1864. Worse, warlike tribes already mocked them for following the sedentary life, and they might just quit agriculture if they failed again. De Smet explained to the Indians that though he desired it, he alone could not bring rain. But if they prayed with him, he would say a Mass for their special intention. Sure enough, on the day following the Mass "the sky clouded up for the first time in a long while, and a gentle and abundant rain fell at intervals for about twenty-four hours." Four days later De Smet said a second Mass, "and the Lord granted us a second rain, which did much good. These favors from on high made a deep impression on these simple-minded Indians." De Smet did not say how many times he prayed for rain at other villages and it did not come.

About that same time, the runner to the hostile Sioux bands returned to Fort Berthold with news. Some Lakotas were camped in a valley to the south and west of the post, they said, tantalizingly close to General Sully's command. Alarmed that the two opposing forces might inadvertently surprise each other, De Smet decided to go immediately to the Indian camp. Unfortunately, neither guides nor interpreters at Fort Berthold would go with him: "The few whites at Berthold were all in the greatest dread of the hostile Sioux, and looked upon the undertaking as altogether dangerous, if not rash, in which none could escape with his life." Unable to proceed, De Smet could only sit at the fort and hope the Lakotas came to him before they clashed with General Sully.

Meanwhile, another tribe of the Sioux nation contacted De Smet. A pair of British traders informed De Smet that some four thousand lodges of Santees, some of them renegades from the uprising in Minnesota, lived close to the Canadian border. The traders said the Indians wished to square accounts with the federal government, if circumstances would permit. Such an offer intrigued De Smet, but he dared not leave Fort Berthold to talk to the Santees while his messenger sought out the Lakotas. So he wrote the Santees a letter instead, dating it June 26. In it he voiced the usual appeals for peace and expressed his "wish to see you and give you all the explanations that you wish to have about your present situation." For the moment he could do no more.

When thirty-five Indian men took up a position outside Fort Berthold on June 29, De Smet hoped he had won the race with time over General Sully for the opportunity to confer with the Sioux. But were these braves friend or foe? "It was clearly a risk to cross over to their side," De Smet acknowledged, but how else could he find out their intentions? Perhaps encouraged by his experience the previous summer at the Milk River, when he boldly advanced on a band of Indian horsemen, De Smet left the safety of the fort to meet the warriors on their own turf. No one else at the fort volunteered to accompany him.

Perhaps it was a foolish stunt, but for the second time in as many tries De Smet got away with it. The Indians, he later informed the commissioner of Indian affairs, watched him approach and then "received me with unmistakable tokens of friendship and respect." Together they "repaired to the spot for the

express purpose of having a conference with me." The Indian
delegation turned out to be not the Lakota tribesmen he so desired to meet, but instead some Yanktonai headmen from a large
camp of about five hundred lodges located on a branch of the
Heart River. De Smet convened a council anyway, one in which
both sides used the word "peace" many times during the next
three hours. Ultimately, De Smet urged the chiefs to contact
other holdout bands and encourage them to come to Fort Berthold and smoke the pipe of peace with him. He sealed his offer
with a present of tobacco.

A year after the incident, De Smet wrote to another Jesuit
missionary a letter in which he said that the Indians harbored a
plot to murder him, possibly because he acted in the capacity of a
government agent, though they did him no harm. Such a statement is a good example of the manner in which De Smet exercised his talent for making a good story better. After the event,
De Smet learned that only two days earlier three Sioux warriors
had killed an army officer from an ambush and then were themselves killed by a cavalry unit attached to General Sully's command. De Smet suggested that the Yanktonais could have been
part of that war party, and he attributed the salvation of his life
to the chief who "recognized me and attributed to me the de-
liverance of his daughter, a captive among the Crows." Thus, for
the third time De Smet dredged up the Red Fish connection. It
did not seem to matter that Red Fish belonged to the Oglalas
and that it was Yanktonais who had approached the fort. De
Smet termed this sequence of events at Fort Berthold a miracle
of the first order. More likely it is evidence of a fading memory;
De Smet must have forgotten that he had already told the Red
Fish story before in both 1848 and 1863.

More than a week passed before the next group of Indians
appeared as silhouettes on the hills across the Missouri from Fort
Berthold. This time the delegation consisted of from two hundred to three hundred Oglala and Brulé warriors under Chiefs
Black Eyes and Red Dog. Once he realized the significance of
the visitors, De Smet made immediate preparations to meet
them. As if by prearrangement, but in fact quite by accident, the

steamer *Yellowstone* reached Fort Berthold at almost the same time, so De Smet pressed Captain Charles Chouteau into his service. Using two small boats from the decks of the *Yellowstone* to cross the river, De Smet and Chouteau entered the Sioux camp, where the chiefs met them with tokens of kindness and confidence. After a ceremonial smoke, the Indians agreed to re-locate to more comfortable quarters on the steamer. Chouteau showed himself to be more than a silent partner during the long discussions on board the *Yellowstone*, De Smet reported, for he, too, addressed the Indians in a "most appropriate discourse." Several Indians rose to make statements in reply to De Smet, though none manifested a desire to do the same with General Sully at another meeting. The conference broke up as abruptly as it began, with the Indians leaving suddenly .

The next day De Smet himself left Fort Berthold for Fort Rice, General Sully's newest cantonment on the Missouri, where he hoped to find the general. He needed to tell Sully about his re-cent conferences with the Indians; that, after all, formed part of his agreement with Commissioner Dole. By the same token, De Smet needed to learn the general's "dispositions toward the savages." When the two men finally did meet at the cantonment, De Smet provided Sully with an extensive account of his inter-views, emphasizing the Indian desire for peace. The general re-vealed little interest. "He told me plainly," De Smet recorded in his letter book, "that circumstances obliged him to punish by force of arms all the Sioux tribes that harbored in their camps any murderers of white men. 'Unfortunately,' he added, 'all the In-dian camps harbor some of these desperate ruffians, over whom the chiefs have little or no power.'"

Sully's attitude seriously crippled De Smet's hopes for a recon-ciliation between the government and the Lakotas. He could not ask the Indians to deliver up any tribesmen, especially those im-plicated in the Minnesota war, while popular sentiment still ran high against them. He thought Sully's stance "altogether impracticable, or rather impossible," and regrettably came to the conclusion that "in consequence of the general's declaration and the circumstances of my case, my errand of peace, though

194 FATHER PETER JOHN DE SMET

sanctioned by the Government, became bootless and could only serve to place me in a false position; namely that of being face to face with the Indians without being able to do them the least service." Disgusted, De Smet abandoned his peace mission and returned to Saint Louis.

Sometime later De Smet learned, much to his horror, that after his departure Sully marched to the vicinity of Fort Berthold, where, on July 28, he engaged about sixteen hundred warriors of both the Santee and Lakota Sioux at Killdeer Mountain. The Indians gave way to artillery during Sully's relentless assault, but not before losing more than a hundred warriors. Sully burned the Indian village and ordered his men to pursue the hostiles through the Badlands, all the way to the Yellowstone River if necessary. Further skirmishing continued in August.

Outraged by Sully's aggression, De Smet took a train to Washington, D.C., where he delivered his complaint to Commissioner Dole. Lamenting his inability to work with General Sully, De Smet could, nevertheless, point out to the commissioner that his presence at Fort Berthold strengthened the resolve of roughly three thousand Indians to continue to resist the threats and enticements of the hostile Sioux. The recent events of the summer, he said, only proved what he had said all along about the need for more missionaries—and fewer army officers—in the West. Once again De Smet pressed Dole to allow the Jesuits to establish one, or perhaps two, new missions on the upper Missouri, presumably one for the Sioux and another for the triumvirate of peaceful tribes at Fort Berthold. De Smet, however, cautioned Dole that he, personally, did not have the authority to commit the Society of Jesus to such an obligation, and, moreover, his order would require an endorsement by the government before it would proceed.

Taking further advantage of his time in Washington, De Smet decided to confer with Secretary of War Edwin M. Stanton regarding his earlier appeal for the release of Jesuits from the Draft Act of 1863. De Smet hoped that his correspondence with Thurlow Weed in April would have ended the matter, but that, he subsequently learned, proved not to be the case. Apparently, while

This photograph of De Smet in 1864 is believed to have been taken by Matthew Brady in his Washington, D.C., studio. Courtesy of Oregon Province Archives of the Society of Jesus, Gonzaga University.

De Smet sought peace on the upper Missouri during the summer of 1864, nearly twenty Jesuit faculty members at Saint Xavier College in Cincinnati registered for the draft under duress, and in Missouri five fathers, two brothers, and a scholastic also enlisted under similar circumstances. Stanton proved to be a willing listener, especially to a man as respected as De Smet, and after hearing his arguments he asked the priest to give him a week to follow up on the matter. True to his word, in a letter dated September 29, 1864, the secretary promised that henceforth he would exempt all Jesuits called up for military service. As a result, no Jesuit was ever drafted into the Union army.

One final governmental matter occupied De Smet's attention during his brief stay in the capital, and that matter concerned money. Once again the government fell in arrears in its payments for the Potawatomi and Osage schools operated by the Jesuits, this time in the amount of $13,810.60. De Smet wasted no time marshaling the support of high government officials to his cause before he went to see the secretary of the interior. As a result, when he did make his demand he obtained an immediate payment of $10,197.06, with an assurance that the balance would follow within a month.

Toward the end of September, De Smet returned again to Saint Louis. He needed to write a series of letters to local military commanders clarifying the draft issue, but in general he looked forward to resting and answering some long overdue personal correspondence from Belgium. His superiors, however, made other plans and handed him an itinerary for another trip to Europe. It was time to go begging again. And this time De Smet should not restrict himself to Belgium, Holland, and France, all generous but overworked areas; he should include on his schedule any and all Catholic colleges and Jesuit houses from Paris to Rome.

The lateness of the season required De Smet to hurry to New York City to catch the steamship *China* bound for Liverpool. From there he worked his way to the south of France, begging all the way. Later he took a boat from Marseilles to Civita Vecchia in Italy. Writing to his nephew Charles from Rome in mid-November, De Smet proclaimed a miraculous restoration of his health following a visit to Vatican City: "Headache, blood-spitting, lack of appetite, etc., disappeared upon my arrival in Rome. . . . I have spoken to you about my fever, and now I will tell you how I got rid of it. I climbed to the dome of Saint Peter's. The remedy, though most fatiguing, was salutary, and since then my pulse has not been so rapid."

While in Rome, De Smet witnessed the beatification of a saint, visited several basilicas and catacombs, and three times conferred with Pope Pius IX, doubtless about the Indian missions. From Rome, De Smet worked his way north, speaking to school-children, begging from patrons, and exhorting the seminaries for vocations to the missionary life. He eventually collected more than 86,500 francs in cash and merchandise. Whenever possible, he returned to Belgium to spend time with his family.

In the course of these European travels, De Smet received accolades as well as monetary contributions. Chief among them was a knighthood in the Order of Leopold conferred by the Belgian government. Still, by the spring of 1865, De Smet longed to return to America, and in early June he did just that. "I always miss something when I am not among my good Indians," he told the twelve young men he enlisted for the society; "I am conscious of a certain void where ever I go, until I come again to my dear Rocky Mountains. Then calm comes back to me; then only am I happy."

CHAPTER 7

Peacemaking during the Sioux War, 1866–1868

FATHER De Smet left Europe in 1865 a troubled man. He feared he might never see his family again: "Here I am once again leaving my country, my family, my friends, benefactors, and brothers in religion. A fond farewell to all, perhaps forever, until the last meeting in heaven. This separation—and why should I not admit it?—is for me a painful sacrifice." He also worried that he might never accomplish all the things he set out to do as an Indian missionary. Later that summer, when Catholic prelates sought De Smet's permission to nominate him for a bishopric in Montana Territory, he scarcely even considered the honor, because he wished nothing to interfere with his goal of establishing Indian missions on the upper Missouri River. Admittedly, as a bishop De Smet could play a pivotal role in influencing the Catholic character of a large territory, but after his return to Saint Louis, he devoted himself to but a single purpose. To lay the foundation for a pair of upper Missouri Indian missions would complete his life's work among the western tribes.

During De Smet's European sojourn, the Sioux War continued unabated. The fact that it did not end at the same time as the Civil War made it that much more difficult for De Smet to fulfill his dream, because the U.S. Army then had no shortage of experienced soldiers to throw against the Indians. Hostile war parties, a seemingly large number now being led by Sitting Bull of the Hunkpapas, continued to threaten settlers on the northern Great Plains after Appomattox, making it dangerous, if not impossible, for whites to travel on the Missouri River.

Early in 1866, while De Smet weighed his options, the commissioner of Indian affairs urged the missionary-priest to use his influence with the upper Missouri tribes to seek a reconciliation between the government and the warring Sioux. General Sully, De Smet's old nemesis, seconded the motion in a highly solicitous letter on February 28. After three years of nearly constant warfare against the Sioux, Sully had mellowed. Perhaps Christianity could accomplish what his units of armed soldiers could not. He regretted any unpleasantness toward De Smet during the summer of 1864 and now suggested that much good could come from locating one Catholic mission at Fort Berthold and another at the Yankton Agency below Fort Randall. He conceded that the Indians "are decidedly in favor of the Catholic religion to the exclusion of any other."

De Smet replied to Sully in mid-March, stating that the idea of two missions had been his goal for some time. But, he cautioned the general, "owing to our numerous establishments and the great want of personal means, the design may not be immediately acted upon" by his society. In any case, he made up his mind to leave Saint Louis in April 1866 to deliver the annual supply shipment to the Rocky Mountain missions. Then, on his return journey, he would consider sites for Indian missions on the Missouri. Such had been his plan in years before; this time he hoped it would work.

The *Ontario* left Saint Louis on schedule, bound for Fort Benton. De Smet loved steamboating on the Missouri River, and this experience only furthered his enthusiasm. The captain assigned him to a large cabin, and from it he passed the day in social conversations with fifteen gentlemen and twelve ladies who shared first-class accommodations on the same deck: "Storytellers or jokers are never lacking in an assemblage of American travelers. Some read, others play at cards or dice, or perhaps checkers or other games of chance, the names of which are unknown to me. Evenings, we amuse ourselves by proposing charades—somebody imitates some animal or other, as the antelope or buffalo, or suggests some word or question, and the audience guesses. But the principal amusement, in the main cabin, appears to be dancing to the sound of music, and on moonlight nights there are concerts out on deck, with mirth and refreshments."

During more than a quarter of a century of travel on the Big Muddy, De Smet never bored of watching the passing panorama. In 1838 he had described the character of the river and the region with the enthusiasm of a tenderfoot in letters to his Jesuit confreres. On subsequent trips he made so many notes on the river and its environs—he collected so many anecdotes—that he had enough material to write a fifth book. But *New Indian Sketches,* published in 1863, remained De Smet's fourth and final book. It seemed anemic in size compared to the hefty volumes he published in the 1840s, but Indians no longer fascinated either European or American audiences to the same degree they once did, so De Smet adjusted his sights appropriately downward. He could still write for his own pleasure, however, and continued to do so.

Marine engineers shaped the *Ontario* to draw only thirty inches of water, making her an excellent choice for a summer trip up the shallow Missouri River. But when the river swelled bank-full with the runoff from a heavy winter snowfall, the *Ontario* bobbed like a cork against the pull of the mighty Missouri. In spite of maximum steam from three boilers and full throttle on the boat's twin 132-horsepower engines, the ship sometimes slid backward in the water. A cable winched the boat forward at especially treacherous locations, but even that device snapped once under the strain. Then, as is frequently the case on the upper Missouri, one afternoon the runoff ceased and the river fell into quiet repose. Sandbars, mud flats, snags, and sawyers surfaced to hazard the *Ontario* for the rest of its voyage. Once the steamboat struck a submerged rock so violently that De Smet feared the boat might sink. The vessel teetered under the force of the blow, causing several officers to call "for abandoning her, but others redoubled their efforts to repair the injury, and with the aid of pumps they kept her afloat, and she resumed her course."

Despite an especially arduous winter on the northern Great Plains, where temperatures dipped to double digits below zero for weeks at a time in some locations, wild game still managed to flourish when spring arrived. Passengers watched from the upper decks of the *Ontario* as hunters on shore bagged antelope, deer, and other game, seemingly at will. Buffalo herds provided the greatest entertainment for the travelers. Ever ready to tell a good story, De Smet fashioned one buffalo encounter into a theatrical metaphor.

"Yesterday we were all spectators to a striking scene in which buffalo alone were the actors," he began; "The theatre was the most wonderfully wild and picturesque part of this region." As the *Ontario* labored upstream, its boilers gasping and wheezing, it startled a small herd of buffalo, and the animals bolted for the nearest bluffs. Zigzagging to the crest along well-worn switch-backs, most of the bison made it to the summit without any difficulty. "The dark, living, winding lines, the columns of dust that followed them, from the bottom to the top, and the noise of their tread and their dull bellowing, furnished the spectators a most charming and imposing spectacle," said De Smet, "a revelation concerning the agility, muscular strength and capacity for endurance of this mighty animal of the American desert." But "as in all spectacles a farce is usually the closing piece, so here three old buffalo bulls gave us one." Sprinting to the next rise on the landscape, a thousand-foot-high bluff with an extremely steep incline, the bulls reached the middle of the slope just as the steamboat caught up to them, whistles piercing the air.

> At the approach of the boat they made prodigious efforts to clamber up and gain the top. All eyes were fixed upon them; our cheers were a powerful encouragement to high speed. One reached the goal, and received the applause of the spectators; his two companions strained their best, but still they slipped down; and beginning to slide with their enormous weight, they rolled head over heels, and by a long series of bumps and pirouettes, at a height of 400 or 500 feet, they came tumbling into the river within a few yards of the boat. The entire descent was accomplished in less than a minute. We supposed they were killed; but not the least in the world—to our great astonishment and admiration they rose to the surface and, snorting, blew the water from their nostrils. Their life was granted them—for the reason that our larder was well stocked. We saw them both reach shore, shake the water from their shaggy heads and necks, and each triumphantly hoisting his standard (his tail), they disappeared at full gallop.

Entering buffalo country also increased the likelihood of seeing Indians. The question now would be whether the *Ontario*

could outrun an Indian war party as easily as a buffalo herd.
"Upon entering the Sioux country," observed De Smet, "the *On-tario* was put in fighting trim. The pilot-house was planked over
and made safe against bullets or arrows, the cannon was mounted
in the bow, all the carbines, guns and pistols were inspected and
loaded, and above all, sentinels were posted by night to keep
guard against any surprise by the enemy." Happily, the boat
arrived unmolested at Fort Sully on May 8, all of the defensive
preparations having been made for naught.

Fort Sully had the appearance of a refugee camp. Several
hundred lodges of neutral Sioux crouched in the shadow of the
post seeking protection from the two warring factions, the un-repentant Lakotas and the persistent U.S. Army. "We had a long
talk," De Smet said of his conference with the Indians, "in the
course of which their miseries, sufferings and griefs came to
light. For several months the Indians had subsisted on the flesh
of their lean dogs and horses, together with a pittance of wild
roots." The Indians' tragic situation pained De Smet more and
more with each visit to the upper Missouri. "In my quality of
Black-robe I did my best to give them salutary counsels, as well
as to console them," De Smet explained to his superior, but
inwardly he felt unchristian anger toward the whites who pro-voked the tribes into vengeance that subsequently opened the
Indians to retaliation by federal forces. De Smet laid the blame
for 90 percent of the Indians' troubles on "the scum of civiliza-tion, who bring to the Indians the lowest and grossest vices,
and none of the virtues of civilized men."

The schedule of the *Ontario* determined how long De Smet
could stay with the tribesmen at Fort Sully, so after a brief two-day visit he had to leave them. The condition of the Arikaras,
Mandans, and Gros Ventres at Fort Berthold, when he got there,
seemed even more desperate to De Smet than that of the Sioux at
Fort Sully—if that was even possible. "During the rigors of last
winter," De Smet learned from the headmen of the tribe, "the
famine and misery were so great among them, that some fifty
persons died of starvation." There were additional Indian camps
farther upriver at Fort Union, plus several large villages secreted

in the adjacent valleys, but "despite their pressing invitations, the *Ontario* did not slacken speed" until it reached Fort Benton on June 7, fifty-seven days out of Saint Louis.

Much to De Smet's disappointment, the Jesuits from Saint Peter's Mission failed to meet him at Fort Benton. Father Giorda relayed word to De Smet that he had been forced to move the Blackfeet mission to the Little Belt Mountains earlier in the spring, and then he had closed it altogether. Gold miners on their way to the rich digs at Alder Gulch kept the Indians in a constant state of siege by their trespasses, so Giorda did not expect to get to Fort Benton for some time. If De Smet could just leave the cargo at the house of some inhabitant, Giorda would get it later. This left De Smet in a quandary, because a good portion of the supplies he brought consisted of sacred vessels, church orna- ments, and religious items. Angry as much as frustrated by this development, De Smet had few options. Fortunately, General Thomas Meagher lived at Fort Benton, and since De Smet knew him to be a good Catholic, he asked the Irishman to take respon- sibility for the cargo. Thus, when the *Ontario* headed down- stream a few days later, De Smet went with it, and his supplies remained behind.

The mix-up at Fort Benton did have a good side, inasmuch as De Smet could now spend more time ministering to the upper Missouri tribes. That is, he could disembark at Fort Berthold without fear of being stranded, because he knew from personal experience there were still steamboats unloading at Fort Benton, and eventually they would have to pass Berthold on their way back to Saint Louis. For two fruitful weeks De Smet reveled in his return to the life of a missionary, baptizing Indian children— 150 of them conveniently godfathered by his interpreter, Pierre Garreau—comforting adults, and exploring potential sites for a permanent mission. At the end of June, De Smet boarded the steamboat *Minor* and shuttled to the Yankton Agency near the mouth of the James River.

De Smet considered himself a veteran of veterans among frontier travelers. On many occasions he had endured the hard- ships of the trail, including many nights in Indian camps. But the

Fort Benton, Montana Territory, was the head of steam navigation on the Missouri
River. In De Smet's time steamboat captains estimated it to be 2,302 miles from Saint
Louis. Courtesy of *Harper's New Monthly Magazine.*

silver-haired priest rued the day he asked the Yanktons for sleeping accommodations, "some little private abode, in whatsoever
condition, where I might discharge in quiet my spiritual duties."
He quickly realized his mistake:

> Worn out by the heat of the day and the fatigues of the journey, I
> expected to enjoy a good sleep. I had reckoned without my hosts.
> I had been perhaps ten minutes in bed and was almost asleep, when
> I was awakened with a start. The dugout was swarming with fam-
> ished rats; they came and laughed in my very face. Night is their
> particular domain and they make the best use they can of it in their
> own behalf. They carried on at a shocking rate. They were rummag-
> ing all my bags of provisions, and were about in earnest the transpor-
> tation of such of their contents as suited their purposes to the caves,
> when I stopped them short. To prevent the depredations of the rats, I
> hung my sacks on the posts of my mansard out of reach of any
> attempts on the part of these highwaymen. During this labor I felt
> myself assailed by another enemy, the flea. If he is not so formidable
> as the rat, he is more importunate and he attaches himself to his prey
> in a most tenacious manner. . . . I was awake and up all night, making
> play with my hands, fingers and nails to defend myself against the

fleas and their comrades in evil-doing, the mosquitoes, the bed-bugs, the ants, the spiders, etc."

Cutting short his visit, De Smet hurried to Saint Louis on the next steamboat.

Keenly aware of the benefits of publicity, and more convinced than ever of the necessity to establish missions on the upper Missouri, when De Smet returned to Saint Louis he satisfied a long-standing request by his old friend, Father Terwecoren, editor of *Précis Historiques,* to write an article on the condition of the western Indians. If De Smet himself sometimes viewed the Indians from the perspective of a European, consistently referring to them as "savages," for example, it nevertheless offended him when others perceived them as incapable of either salvation or civilization. He decided to set that record straight: "By most persons the capacity of the Indians has been greatly underrated. They are generally considered as low in intellect, wild men thirsting after blood, debased in their habits and groveling in their ideas. Quite the contrary is the case. They show order in their national government, order and dignity in the management of their domestic affairs, zeal in what they believe to be their religious duties, sagacity and shrewdness in their dealings and often display a reasoning power far above the medium of uneducated white men."

De Smet also wrote a second treatise for Father Terwecoren, this one about the deplorable condition of the Yankton Sioux. And he did not stop there. Before the year 1866 closed, De Smet rewrote that same piece and directed it to two other persons. Virtually the same material went to De Smet's provincial, accompanied by a plea that the society's board of missions honor the Yankton request for a Jesuit mission, and, finally, De Smet sent a variation of the same letter to the new commissioner of Indian affairs, L. V. Bogy. To the commissioner De Smet asked pointedly: "Should our Board of Missions agree to grant a Catholic missionary establishment, as expressly desired by the chiefs of the Yankton tribe, will it meet with the approbation of the Indian Bureau in Washington?"

While the Missouri Province and the government mulled

over De Smet's recommendation, he turned his attention to another urgent matter. Although it had never been his formal responsibility to provide the annual shipment of supplies to the Pacific Northwest missions, De Smet had done so for two decades as a labor of love. Raising the money and making the purchases occupied only half his time. He also had to arrange for the delivery. For a while De Smet complied with Roothaan's credit-and-debit arrangement between Fort Vancouver and the London office of the Hudson's Bay Company, but after the mid-1850s he found it more convenient just to ship the mission supplies to Fort Benton from Saint Louis on American Fur Company steamboats. The Chouteau family not only transported the goods free of charge, but they even provided men, wagons, and mules to move the cargo 350 miles to Saint Ignatius Mission, an enterprise that sometimes extended beyond a month. This fifteen-year arrangement, however, ended in 1866 when the Chouteau family sold their interest in the American Fur Company. Henceforth, not only would the Jesuits have to pay for their freight at the rate of 15–20 cents per pound, but also De Smet himself would have to purchase a three-hundred-dollar ticket just to escort the supplies to Fort Benton. De Smet blamed the high tariff on what he considered an unsavory "Protestant takeover" of the steamboat business. There had to be a better way.

De Smet thought it probable that Captain Joseph La Barge would grant free passage on any of his steamboats to Missouri Jesuits; the consignment of several tons of freight would be too much to ask, however. De Smet therefore decided to reconfigure the route of his next shipment of mission materials to the Pacific Northwest. Accordingly, a train took the cargo from Saint Louis to New York; a steamship moved it to San Francisco by way of Panama; and an ocean liner completed the delivery to Fort Vancouver on the Columbia River. From there contractors redirected the supplies to individual missions. Such a route involved more miles, but in De Smet's calculations, "it is easier and more sure and is made in less time than by the Missouri River," especially considering the uncertainty of Indian affairs. De Smet reckoned that the voyage up the Missouri, under even the most favorable circumstances, took three months to deposit supplies at Sacred Heart Mission; the new route got the same materials to the parish house in just six weeks.

Meanwhile, news of the Sioux War continued to disturb the American public, few more so than Father De Smet. In October 1865 a smattering of chiefs counciled with federal peace commissioners at Fort Sully, and for a brief moment a peaceful settlement to the war on the plains seemed possible. The Hunkpapas under Sitting Bull, however, dashed all hopes when they blockaded Fort Rice in the spring of 1866 and later that summer turned their wrath on Fort Buford, a permanent military post being built two miles away from old Fort Union. Then the government announced a plan to build three new forts on the Bozeman Trail, a popular shortcut connecting the Oregon Trail at Fort Laramie to the Montana gold fields, and Chief Red Cloud of the Oglalas opened a second front of the war. In the five months between August 1 and December 31, 1866, Oglala war parties killed 154 persons in fifty-one encounters along the Bozeman Trail. One could only presume that similar occurrences would take place in the spring of 1867.

In an effort to control the escalating Sioux War, Secretary of the Interior O. H. Browning decided to reopen talks with Father De Smet regarding the feasibility of a mission for the Yanktons. The idea was not wholly his own. In the first place, the U.S. Senate Committee of Indian Affairs presented its report on the condition of Indian affairs in January 1867, and it flatly demanded that the government spend more of its time and resources in seeking peace with the Indians. A humanitarian movement in the United States greatly influenced the congressional committee, and their report, in turn, seriously influenced the secretary of interior.

Second, the Yanktons themselves encouraged Secretary Browning to follow up on the mission concept. In February 1867, De Smet's friend Man Who Strikes the Ree led a delegation of headmen from the Yanktons and various surrounding tribes, a total of twenty-eight persons, to Washington, D.C., to meet with the commissioner of Indian affairs. In the course of their meetings the Indians universally endorsed De Smet's proposal for a Yankton mission. Even a bureaucrat like Browning could recognize a pattern here. A year earlier, General Sully encouraged the idea of a Yankton mission. Then followed the unsettling events of the summer and winter on the Great Plains. Clearly the Sioux War needed to be defused by some moderating force. Just as clearly, De Smet's proposal for a Yankton mission had support from the peaceful Sioux.

But Commissioner of Indian Affairs L. V. Bogy changed the agenda when De Smet reached Washington. Instead of discussing a new mission for the Yanktons, Bogy really wanted to probe De Smet's knowledge of the Oglalas, specifically the validity of their complaints about forts on the Bozeman Trail. Such information could be useful to the newly empowered U.S. Indian Peace Commission that Congress formed in June 1867. De Smet reacted with incredulity, for his opinions on Indian matters should have been well known in government circles by this time. The current unrest of the Oglalas, indeed of all Indians, he stated, resulted from "incessant provocations and injustices on the part of the whites. When the savages raise the hatchet to go on the warpath, it is because they are pushed to the limit of endurance, and then the blows that they deal are hard, cruel and terrible. . . . It is always true that if the savages sin against the whites it is because the whites have greatly sinned against them."

The commissioner extended to De Smet an invitation to meet with the Sioux in the spring of 1867 as an "envoy extraordinary," or official peacemaker. The peace offensive of 1867 focused particularly on the central plains and Red Cloud's war. "Your relations with the Indians and your marvelous influence over them are well-known facts," Bogy said, perhaps not realizing that De Smet held no special sway with the Oglalas. Perhaps he assumed that they would honor Black Robe because of his reputation. "No special instructions will be given you and I leave you at liberty to take your own measures," he promised. De Smet would have preferred a pledge to assist the Jesuits in founding missions, but, obviously, the commissioner did not place that item on the agenda. Still, De Smet agreed to accept the assignment. He would go to the warring Sioux because he could do more good for the Indians by being in the field with them than he could by just watching events unfold from afar. De Smet specified that "I shall not accept any remuneration for my personal services." He did, however, receive a cash advance of twenty-five hundred dollars to cover government-related travel expenses.

Commissioner De Smet—officially, Major Peter De Smet of the U.S. Army—left Saint Louis by train on the afternoon of April 12, 1867. Earlier that morning he loaded one wagon, two mules, a saddle horse, several trunks, and some camping equipment onto the steamboat *Bighorn*. Theoretically the train carrying De Smet would reach Omaha at the same time as the *Bighorn*. De Smet loved to travel by steamboat, but as a man with a lifelong curiosity about the unknown, he decided to test out a new route on a modern mode of transportation. He expected to arrive in Omaha in time to meet the Yankton chiefs making their way home from Washington, D.C. Together with the Indians he would board the *Bighorn* and steam upriver to the Yankton Agency, sending out messages of peace to the warring Sioux bands. If need be, De Smet would even "penetrate into the interior of the country in search of the Sioux tribes."

At first everything proceeded according to plan. De Smet's train made fifty-three stops on the way from Saint Louis to Chicago; still, it remained on schedule. After the train left Chicago, however, delays became commonplace, a good number of them caused by heavy rains that washed out railroad bridges and turned bottomlands into mud flats. Some interruptions of service lasted for more than a week. De Smet finally reached the Missouri River by riding the final twenty-seven miles to Sioux City in a wagon. Fortunately, Man Who Strikes the Ree and his community of headmen also had experienced delays, so they, too, ended up in Sioux City. When the *Bighorn* failed to appear after several days, De Smet revised his plans and placed everyone on another steamboat, the *Guidon*. A full complement of passengers made the trip crowded, uncomfortable, and slow, but the *Guidon* nevertheless made the 155 miles from Sioux City to the Yankton Agency safely in six days.

A great celebration welcomed Man Who Strikes the Ree when the *Guidon* docked at the Yankton Agency. The Indians looked upon De Smet's simultaneous arrival as a bonus, and he, too, became the object of the tribesmen's friendly demonstration. Remembering his distasteful experience with rats and spiders the previous July, De Smet this time arranged to stay at the home of Alexis Giou, the agency interpreter. "He put me in possession of a nice little closet or attic, the only place available, where my altar, bed and all my things were straightway arranged, and in a few minutes I found myself in a real little *chez moi*, glad and happy to have escaped from the noise and tumult of the boat." Although he lacked supplies—the *Bighorn* inched forward in low water and would not reach Yankton until May 17—De Smet occupied his time by preaching to the Indians both at the agency and in the outlying areas for a distance of thirty miles.

When the *Bighorn* finally docked at the Yankton Agency and unloaded De Smet's equipment, Black Robe turned his attention to locating the interior Sioux. For that he would need help. Man Who Strikes the Ree volunteered some Yankton warriors to serve as escorts. Meanwhile, De Smet recruited interpreter Alexander Rencontre, guide Joseph Picotte, and a half-blood simply referred to as Pratt. After assembling everyone, De Smet headed straight for Fort Thompson, where, word had it, approximately 120 lodges of noncombatant Brulés, Two Kettles, and Yanktonais camped. He hoped that from them he would learn the location of the belligerent bands of Oglalas and Miniconjous who made travel so dangerous on the Platte Road and the Bozeman Trail and to the Union Pacific construction crews.

Thirty-six chiefs and braves attended De Smet's first council at Fort Thompson. Following his time-tested format, De Smet opened the proceedings with a short statement recounting the desires and wishes of the government. Then the Indians responded. Several Indian orators addressed the assembly, laying before De Smet their critical position:

On the one hand, they alleged their nearness to and relations with the fighting bands, who are their own blood and kin; and the invitations of the latter to take up the hatchet against the whites in defense of the land of their birth; invitations always accompanied with insults and menaces. On the other hand—I will quote their own words: "Commissioners and agents of the Government come to us every year; they are affable and prodigal of speeches and promises in behalf of our Great Father. What is the reason that so many fine words and pompous promises always come to nothing, nothing, nothing?" Then they entered into a series of details concerning the injustices and misdeeds of the whites.

De Smet knew the Indians spoke the truth, and they instinctively understood that he felt as they did.

Two days later De Smet followed a well-worn path to Old Fort Sully, long since abandoned by soldiers and now home to 220 lodges of peaceful Sioux. Again, De Smet convened a council, and again the Indians "complained bitterly of the bad faith of the whites, of the commissioners and agents of the Government, always so prodigal of promises and always so slow in fulfilling them, if they ever do so. This conduct sticks in their minds." De Smet feared that these bands might join the hostiles.

During this time at Old Fort Sully, General Alfred Sully and Ely S. Parker, also envoys extraordinary of the government, caught up with De Smet. Their credentials, like De Smet's, empowered them to "take special information in regard to the complaints of the Indians against the whites, and the injustices of which they continually have been victims." General Sully still professed an interest in the missionization and Christianization of the Plains Indians, but the fact that he brought with him five companies of soldiers also said something about his basic attitude toward finding a solution to the conflict between the races. In his view the Indians' continuing war against whites made soldiers necessary, and he would withdraw them only when peace returned to the plains. On several occasions chiefs told Sully, as they also informed De Smet, that there could be no peace until the soldiers departed from the plains, but the general always shot back that his men would continue to increase like grasshoppers until they covered all the fields. Bury the hatchet, the general commanded, and then the soldiers would leave. The Indians' other demands included the closure of the public roads and the cessation of riverboat traffic on the Missouri. Sully would not even debate those ideas.

De Smet does not indicate the level of cordiality between the commissioners, or to what extent he attempted to convert Sully to his views, but the priest secreted nothing in his official report to the commissioner of Indian affairs:

> This far, all that I have observed and been able to learn among the different bands of Indians makes me augur favorably of their good dispositions to live at peace with the whites, and to make efforts to withhold their young men from committing depredations. They ask, and have a right to demand, to have justice done them; that the annuities granted them by treaty should come to them; that the practice of putting them off with fine words should cease once and for all; that they be protected against the whites who come to sow iniquity and misery in their country; and in conclusion, they humbly beg their Great Father the President to grant them agricultural implements, seeds, plows and oxen to till the soil. I repeat it, if our Indians become enraged against the whites, it is because the whites have made them suffer for a long time.

For decades De Smet fretted about the worsening condition of the western Indians. He watched their numbers diminish yearly. Those who survived often did so in humiliating fashion, and De Smet could foresee no respite. He favored instructing the Indians not only in Christianity, but also agriculture, domestic arts, and a European-style educational system. How he intended to achieve those goals is not clear, except that missionaries and missions would play a central, rather than supporting, role. If his thoughts on the matter are confused and sometimes redundant, it is because he could never separate the reality of the abusive, inexorable advance of white pioneers, pressing ever deeper into Indian lands, impoverishing the natives and destroying their environment, from his emotional attachment to the Indians and the life they led. De Smet's greatest sadness was the demise of the Indians during his lifetime.

Whatever their differences or common understandings, the three commissioners resolved to remain together at least as far as Fort Union. Before they left Fort Sully, De Smet wrote several messages for Indian runners to carry into the interior. He announced to all warring bands of Sioux that he would soon return to Old Fort Sully, and when he did he wished to meet with them. The *Graham* transported everyone to Fort Union.

Fort Union had ceased functioning as a private, commercial fur trade post after 1867. The government purchased it and used its materials to enlarge an adjacent military post named Fort Buford. Again, De Smet sent out appeals to the Indians, this time to the allies of the hostile tribes. "We are waiting for the arrival of the Crow and Santee chiefs, to announce and explain to them the wishes of the Government," De Smet penned in his journal; "After that, I shall go down the river to Fort Rice or Fort Sully, and set out into the interior to visit the hostile bands, if the thing is practicable." But the scouts never managed to locate either the Santees or the Crows, so the commissioners decided to go back downriver. De Smet knew from his experiences in 1851 that it would be futile for him to attempt to locate the tribes in the broken and pockmarked landscape of the Yellowstone Desert by himself, so he had no choice but to comply with the majority decision of the commissioners.

On the way downriver De Smet received some shocking news at Fort Rice. To his dismay he learned that upward of one hundred Sioux chiefs and warriors had come in to council with him; they had waited for ten days and had then left to hunt buffalo. Before departing, they told the fort interpreter "that they greatly desired to see the Black-robe and talk with him." De Smet reeled under the disappointment. For years he had hoped to entice the most destructive bands of Sioux to a conference, and now he had missed his opportunity by mere days. Perhaps he could chase after them as they followed the buffalo herds south.

Endorsing his suggestion, all three commissioners hurried downstream to pick up De Smet's traveling wagon, a concession to frontier travel the missionary accepted when his aging body rebelled against the strain of endless hours in the saddle. Alas, when they arrived at Fort Sully, De Smet learned that his mules and his wagon had been heavily used by others during his absence and were currently unfit for an extended journey. Thus, for the second time in a week De Smet suffered an annoying setback. Since he could not chase after the Indians, he would just have to remain with Sully and Parker as far as Fort Leavenworth and from there proceed to Saint Louis. But, he vowed, he would return to the upper Missouri again in the spring of 1868.

On the way downriver the commissioners compared notes on what they had learned regarding the attitude of the Indians and what should be reported to the commissioner of Indian affairs. Together they had heard the opinions of some fifteen thousand nonwarring Indians. The claims of the Indians convinced De Smet that

> if their annuities are paid them at the proper time and pace; if the agents and other employees of the Government treat them with honesty and justice; if they are supplied with the necessary tools for carpentry and agriculture, the Indian tribes of the upper Missouri . . . would maintain peace with the whites; and the war-like bands who to-day infest the plains of the Far West and the valley of the Platte, where there is so much destruction of property and loss of life, would promptly cease their depredations and would not be long in joining the stay-at-home tribes.

De Smet considered his government service ended when he reached Fort Leavenworth. At any rate, a new seven-member government peace commission had already assembled at the fort. They came because while De Smet, Sully, and Parker listened to Sioux complaints on the upper Missouri, elsewhere on the plains a large war party of Oglalas attacked Fort C. F. Smith. On the day following, another band of Indians, this one under Red Cloud, killed a detachment of woodcutters from Fort Kearny. Since the Sioux War did not seem to be winding down, President Andrew Johnson, bowing to humanitarian demands, authorized a new Indian commission, ordering this panel to write a final, lasting peace between the tribesmen of the Great Plains and the whites.

In October 1867 government negotiators settled matters with the Southern Plains tribes when it concluded a series of treaties at Medicine Lodge Creek, Kansas. There still remained, however, the war on the Northern Plains, specifically the two prongs of the Sioux War, one led by Red Cloud and the other by Sitting Bull. The members of the newest commission unanimously invited De Smet to join them on their peace mission, an arrangement he readily accepted for two reasons. First, he could return to the tribes that waited for him beyond Fort Rice. Second, membership on the panel would provide him with a second opportunity to present his views on Indian affairs to cabinet-level officials in Washington, D.C. But first De Smet needed to hurry to Saint Louis to retrieve his wagon, livestock, and camping equipment, all of which continued on without him when he got off the steamboat at Fort Leavenworth.

As events turned out, De Smet did not return to Leavenworth again that summer. Once in Saint Louis, the oppressive heat and humidity of the Mississippi Valley completely wearied the elderly priest. Following orders imposed by his physician, De Smet sent his regrets to the commissioners at Leavenworth and remained at Saint Louis University for the rest of the year convalescing. "More and more I feel the weight of years," De Smet confided to his old friend Father Terwecoren; "My strength is failing and I am getting thin." His weight had, in fact, dropped from a once robust 210 pounds to about 167. Diagnosis in Saint Louis confirmed that De Smet suffered from Bright's disease, a kidney ailment.

Before he wrote his report on Indian matters to the secretary of the interior, De Smet attended to a personal matter so distasteful to him that he said he would have just preferred to avoid it, but he could not in justice to himself and others of the Missouri Province of the society. In the course of his return trip down the Missouri River in July, De Smet had chanced to meet at Omaha one Father John Anthony Gaes of Freiburg, Germany, a cousin of a German Jesuit. During the course of their brief conversation, De Smet read to Gaes several passages from his three most recent letters, all of which he planned to send to the *Précis Historiques*. Gaes exhibited obvious surprise, remarking that German Jesuits commonly held that Father De Smet merely lent his name, as a sort of universal nom de plume, to all of the articles and books

collectively written by the missionaries of the Society of Jesus in
Missouri.

This revelation grievously offended De Smet. He prayed over
the matter, consulted with his superiors, and then wrote an in-
dignant letter to the provincial of the German Jesuits. "I will
admit," he began, "that I am sensitive to a personal attack which
I have in nowise deserved, and which has cost me much labor."
De Smet declared emphatically that "the printed letters bearing
my name are due to no other person, and permit me to protest to
your Reverence against those of your province who advance the
contrary." He stated further that during thirty years as an Indian
missionary he had dutifully followed the instructions of his superiors to "enter into minute details upon everything that concerned the Indian missions, the diverse countries inhabited by
the Indians, the manners, customs, beliefs, etc. of these strange
and unfortunate tribes." The charges advanced against him are
hearsay, De Smet asserted, and "that hearsay is false." At the
same time, De Smet asked Father Edward Terwecoren, the publisher of so many of his letters in *Précis Historiques,* to expose and
correct the rumor in his magazine. Terwecoren responded affir-
matively and in 1868 condemned the unwarranted "false beliefs"
cropping up against Father De Smet. Terwecoren stated for the
record that the only corrections or additions anyone ever made
to Father De Smet's manuscripts were those of grammar, not
substance.

It is absolutely true that the Missouri Province Jesuits did not
collectively author De Smet's books and articles. On the other
hand, sometimes De Smet did write essays with information he
received from others. His dissertations on the Blackfeet, for example, strongly reflect the input of Father Nicolas Point, who
understood those tribesmen far better than De Smet. Similarly,
interpreters and agents at fur posts along the Missouri supplied
De Smet with anecdotes about the upper Missouri Indians that
later found publication under his name. In particular, Edwin T.
Denig, longtime post trader at Fort Union, provided De Smet
with extensive insights into Assiniboin life and customs, thereby
allowing De Smet to illuminate the tribe with a greater depth of

knowledge than he ever could have gained during the fleeting stops he made to their camps. Alex Culbertson furnished similarly perceptive observations for De Smet on the Mandans and Arikaras, and Zephyr Rencontre, F. F. Gerard, and C. E. Galpin assisted him in understanding Sioux culture. De Smet certainly did not plagiarize material from any of these informants, though it also cannot be said that all of his ethnographic conclusions came entirely from his own surveillance.

Likewise, though De Smet's maps provide expert assessments of many rivers he knew intimately, such as the Columbia and the Missouri, some of his cartographic work relied on information provided by Indian informants, guides such as Jim Bridger and Andrew Drips, and fellow Jesuits. Among the most significant of the De Smet maps are those detailing the "boiling fountains" of the lower Yellowstone River, antedating by some twenty years charts that would be made by the Washburn Expedition of 1870, yet there is no evidence that De Smet himself actually ever visited the future Yellowstone National Park.

Turning now to Indian affairs, De Smet used his period of recuperation to write several letters to the secretary of the interior about his recent contact with the upper Missouri tribes. In measured phrases he summarized his position on the Indians yet one more time: "It is my candid opinion, should due regard be paid to the just complaints of the Indians, should their annuities be delivered in due and proper time, and implements of agriculture be supplied to them; should they be dealt with honestly and kindly by agents and other persons in the employ of the Government, the bands mentioned will be kept friendly to the whites, and the warrior bands in the upper Missouri plains will soon cease their depredations."

In conclusion, De Smet offered his services to the secretary in the spring of 1868, providing that the government would again defray his travel expenses. During his recent journey he had spent a total of $1,576.30 of the $2,500 he had been given, and he proposed to hold the balance in his own account until further notice. The secretary of the interior agreed to De Smet's proposition, telling him further that the government decided to honor a request by Man Who Strikes the Ree that up to $3,000 per year should be taken from tribal annuities to assist in the establishment and maintenance of a Catholic mission for the Yanktons. Now more than ever, with this success under his belt, De Smet resolved to return to the upper Missouri in the spring of 1868 and do the same for another tribe.

All through the winter of 1867–68, De Smet laid plans for his return to the upper Missouri in the spring. Could Charles Galpin, the post trader at Fort Rice, obtain an interpreter, wagon, mules, and a driver for him? De Smet also quizzed General William Tecumseh Sherman about the success of the most recent peace commission to the tribes. Sherman considered the mid-September meeting with delegations from the Oglalas and Brulés at North Platte, Nebraska, a success, but, to his regret, only one chief came to a second scheduled meeting on November 5, and no chiefs attended a later Fort Laramie conference. Sherman urged De Smet to join the re-forming peace commission in the spring, a sentiment enthusiastically endorsed by General Harney. Speaking of the relationship between De Smet and the hostile tribes, Harney wrote to the commissioner of Indian affairs: "It is well known that he has almost unbounded influence over them, and his sole object in going among them is to prevent further hostilities." Besides, General Harney knew from past experience that De Smet "charges nothing for his individual Services—the Priests never do."

De Smet disliked personal titles, be it chaplain, major, envoy extraordinary, or commissioner—the only designation he wished was an "S.J." for Society of Jesus. Still, his formal governmental connection provided him with an official status that permitted immediate access to high-level policy makers, a privilege De Smet used on more than one occasion to the advantage of the Indians and the Jesuits. And he appreciated the minor financial advantage of traveling at government expense. Most important of all, participating on peace commissions enabled De Smet to advise the Indians as well as the government. De Smet believed that the Indians placed themselves in a precarious position when they chose to match themselves against the military might of the

U.S. Army, and he tried to convince the warring tribes of that fact. "I desire much to see the hostile tribes," De Smet told his friend Charles Galpin; "For their own good they must come to a good understanding with the whites and accept the peaceful measures the Government proposes to them." If his recommendations made him appear to be a government operative, so be it. The truth was that the Indians were in danger of extermination, and they must yield—an unpleasant message to be sure, but one which De Smet hoped the tribal headmen would accept.

The Peace Commission of 1868 assembled in Omaha, a growing railroad center, rather than Fort Leavenworth. De Smet took the train from Saint Louis, joining generals Sherman, Harney, Alfred Terry, and several other envoys. General Christopher C. Auger; Senator John B. Henderson, chairman of the Senate Committee on Indian Affairs; Commissioner of Indian Affairs N. G. Taylor; attorney J. B. Sanborn; and trader S. F. Tappan joined them at Omaha on April 2. From there the entire group boarded Union Pacific Railway cars for Cheyenne. The peace commissioners divided into two groups, one going south to deal with the tribes living below the Platte River and the other continuing west to Fort Laramie for a prearranged council with the Sioux and Northern Cheyennes.

At this point De Smet decided he could be most effective operating as an independent, so he volunteered to return to Omaha, take a steamboat to Fort Rice, and from there attempt to contact those Sioux bands not planning to attend the conference at Fort Laramie. Specifically, he hoped to link up with the so-called Sitting Bull bands of the Hunkpapas, who secluded themselves in buffalo-rich territory in the Yellowstone Valley between the Powder and Bighorn Rivers. If successful, De Smet would bring leaders from these tribes to a meeting with Commissioners Harney, Sanborn, and Terry, probably at Fort Rice. And so they all agreed.

Low water on the Missouri River forced the steamboat *Columbia* to crawl upriver over sandbars and snags at such a slow pace that it took thirty-three days to reach Fort Rice. As a result, word of mouth preceded De Smet upriver, and by the time he reached Fort Rice on May 24, thousands of Indians already knew Black Robe's intentions. Several tribes wanted an immediate meeting with De Smet, anxious to hear the latest government proposal. But De Smet postponed such a council, preferring that everyone wait until the warring bands came in, and then all of the upper Missouri tribes could come together to hear the words of the peace commissioners at a single sitting. De Smet did not have a timetable in mind, but a fair guess might be that it would take several months to bring the warring bands back to Fort Rice. Common knowledge placed the Hunkpapa bands approximately 350 miles due west of Fort Rice.

Headmen and warriors at Fort Rice tried valiantly to dissuade De Smet from disturbing the Hunkpapas. "My plan seemed to astonish them," said De Smet, "and they hardly concealed from me the dangers that were involved in it, even touching the security of my scalp." De Smet told them truthfully he had nothing to fear, for he trusted completely in the power of the Great Spirit, and so sincerely did he state his convictions that eight Lakota and Yanktonai chiefs agreed to join him on the expedition. Because each chief took with him his own guard, the escort eventually totaled about eighty people. Charles Galpin, a thirty-year resident with the Indians, "volunteered" to assist De Smet as his interpreter. Galpin brought along his wife, Matilda, known to the Hunkpapas and Two Kettles, the tribes of her parents, as Eagle Woman.

Heading directly toward the Dakota Badlands, De Smet and his entourage experienced hot, windy weather. Before long De Smet looked tired and drawn. For perhaps the first time the Indians realized the strain placed on Black Robe by these long marches. On June 8, after only six days on the trail, De Smet called a halt, ostensibly to check his position on the map, but more likely to rest his weary body. He asked for scouts to move out independently, to "beat up the country" in search of Hunkpapa villages while he and the main party continued at a slower pace along a prearranged route. He selected four braves and gave to each a small carrot of tobacco. "I should mention that sending tobacco is the same thing as a formal invitation, or the announcement of a desire to meet to confer upon important affairs," De Smet informed his superiors in a letter; "If the tobacco is accepted, it is a sure sign that you will be admitted among them; if on the contrary, it is refused, you may understand that all communication is forbidden, and govern yourself accordingly."

The days dragged on. "All are anxiously looking for the messengers we sent to the Camp; they should be back today," Galpin recorded in his journal for the night of June 13; "The heat is almost insufferable. Father De Smet shows more fatigue than at any time before." Two days later De Smet halted the main party on a fork of Beaver Creek in the hope that the scouts could more easily find them if they just stayed still. About midday on June 16, De Smet spotted a large band of horsemen through his field glasses. To his immense pleasure, it turned out to be his scouts, and they were accompanied by an escort of eighteen other braves. After handshakes all around, everyone sat down to smoke the pipe, a universal sign of good will. The scouts reported that Chief Four Horns, the principal spiritual and political leader of the Hunkpapa village, accepted the tobacco. He and his headmen waited for Black Robe near the confluence of the Yellowstone and Powder Rivers. "The night was spent in feasts between the Indians of my escort and the newcomers, mingled with joyful songs and fraternal rounds of the calumet. They were uproarious reunions, *a la sauvage,* but harmony and cordiality prevailed," De Smet fondly recalled.

For three days, while he and his escort struggled across the rugged divide to the Yellowstone Valley, De Smet mentally rehearsed his message to Four Horns. By noon on June 19 he could see the Indian camp in the dusty haze that lay across the Powder River valley. Apparently the Hunkpapas could also see the approaching visitors, for De Smet observed a large band of warriors leaving the camp and riding directly toward him and his escort. Black Robe had no reason to suspect treachery; still, the colorful sight unfolding before his eyes carried with it a certain fearsome quality.

When the Indian contingent, estimated by De Smet to be five hundred horsemen, came within one-half mile of convergence,

De Smet unfurled his personal banner of peace, a billowing flag embossed with a likeness of the Sacred Heart of Jesus on one side and the Virgin Mary surrounded by a heavenly halo on the other. But when he did so, the advancing warriors abruptly reined in their horses and spread out across the plains as if preparing for an attack. Too late, De Smet realized the Indians believed his banner to be the flag of the United States, and they feared a trap of some sorts. Tension filled the air. Fortunately, four chiefs demonstrated their bravery by riding at full gallop right up to the banner, and they circled it in a show of bravado and inspected the insignia. As soon as they learned what it represented, De Smet recorded, "they shook hands with me and signaled to their warriors to approach. They all drew themselves up in a single line and we did the same. Then the two lines approached each other. On both sides rose cries and shouts of joy. I was moved to tears by the reception those pagan sons of the desert gave me."

Once inside the main Sioux camp on the Powder River, throngs of warriors and women pressed forward to examine the man known across the plains as Black Robe. The rush of inquisitive faces, many of them streaked with black, yellow, and blue paint, so overwhelmed De Smet that he playfully renounced any previous intentions to convert the northern Sioux bands to Christianity. These were truly wild Indians! Sitting Bull stepped out of a lodge to meet De Smet. Without ceremony, but with distinct implications to his tribesmen, Sitting Bull, the ranking war chief of the village, placed Black Robe and the Galpins under his personal protection by opening his lodge to them. Such an action was necessary, De Smet later learned, "to prevent any perfidious attack by secret traitors who might be determined to take vengeance on the pale-face." By the honor code in force among the Indians, any brave "who has lost a member of his family at the hands of the whites is obliged to avenge himself on the first white man he meets. Well, there were a good many of them in this position at the time of my arrival among them." Physically drained by the travel and excitement, De Smet entered the tent, laid down, and almost immediately fell into a deep sleep.

When he awoke several hours later, De Smet found Sitting

Bull, Four Horns, Black Moon, and No Neck watching over him. The "generalissimo of the warriors," Sitting Bull, asked the Black Robe what could be accomplished by his visit. De Smet slowly, precisely explained his mission of peace, after which Sitting Bull replied, according to the priest, "I will listen to thy good words, and as bad as I have been to the whites, just so good am I ready to become toward them." Sitting Bull further indicated that he would listen to De Smet's full message at a great council planned for the next day.

The Great Powder River Council, as De Smet named it, opened at 1:00 P.M. on June 20, 1868. Crews of workers spent the morning readying ten tepees on a half-acre site large enough to accommodate hundreds of spectators because no one among the six hundred lodges in the village wanted to miss the oratory. "The banner of the holy Virgin occupied the centre" of the council site, "and on one side a seat was prepared for me of fine buffalo-robes." The council opened with songs and dances. Then "Four Horns lighted his calumet of peace; he presented it first solemnly to the Great Spirit, imploring his light and favor, and then offered it to the four cardinal points, to the sun and the earth, as witnesses to the action of the council." The calumet passed to Black Robe and then in descending rank from the spiritual and political chiefs in the front row to the war chiefs, like Sitting Bull, seated in the second row. At length Black Moon introduced De Smet, and the priest stood up to address the crowd. A profound sense of respect hushed the spectators.

For about an hour De Smet spoke to the leaders through his interpreter, Charles Galpin. Drawing on his years of experience at similar councils, De Smet phrased his statements at just the proper cadence so that the words could be simultaneously translated by an aide. Indians loved metaphors and imagery in their speeches, so De Smet appealed to his listeners with all the pageantry and drama of an actor. "Especially I spoke to them of the dangers with which they were surrounded, and of their weakness beside the great strength of the whites, if the 'Great Father' were forced to use it against them," he explained to the commissioner of Indian affairs. The Sioux have shown themselves to be a formi-

This watercolor of De Smet attending a council of Sioux chiefs in June 1868 at Sitting Bull's camp on the Powder River is attributed to Matthew Hastings. De Smet sits under his banner of the Blessed Virgin Mary. Courtesy of De Smetiana Collection, Jesuit Missouri Province Archives, Saint Louis IX-C7-141-Linton Album.

dable opponent, De Smet congratulated the Indians, but now they must accept the admission of the Great Father that harm and injustice has been done to men on both sides and respect his desire "that all should be forgotten and buried." They should meet the commissioners at Fort Rice; they should accept the Great Father's offer to provide agricultural implements to feed their families and schools to teach their children.

Black Moon, the best of the Sioux orators, replied to De Smet after another ceremonial passing of the pipe. Sitting Bull followed, speaking on behalf of the warrior element. He professed friendship to the whites, but he also made clear that he would neither sell any lands nor allow his braves to rest easy until the white soldiers quit his country. Two Bears, chief of the neutral Yanktonais, and Running Antelope, of the Brulé Sioux, both part of De Smet's escort, also voiced their opinions. De Smet listened intently as Charles Galpin translated every word, later committing it all to paper for the benefit of the commissioner of Indian affairs. Nevertheless, it is likely that the nuances, if not the substance, of what the Sioux had to say somehow got lost either in the translation or in De Smet's dramatic prose style. At the end of four hours the council proclaimed its decision: the Hunkpapas would send a delegation to meet the peace commissioners at Fort Rice.

In the emotional moments immediately following the conclusion of the conference, several Indians overcame their shyness and inquired if De Smet would leave his beautiful banner of peace with them as a souvenir of his visit. "I gladly acceded to their wish. I presented the banner to them in sign of gratitude for the confidence with which they had inspired me in all their behavior toward me and the speeches that they had just uttered." As standard bearer for this precious sign of peace, the chiefs chose a warrior with seven scalps to his credit, an incongruity De Smet pretended not to notice. De Smet also presented to Sitting Bull a crucifix; the Indian promised to wear it around his neck for all time.

Spontaneous songs and dances energized the Indian camp that evening. De Smet, proud of his accomplishment but exhausted by the effort, sequestered himself in Sitting Bull's lodge for a well-deserved night's sleep. He did not even awaken, Galpin reported, when "at a late hour we were somewhat alarmed by a great yelling and firing of a gun in close proximity to our lodge." Fearing the worst, the interpreter slipped out of the tepee to investigate the commotion and found to his relief that "it was caused by a mule trying to kill a colt. As it could not be driven off with clubs they had to use extreme measures: thus the firing of the gun. . . . After a while the cause of the alarm was known to all, when they sang and enjoyed themselves till morning."

De Smet said Mass at 4:30 A.M. on Sunday, June 21, so as not to delay an early departure of the peace delegation. Sitting Bull and three other chiefs escorted De Smet a portion of the way down the Powder River valley, but the great war chief chose not to go all the way to Fort Rice; eight Hunkpapa deputies, led by Gall, assumed that obligation. Thirty Indian families, an additional 160 persons, swelled the traveling party to nearly 250 men, women, and children, clearly identifying it to observers as a peace party, not a war party.

For ten days De Smet's escort marched uninterrupted, straight as an arrow, to Fort Rice. The weather held, buffalo and antelope provided plentiful food, and the travelers averaged 35–45 miles per day. On June 25, De Smet sent an advance messenger ahead to Fort Rice to announce the favorable results of his meeting with the Hunkpapa chiefs. General Terry accepted the good news with both surprise and relief, immediately sending a messenger of his own to tell De Smet that he, Harney, and Sanborn anxiously awaited his arrival. They carried with them the most recent Fort Laramie treaty document and would read it to the Hunkpapa delegation. General Terry, meantime, dressed the entire garrison at Fort Rice in full uniform to welcome De Smet and his Indian emissaries. General David S. Stanley re-created the scene for his friend, the bishop of Cincinnati: "The warriors formed a long file and marched with true precision. It was a really remarkable spectacle, though little in accord with the tastes of the good Father, who does not love the sound of trumpets and the glare of parades."

A second great council for the Sioux, this one at Fort Rice, took place on July 2. De Smet attended the meeting, proud to play a role in what he estimated to be "the greatest council that had been held on the Missouri in fifty years." The generals permitted each chief to make a speech, then all present "touched the pen" and agreed to the provisions of the Fort Laramie Treaty previously signed on May 11 by other Sioux chiefs. According to the terms, the tribesmen received a "Great Sioux Reservation," essentially all of the present state of South Dakota west of the Missouri River, and for thirty years the government pledged to maintain an agency and issue rations. In addition, the government guaranteed the Indians' right to hunt on the North Platte "so long as buffalo may range there in numbers sufficient to justify the chase." The Powder River country in which the Hunkpapas lived fell under a special provision in the treaty referred to as "unceded Indian territory." The government promised to abandon the Bozeman Trail forts, though it said nothing about the posts on the upper Missouri River.

Gall signed the treaty, but only after stating for the record his nonnegotiable position that in order for there to be peace on the northern Great Plains the whites must abandon all forts, halt steamboat traffic on the Missouri River, and recall the white settlers. Obviously, he did not understand the gist of the treaty provisions. De Smet also signed the Fort Laramie Treaty, but he, too, probably did so in ignorance. For the moment peace reigned on the plains. But the Sioux War did not really end on July 2 at Fort Rice any more than it ended on May 11 at Fort Laramie. De Smet probably knew that—though he did not want to admit it just now.

Terry, Sanborn, and Harney expressed their personal thanks to De Smet in an official letter the very next day: "We are satisfied that but for your long and painful journey into the heart of the hostile country, and but for the influence over even the most hostile of the tribes which your years of labor among them have given to you, the results which we have reached here could not have been accomplished." General David S. Stanley went even further in lauding the conduct of De Smet in a letter that stated:

> Without doubt the fulfillment of the provisions of this treaty will assure peace with the Sioux. But whatever may be the result, we can never forget, nor shall we ever cease to admire the disinterested devotion of the Rev. Father De Smet, who, at the age of sixty-eight years, did not hesitate, in the midst of the heat of summer, to undertake a long and perilous journey across the burning plains, destitute of trees and even of grass; having none but corrupted and unwholesome water, constantly exposed to scalping by the Indians, and this without seeking either honors or remuneration of any sort; but solely to arrest the shedding of blood, to save, if it might be, some lives, and preserve some habitations to these savage children of the desert.

Quietly, without fanfare, De Smet departed Fort Rice on the Fourth of July. As this was the day for the Indians to collect their presents at the peace council, most of them did not even notice. Because many months had passed since his last visit to the Potawatomi mission in Kansas, De Smet made his way down the Missouri River to Saint Mary's Mission, a decision he soon regretted. "After a few days," he said, "I found myself really, as you might say, demolished, panting with open mouth for the slight breeze. . . . This was the 29th of July. Every one was languishing. I was under a burning sun, with the thermometer ranging from 104 to 109 degrees in the shade, and up to 130 in the sun. I shall, I doubt not, feel the effects for a long time."

Exhausted, moving as if in slow motion, De Smet completed his journey to Saint Louis at the end of August. Fearful that he would die before he could jot down the history of what he now considered his finest moment as a peacemaker, De Smet spent his first week back at the university composing an extended dissertation about what he had done and with whom he had done it. When at last he mailed it to Father Terwecoren, he informed his editor that this would probably be his final article: "This letter may well be my last. My health is very much undermined in consequence of my late painful journey of about six thousand miles, but still more by the shocking heat that we have suffered for three months past. In proportion as I advance in age, heat becomes more and more insupportable to me. Very often one would say that I resemble a man whose end is at hand."

A short time later De Smet heard the news that Sitting Bull waited less than two months for the ink to dry on Gall's signature at Fort Rice before he attacked Fort Buford with 150 warriors, killing three soldiers and making off with the army's horse herd.

CHAPTER 8

"A Saint, but a Saint According to His Own Way," 1869–1873

WHEN the summer heat of 1868 gave way to cool October days, De Smet's health rebounded. Except for a partial loss of hearing, the result of a painful tooth extraction two years earlier, the old priest felt good. Unfortunately, the hearing condition worsened at the onset of winter, so the provincial, who knew De Smet had little tolerance for American physicians, urged him to seek medical treatment in Belgium. De Smet went, but only reluctantly. He still planned to establish a Jesuit mission in the upper Missouri country, and medical distractions interfered with his goal.

De Smet spent the first six months of 1869 in Europe, but he enjoyed it very little. In the first place, he slipped on deck during the steamer trip to Liverpool, breaking two ribs. Then Belgian doctors failed to rejuvenate his hearing. Still, he did not regret having made the trip, because it furnished yet another opportunity to visit with his nieces and nephews and to contact some benefactors. The ocean voyage back to America on the *City of Dublin* in late June dangerously wearied De Smet even more than the voyage over, and in addition to the general maladies of old age and enfeeblement, De Smet also continued to suffer from Bright's disease. This combination of reoccurring illnesses kept him in his room at the Jesuit residence of Saint Louis University for long weeks at a time. Even worse, it forced him to postpone, and ultimately cancel, his Missouri River trip.

When he did finally return to an active life, De Smet permitted himself only a few short trips. The most satisfying of these excursions took place when he escorted six Sisters of Charity to Omaha. The least satisfying of his outings occurred a month later, in November 1869, when he visited Saint Mary's Mission in Kansas. It greatly pained De Smet to see the Potawatomis so demoralized by the influence of whites. De Smet scolded state authorities for being even less vigilant than federal marshals in halting the whiskey trade among the Indians. Sellers "swooped down like vultures on these savages, and made unheard-of efforts to ruin and destroy these innocent creatures, once so happy," he complained, repeating phrases like "terrible scourge" and "destroyers of civilization" to emphasize his point. A quick trip to Chicago and Milwaukee in December raised more money for the ever-needy missions.

After several false starts, in June 1870, De Smet embarked on his long-anticipated journey up the Missouri River to finalize arrangements for a new Indian mission. Because of his infirmities De Smet required the assistance of another Jesuit, in this case Father Ignatius Panken, S.J., a Dutchman who had immigrated to America in 1857. It is not possible at this late date to understand the methods by which the two priests selected or rejected potential sites, but for some reason they purposely overlooked two locations that De Smet had previously favored, one at Fort Randall and another at Fort Berthold. For reasons best known to themselves, they selected as the site of the mission a spot in the Grand River country near present-day Mobridge, South Dakota.

De Smet initiated preliminary negotiations with the Indian agent in charge at Fort Stevenson and then announced his intentions to the local chiefs. The Sioux leaders responded with heartfelt gladness, but the thrill of this achievement dimmed for De Smet as his physical condition continued to deteriorate. Dizzy with fatigue, in August he abandoned his original plan to visit other tribes and returned to Saint Louis as quickly as possible. For the rest of the year De Smet occupied himself with projects that could be done from his room at Saint Louis University. He expressed a special interest in writing a history of the Missouri Province of the Society of Jesus.

Toward the end of 1870, De Smet rekindled his interest in government service. Immediately before his election, President U. S. Grant fell under the influence of humanitarians who formed a powerful lobby for Indian interests in the United States. The corrupt state of Indian affairs in the Department of the Interior offended them, and they pestered Grant to reform the system. To mollify them, in June 1869, President Grant appointed ten philanthropic citizens to a board of Indian commissioners. Members served without pay, but oversaw the activities of federal agents on the Indian reservations. About the same time, a group of Quakers persuaded President Grant to raise the moral level of the Indian service by allowing them to nominate men—presumably morally strong, religiously oriented Friends—for agency appointments. Congress, in the meantime, joined in the reform movement by passing a law that denied Indian agency appointments to army officers.

These were busy times, and they got even more hectic after the Union Pacific and Central Pacific Railroads joined together at Promontory Point, Utah. A relentless westward migration followed, placing new pressure on Indian lands and reservations. Hoping to head off trouble before it got out of hand, President Grant invited other denominations to follow the Quaker example and make their own nominations for Indian agents or superintendents. Their advice would be particularly welcome on reservations where they had already made their presence felt among the tribesmen. De Smet believed he could help Grant.

The Catholics, with forty-three Indian missions under the guidance of Jesuits, Oblates of Mary Immaculate, Franciscans, and other orders, served more than a hundred thousand Indians at various locations in the trans-Mississippi West. De Smet naturally assumed Grant's new Indian policy would rely heavily on Catholic input. Moreover, he believed the Grant administration would provide desperately needed federal assistance for all Indian missions, including those of the Jesuits. The foundation of the Grand River Agency mission for the Sioux was virtually assured by now, but De Smet knew the society would need fresh dollars to establish additional missions at or near forts Berthold, Randall, and possibly even Sully. It all seemed very hopeful to De Smet, so when Secretary of the Interior Columbus Delano invited him to assist in the assignment of federal Indian agents, De Smet accepted immediately. Delano told De Smet that Catholic

Church officials the secretary had contacted chose him unanimously.

The first commission meeting De Smet attended took place in February 1871 in Washington, D.C. About thirty other persons, each of them representing religious denominations, also took part. Buoyant at the start, De Smet eventually sat in silence as politics and religious bigotry overwhelmed the meeting. Little by little he saw his hopes for federal assistance to Catholic missions dashed. He was partly at fault. Where once De Smet had been the Catholic Church's most eloquent spokesman for the Indian missions, a virtual encyclopedia on the breadth and depth of Catholic missions on the western frontier, now he could no longer rebut what he considered false and misleading statistics proclaimed by others. Under interrogation he could not speak with authority about the number of Catholic converts among the Indians, and he did not even know the number of missions and schools currently operated by the Society of Jesus, much less by all Catholic orders. In the end, the Catholics received the right to recommend the agent at only four reservations; they lost their influence with thirty-nine tribes.

Eventually the Catholics would gain an additional four reservations, but by then it made little difference to De Smet. "Neither my presence, nor my demands on behalf of the Catholic missions," he confided to his close friend Dr. Linton, "produced any effect. The plan for civilizing and evangelizing the Indians had already been decided upon by the President and approved by the Senate." In short, he felt powerless to thwart the predisposition of Grant and the Congress, and in a single executive department action he saw some eighty thousand Catholic Indians torn from their adopted religion without any consideration for their desires. De Smet thought it incomprehensible that henceforth agents for the Coeur d'Alenes, Blackfeet, and Potawatomis, among others, would be recommended by Protestants. "One can scarcely believe that such a state of things could exist in the republic of the United States, so much vaunted for its liberty," De Smet lamented. That the Methodists, President Grant's church of choice, received the lion's share of the assignments could not have displeased De Smet more—he considered them the least educated of all the denominations and the most spiteful toward the Jesuits—but his complaints to Commissioner Ely Parker fell on deaf ears.

Meanwhile, in January 1871 the board of consultors for the Missouri Province had announced that the father general approved of locating a Jesuit mission at the Grand River site. Happily, Grant's Board of Indian Commissioners concurred in the same plan; the mission would be entrusted to the Catholics. The Missouri Province consultors next considered who would be the superior of the new mission. At its March board meeting the consultors considered the names of six priests, but not De Smet's in view of his advanced age and worsening physical condition. They selected Father Francis Kuppens, S.J., to be the superior, with Father Peter De Meester, S.J., as his assistant. De Smet could, however, still oversee the actual foundation of the mission. "Two fathers will accompany me," De Smet proudly informed his niece in Belgium, "and we intend to establish a mission for the Sioux. The head chiefs of the tribe are expecting me, and I have just written to inform them of my plans and to ask them to prepare a cabin for us in their camp."

Unfortunately, just before De Smet's embarkation for the upper Missouri the plans to open the Sioux mission fell through. In spite of earlier, favorable calculations, Jesuit consultors suddenly changed their mind and decided they would not proceed with a Grand River Agency mission. For one thing, the province could not count on the increasingly scandalous and unreliable Grant administration for financial assistance. Devastated by this turn of events, De Smet decided to return to Europe and raise his own money. Shaking their heads in disbelief, De Smet's superiors nevertheless yielded to the old man's request. Accordingly, De Smet took the *City of New York* to Liverpool during July and stayed the rest of the summer in Europe, plus the fall and winter, raising money on behalf of the Missouri Province Indian missions.

Kuppens and De Meester, meantime, spent their time with equal profit at Grand River, Dakota Territory, learning bits and pieces of the Sioux language from Two Bears, a Yanktonais chief.

The debilitating effects of Bright's disease can be seen in this photograph of De Smet that appeared in an 1872 issue of *The Central Magazine*. De Smet died only a few months later, on May 23, 1873. Courtesy of Oregon Province Archives of the Society of Jesus, Gonzaga University.

They also met Sitting Bull and Major John C. Connor, the agent in charge at Grand River, one of the few appointments De Smet accomplished under the Grant peace plan. Connor told Kuppens that, in his opinion, the elders of the Sioux tribes would not be able at this point in their lives to grasp the cultural or religious changes embodied in Christianity. He suggested that the missionaries concentrate on educating the children.

By January 1872, De Smet had worked himself into a state of complete fatigue in France. "I am so weak," he informed his nephew Charles, "that even a short conversation tires me. The doctor orders complete rest and forbids all work or preoccupation for the missions." During his convalescence in Belgium, De Smet mulled over several ideas, at least one born of despair and sheer desperation. He told his family that he wanted to establish a seminary in Belgium dedicated exclusively to training European clerics for service in the American Indian missions. He even knew a good site for the school. But the idea went no farther than his family; on second thought, he never mentioned the plan to his Jesuit superiors.

A second notion held greater promise. With De Smet's encouragement, Father Francois Deynoodt, S.J., a Belgian Jesuit, set about to accumulate all of De Smet's letters and papers. Hopefully, at some time in the future, Deynoodt would prepare a complete edition of De Smet's writings from both published and unpublished manuscripts. De Smet advanced the idea because he feared he could not do the task himself as his health grew ever worse. Indeed, by February 1872 the old priest began to hemorrhage so badly that his family made a pilgrimage to Lourdes to pray for him.

De Smet felt well enough to return to America in April. Ever the campaigner for the missions, he brought with him nine priests and novices, plus sixty-six thousand francs (twelve thousand dollars) in cash and supplies, more than enough to ensure the establishment of the Sioux mission on the upper Missouri as an independent Jesuit agency. During the past half-century De Smet had crossed the Atlantic Ocean eighteen times, but this would be his final voyage. Appreciating the marvels of modern transportation, only eighteen days after the *City of Paris* left Antwerp on April 7, De Smet settled into his room in Saint Louis. He would never leave the city again.

During his tenure in Europe, De Smet had received a permanent appointment to Secretary of the Interior Delano's advisory board on the Indian missions. De Smet, however, hardly wished to be reminded of that situation. Still, he accepted so that he would at least have an avenue of direct contact with the secretary. Then he abruptly resigned. Officially, De Smet begged off by saying that he lacked sufficient knowledge about current mission matters. But to Father Deynoodt he further explained: "As regards my health, the machine is completely out of order. For two months I have been confined to my room by order of the doctor, and I have to follow a very strict diet and, for me, quite a new régime. My mantelpiece looks like a drug-shop and the very sight of it takes away my appetite." Six months later De Smet could not even see the mantel, for "my left eye is totally paralyzed, and the sight is gone." The unprecedented cold of the winter enfeebled him even more, he said, and "I await with resignation my last hour."

Although he could not personally go to his Indians at the Grand River Agency, De Smet maintained communication with them through their agent, John Connor. Unwilling to give up hope of making yet one more expedition up the river, De Smet contemplated accepting the offer of Captain Joseph La Barge to go upriver with him in May 1873. It became his fantasy. In his final letter to his beloved sister Rosalie, herself seventy-six years old, De Smet still held hope that a change in the weather might improve his health and allow him to travel once again. For the moment, however, he wrote, "I have been sitting in the chimney-corner, and I find my fire an agreeable companion."

A week later, on May 13, 1873, Father De Smet summoned all of his available strength to take a carriage several blocks to the Saint Louis levee, where he blessed Captain La Barge's newest steamboat, the *De Smet*. It was an honor De Smet could not decline, a request from an old friend he could not refuse. The ceremony was mercifully brief, but the ride back to the university seemed longer to De Smet than any trek he had ever made across the highest summits of the Rocky Mountains, and it left him gasping for breath. By the time he entered his room at the university, De Smet was deathly ill.

Somehow, the next day De Smet managed to say Mass, but at the conclusion he told his server: "This is the end. I shall never again ascend the altar." And he never did. Priests administered the Last Sacrament to De Smet on May 20, and three days later, at 2:15 A.M. on May 23, 1873, Black Robe passed away. When the province superior cleaned out De Smet's room at the university, he found a cash box containing six thousand dollars, a contingency fund the irascible missionary held in reserve for his Sioux Indian mission. The provincial directed that the money be used instead to further the Oregon Mission, De Smet's own, as a remembrance of his accomplishments in that region.

The citizens of Saint Louis paid Father De Smet a great honor in the funeral procession they attended and the obituaries they wrote in area newspapers. Thousands of mourners, including General Harney and two other generals of the army, attended the funeral on May 24 at Saint Francis Xavier Church, where they heard Bishop Patrick Ryan preach the oration. A funeral cortege laid the remains of Father De Smet to rest at the historic Jesuit novitiate in Florissant, a seminary which he had helped to construct more than fifty years earlier.

Meanwhile, a telegraph message raced ahead on copper wires to intercept Captain La Barge on the maiden voyage of the *De Smet*. When he read the message at Sioux City, Iowa, La Barge ordered the vessel's flag flown at half-mast. As the *De Smet* powered its way upstream, the word spread to the military forts, trading posts, and Indian camps that Black Robe had passed away. The man the Indians thought would always be with them would never return.

Father Peter John De Smet may or may not have been the best Catholic, or even Jesuit, missionary in nineteenth-century America, but he was certainly the most famous. Americans and Europeans, Catholics and non-Catholics, white men and Indians all

knew about the man called Black Robe. But which man did they
know, for there are many Father De Smets: priest, pioneer Missouri Jesuit, zealous missionary to the Indian tribes of the Oregon
country and the upper Missouri, fund raiser and recruiter of
men, author and publicist, trusted advisor to the Indians, government envoy, frontier scientist, administrator, affable traveling
companion?

De Smet came to America as a young man for the wrong
reasons, but he stayed for the right ones. He left his comfortable
home in Belgium to satisfy his curiosity about America and to
find adventure, but he merged easily into the religious life and
spent five decades attempting to convert every Indian he met,
even whole tribes, to Christianity. If his life as an Indian missionary also presented him with the opportunity to explore new lands
and to enjoy many unique experiences, so much the better. Along
the way he came to some conclusions about the American frontier, its inhabitants, and its future.

The Potawatomi experience at Council Bluffs pointed out to
De Smet what happened to a tribe when they became too closely
aligned with the boisterous crowd of white men who inhabited
frontier settlements. The Potawatomis disappointed and disillusioned De Smet. Thus, when he visited the childlike Flatheads in
1840, De Smet saw in them the opportunity denied him at Council Bluffs. De Smet knew he had only a short time to convert the
Oregon country Indians to Christianity and the Euro-American
concept of civilization he believed in, so he set a fast pace, starting as many missions as he could, continually exploring for new
sites, raising his own money, and encouraging his fellow Jesuits to join him in the Rocky Mountain Mission. He believed he
needed to move quickly to convert the Indians before white men
corrupted them. It is too bad that De Smet did not sufficiently
understand the Indians' motives for wanting missionaries in the
first place, much less that the tribes did not desire for themselves
all of the elements of Euro-American civilization. De Smet's
talents were in planning, locating, and establishing, not analyzing.

His other great talent lay in promoting the missions, not only
with benefactors, but also in his own order, the Society of Jesus.

Unfortunately, De Smet did not supervise personnel matters carefully. While he exhibited the primary quality to be an Indian missionary—that is, he instinctively loved the Indians with such undisguised admiration and honest feeling that they responded by loving him unconditionally as well—he did not manage other missionaries well. Eventually the father general in Rome heard enough bad reports on De Smet and replaced him as superior of the Rocky Mountain Mission. From 1846 to his death in 1873, De Smet remained in Saint Louis, part of that time brooding in the disgrace of the father general's action.

De Smet restructured his life in three ways after 1846. Principally he redeemed himself by acting as procurator for the Rocky Mountain Mission. Second, he devoted much of his time and energy to the upper Missouri River tribes such as the Arikaras, Mandans, Yanktons, and other units of the Sioux. Third, De Smet dabbled in federal Indian policy as an envoy to the tribes. When his own religious order underappreciated him, he gave his expertise to the government.

De Smet became famous on two continents because he made himself so. He possessed such a rare talent for promoting himself and the Jesuit missions of the American frontier that ultimately the two seemed synonymous. Who in the midnineteenth century could not think of the Potawatomi missions, the Oregon missions or the Sioux mission without simultaneously thinking of Father De Smet. De Smet never apologized for his public relations skill; indeed, he thought it a blessing from God that enabled him, and others, to do the Lord's work with money he raised.

And raise money he did. The most recent research on the subject concludes that in his lifetime De Smet raised 1,225,536.41 francs in Europe, a value in its day of $245,000 and well over $1,000,000 in the currency of the 1990s. No one has calculated how much he begged from American Catholics, though that, too, would be a substantial amount. Add to that the income De Smet received from such sources as the trust funds set up for him by his family; the government expense account he received when he traveled as a federal commissioner; the gifts of clothing, church vestments and the like donated by ladies clubs; and the free passage on steamers he finagled from the Chouteau and La Barge families. No matter how one totals the ledger, De Smet sparkled as a fund raiser.

Of equal importance to the Missouri Jesuits, De Smet also gathered men. Approximately eighty Jesuit priests and brothers from Europe came to America as missionaries after being inspired to follow De Smet's path. The number may even approach one hundred persons if American clerics are included in the totals. Six religious women also went to the Oregon country at De Smet's request.

In addition to raising a sizable amount of money and writing four books, two in the 1840s and two more in the 1860s, Father De Smet earned respect from like-minded colleagues as an ethnographer of some talent. Native Americans never ceased to fascinate De Smet, and in the course of his lifetime he compiled voluminous notes on all manner of influences on their lives. Unlike most explorers of the period, who merely recorded their observations about the material culture of the Indians—the size, weight, color, and so on, of canoes, lodges, etc.—Father De Smet focused his attention on the Indians' life-style and spiritual condition. Simple ceremonies such as the calumet or pipe ritual earned his close observation, but so, too, did burial practices, superstitions, and hunting techniques. De Smet is one of the few amateur ethnographers of the nineteenth century to comment upon the Indians' sense of humor. Admittedly, De Smet accepted as fact the moral superiority of his heritage of western civilization over the primitive culture of his so-called neophytes, and in that he exhibited great prejudice, but even so, his cultural assessments of the upper Missouri and Columbia Plateau tribes are important and useful.

De Smet made nineteen trips across the Atlantic and Pacific Oceans, and in his lifetime he traveled nearly two hundred thousand miles. In half a century of travel in America, De Smet never lost his zest for blazing new trails, locating the source of a river, or crossing the crest of a mountain. His travel narratives of these expeditions took on a personal tone yet remained highly detailed.

In a list of De Smet's accomplishments, one would be remiss not to also include his early maps and his personal depiction of routes across the mountains, deserts, and plains.

It is as a Catholic priest, a missionary to the unconverted, that De Smet is best remembered today. Morally certain that the grace of God would save the Indians from harm, he tried to convert every tribe with which he came in contact. No one has calculated the precise number of children and adults De Smet baptized, but it is certainly in the thousands among the Flatheads, Coeur d'Alenes, Kalispels, Blackfeet, and Sioux alone. He also repaired marriages for both Indians and mixed-bloods, gave comfort to the dying, and distributed First Communion, a sacred Catholic ceremony.

Most history commentators extend to De Smet the title of "peacemaker" to the Indians. A few others believe the work he did at Fort Laramie in 1851 and among the Sioux in the 1860s constitute a failed nineteenth-century attempt to combine religion with politics. In the opinion of early-twentieth-century anthropologist George Hyde, De Smet's forays at federal expense contributed to the dispossession of the Indians by advising them to accept government treaties and take up land on reservations. Indeed, De Smet did do these things in council with the Sioux and others, but to suggest that he did them surreptitiously as a government agent is unfair, for there is no evidence that his actions or advice betrayed any western Indian tribe. Moreover, such an opinion neglects De Smet's personal view that reservations offered a respite to the Indians from the constant badgering of white pioneers. If one or two twentieth-century historians have found duplicity in De Smet's capacity as an advisor to the tribes, let the record show that none of his contemporaries, either Indians or non-Indians, ever did during his lifetime.

After 1851, De Smet wrestled with himself over a solution to the so-called Indian question. In his opinion, immoral and offensive white men badgered and abused the Indians until the frustrated natives struck back with violence. He lamented the fact that the disappearance of buffalo and other game animals caused large and powerful tribes to fall upon smaller, weaker tribes, not only inflicting significant bloodshed, but also simultaneously dissolving whatever Indian unity there may have been in the trans-Mississippi west. If, on the other hand, tribes struck back at the advancing, belligerent whites, the federal officials used this as a justification to unleash the U.S. Army on all the Indians. In De Smet's experience peaceful tribes suffered just as much during these wars, though in different, more subtle ways, as the renegade bands. De Smet rightfully feared that this continuing cycle would result in the extermination of all the Indians.

For De Smet the solution to the Indian question lay in three ingredients: time, isolation, and missionaries. First of all, he hoped to gain some time for the Indians. Ideally, De Smet wished to postpone direct contact between the races for twenty years. Unless the tribes made peace with the federal government and each other, he flatly expected that "the sad remnant of these numerous nations" would be exterminated. Thus, De Smet preferred for them to "find an asylum, a permanent abode, and be incorporated with all the rights of citizens of the Union." To him the reservation became not so much an enforced, arbitrary boundary for the tribesmen as a place where they could be free to enjoy the best of their culture and, at the same time, learn the fruits of the white man's civilization. History disproves his thesis, but De Smet could not see the future.

Finally, De Smet believed that missionaries, preferably Catholic priests, should be the only white people allowed to live among the Indians during their twenty-year interval of isolation on the reservations. Primarily, De Smet wished missionaries to instruct the natives in the tenets of the Catholic religion—food for their souls, so to speak. But the missionaries should also assist the Indians by teaching agriculture and academics—that is, food for the body and mind. At the same time, the missionaries would protect the Indians from the most vile aspects of white society, especially liquor. It could be a little confusing, De Smet admitted, but essentially missionaries saved Indians while neither frontiersmen nor soldiers ever attempted to do so. As noted before, it never occurred to De Smet that in bringing Euro-American civilization to the Indians he tacitly encouraged the destruction of the natives' own culture. Bernard De Voto points out in *Across the Wide Missouri,* "The missionaries thought they were bringing Christ but in thinking so they were deceived. They were agents of a historical energy and what they brought was the United States. The Indians had no chance." While De Smet recognized that change must come, he deplored the fact that it must be accompanied by so much cruelty and injustice.

De Smet could be flexible on some of these points regarding Indian policy. During a half-century of working with the Indians he learned to adjust to change. In the end, however, the federal government never endorsed De Smet's plans for the Indians despite the fact that he had the prestige to command the attention of the top men in the federal government, including even the president.

A true friend to the Indian and an ardent advocate for what he thought best for them, De Smet received in return their spontaneous affection. Everywhere tribes honored him, and even today his memory lives with them in place names, oral history, and religious ritual. Thurlow Weed introduced Father De Smet to President Abraham Lincoln by saying, "No white man knows the Indians as Father De Smet does, nor has any man their confidence in the same degree." Father Adrian Hoecken, who assisted De Smet in the Rocky Mountain Mission, once used similar words to describe the man the Indians called Black Robe: "From the day the Indians first saw Whites, never has any one been so generally known among them, and so sought for and beloved. Certainly no one has ever understood the Indians character better or known so well how to get along with them." Hiram M. Chittenden, the editor with Alfred T. Richardson of De Smet's published letters, echoes those contemporary sentiments when he writes that for the Indians "there was never another White man for whom they felt the deep personal affection and absolute trust that they did for him. Nothing is more remarkable in his eventful life than this fact."

Though he led a charmed life in many ways, De Smet also knew defeat in his lifetime. In 1846 the father general of the Society of Jesus "fired" him as superior of the Rocky Mountain

Mission. Several years later he felt threatened by the radical Know-Nothings. He never actually established a successful mission with either the Sioux or an upper Missouri tribe, though he seemed on the verge of it when he died. And De Smet did little to protect Catholic missions and schools from a Protestant takeover in the Grant peace policy. Throughout much of his lifetime he lacked the respect of many of his brother Jesuits.

No one ever accused Father De Smet of being ordinary. Father John Anthony Elet spoke volumes of truth about De Smet when he stated that the man lived his life "thoroughly good, but a little original," meaning unconventional. Perhaps the best single statement about De Smet, however, and the one to which most Jesuits who knew the missionary would most likely have agreed, came from Father Joseph Joset, who said simply that he believed De Smet to be "a saint, but a saint according to his own way."

Bibliography

THE two best efforts to write a critical biography of Peter John De Smet, S.J., were never completed. The first nonbiography began in 1873, the year that De Smet died. Shortly before his death Father De Smet gave permission to Father Francois Deynoodt, S.J., of Belgium to bring out a comprehensive edition of all his writings, together with a biography. Deynoodt worked diligently at the assignment, and during the next five years he managed to republish two of De Smet's books plus most of the letters he wrote for *Précis Historiques* in France. Deynoodt also prepared *Le Reverend Père P. J. De Smet de la Compagnie de Jésus* (Brussels: Alfred Vromant, 1878), but death overtook Deynoodt before he could complete a real biography of the great American Black Robe. A century later, Father William L. Davis, S.J., of Gonzaga University in Spokane, Washington, assembled thousands of documents for a detailed scholarly biography of De Smet, but he, too passed away before the task could be completed.

Perhaps the most balanced, short treatment of the life of De Smet is contained in the introductory chapters in Hiram M. Chittenden and Alfred T. Richardson, *Life, Letters and Travels of Father Pierre-Jean De Smet, S.J., 1801–1873,* 4 vols. (New York: P. J. Harper, 1905; New York: Arno Press, 1969). Both editions are currently unavailable. Eugene Laveille, S.J., wrote an interesting and useful biography of De Smet in 1913, *Le Père De Smet, apôtre des Peaux-Rouges (1801–1873)* (Musée Lessianum, section missiologique 9, Louvain, [1913] 1928). P. J. Kennedy & Sons of New York published it in 1915 (translated by Marian Lindsay) as *The Life of Father De Smet, S.J.* In 1981, Loyola University Press reprinted Laveille's work, but it is now sold out. John Upton Terrell's *Black Robe: The Life of Pierre-Jean De Smet, Missionary, Explorer, Pioneer* (New York: Doubleday & Co., 1964) is popular and readable, but it, too, is out of print. *"Come Blackrobe," De Smet and the Indian Tragedy* by Father John J. Killoren, S.J. (Norman: University of Oklahoma Press, 1994) emphasizes a single aspect of De Smet's life.

De Smet's original letters and papers are sometimes confusing to use because there is so much duplication. It was not uncommon for De Smet to write the same letter to three or more correspondents on three different dates. Essentially, the most important collections of De Smet materials can be found in Saint Louis, Belgium, and Washington State.

Most of the letters printed in Chittenden and Richardson's *Life, Letters and Travels* are from the De Smetiana Collection in the Jesuit Missouri Province Archives of Saint Louis. See Lawrence E. Edwards, "The De Smetiana of Saint Louis University" (M.A. thesis, Saint Louis University, 1937) to gain an understanding of the sixteen letterbooks that contain copies of hundreds of letters written by De Smet. De Smet also wrote a record of his travels in an album belonging to Dr. Moses Linton.

Laveille's *Life of De Smet* relied mostly on documents from Belgium and Rome; he did not consult the Missouri Province materials. Laveille had access to the private collection of letters owned by the De Smet family, but also the archives for the Belgian province of the Society of Jesus, the repository of the documents collected by Father Deynoodt.

The least consulted De Smet papers are at Washington State University in Pullman, Washington, and Gonzaga University in Spokane, Washington. During the course of his worldwide research on De Smet between 1940 and 1970, Father William Lyle Davis traced approximately three hundred De Smet family letters to Chile, South America. He also found engravings, legal documents, maps, and manuscripts, plus fifty-seven pencil drawings by Father Nicolas Point, S.J. Washington State University subsequently purchased this collection from Paul de Smet d'Olbecke, a great grandnephew of Father De Smet, in 1967. Meanwhile, Davis placed his personal collection of auxiliary documents about the Jesuit presence in the Pacific Northwest at the time of De Smet in the Oregon Province Archives of the Society of Jesus at Gonzaga University. See the article by William Lyle Davis, S.J., "On the Trail of Father De Smet: The Chilean Phase," *The Record of Friends of the Library of Washington State University,* 1968, pp. 21–28, and "The Papers of Father Peter John De Smet, S.J., in the Washington State University Library," *The Record of Friends of the Library of Washington State University,* 1969, pp. 7–40. The papers and transcripts generated by Adelle Knox during the course of her curatorial work on the De Smet collection in the Manuscripts, Archives, and Special Collections section of Washington State University library are well organized and a necessary aid to using the De Smet collection.

De Smet published four books and scores of articles. *Letters and Sketches: with a Narrative of a Year's Residence among the Indian Tribes of the Rocky Mountains* (Philadelphia: M. Fithian, 1843) was De Smet's first and most popular book. It enjoyed numerous reprintings in Europe during De Smet's lifetime, and in the past four decades it has become popular again in America. One of the reasons De Smet's books were reprinted so often, and in so many languages, was that he did not seek royalties, preferring to use the books for their publicity value for the Indian missions and as a gimmick in fund raising. His second book was *The Oregon Missions and Travels over the Rocky Mountains in 1845–46* (New York: Edward Dunigan, 1847; Fairfield, Washington: Ye Galleon Press, 1978). The final two books were both published during the Civil War: *Western Missions and Missionaries* (New York: James B. Kirker, 1863), and *New Indian Sketches* (Boston: D. & J. Sadlier & Co., 1863; Fairfield, Washington: Ye Galleon Press, 1984).

The chief outlet for De Smet's articles—really extended letters he wrote to friends and family—was *Précis Historiques.* It began publication in 1852 and completed forty-eight issues. At the height of its popularity it ran sixty-four thousand copies of separate issues. One of the reasons for its popularity was the large number of articles written by Father De Smet; he authored 101 articles between 1853 and 1870. Many letters first published in *Précis Historiques* were subsequently published in *Western Missions and Missionaries.*

Sometimes *Précis Historiques* would gather up some of the most popular De Smet articles and publish them as their own book. That was the case for the letters De Smet wrote about his experience at the Fort Laramie council in 1851. Other periodicals to which De Smet sent his letters include the *Baltimore Catholic Magazine* and *Annales de la Propagation de la Foi*. Many of De Smet's letters were reprinted without authorization in foreign and American Catholic magazines. A full list may never be compiled, but for a reasonably complete listing see Phyllis R. Abbott, "Publicizing the Missions" (M.A. thesis, Gonzaga University, 1952).

Much of the best literature on De Smet has been in articles by three distinguished Jesuit historians. Father William Lyle Davis, for example, showed what kind of biography he would have written with these three chapters: "Peter John De Smet: The Years of Preparation, 1801–1837," *Pacific Northwest Quarterly* 32 (April 1941): 167–96; "Peter John De Smet: Missionary to the Potawatomi, 1837–1840," *Pacific Northwest Quarterly* 33 (April 1942): 123–52; "Peter John De Smet: The Journey of 1840," Parts 1 and 2, *Pacific Northwest Quarterly* 35 (January and April 1944): 29–43, 121–42. See also William P. Donnelly, S.J., "Father De Smet: A Review," *Historical Bulletin* 19 (March 1941): 57–59; and "Father Pierre-Jean De Smet: United States Ambassador to the Indians," *Historical Records and Studies* 24 (1934): 7–142. Another is Gilbert J. Garraghan, S.J., "Father De Smet, History Maker," *Mid-America* 6 (January–April 1924): 168–80.

Father Garraghan provides a broad view of things Jesuit in the Missouri Province of the Society of Jesus in *The Jesuits of the Middle United States*, 3 vols. (New York: America Press, 1938; Chicago: Loyola University Press, 1984). For the same perspective for the Pacific Northwest, see Wilfred P. Schoenberg, S.J., *A History of the Catholic Church in the Pacific Northwest* (Washington, D.C.: Pastoral Press, 1987), and *Paths to the Northwest: A Jesuit History of the Oregon Province* (Chicago: Loyola University Press, 1982). See also Lawrence B. Palladino, S.J., *Indian and White in the Northwest* (Baltimore: John Murphy & Company, 1894), and Andrew M. Jung, *Jesuit Missions among the American Tribes of Rocky Mountain Indians* (Spokane, Washington: Gonzaga University Press, 1925). See also Claude Schaeffer, "The First Jesuit Mission to the Flathead, 1840–1850: A Study in Culture Conflicts," *Pacific Northwest Quarterly* 28 (July 1937): 227–50. For a newer view, see Francis Paul Prucha, S.J., "Two Roads to Conversion: Protestant and Catholic Missionaries in the Pacific Northwest," *Pacific Northwest Quarterly* 79 (October 1988): 130–37.

For an explanation of the reduction concept that so fascinated De Smet, see Philip Caraman, *The Lost Paradise: An Account of the Jesuits in Paraguay, 1607–1768* (London: Sidgwick & Jackson, 1975). See also William P. Donnelly, S.J., "Nineteenth Century Jesuit Reductions in the United States," *Mid-America* 17 (April 1935): 69–83. Difficult to locate is John Gilmary Shea, *Catholic Missions among the Indian Tribes of the United States* (New York: E. Dunigan & Brother, 1855). Easier to find is Robert F. Berkhoffer, *Salvation and Savage, An Analysis of Protestant Missions and American Indian Response, 1787–1862* (Lexington: University of Kentucky Press, 1965).

Cornelius M. Buckley, S.J., wrote an excellent biography of a De Smet companion, *Nicolas Point, S.J.: His Life & Northwest Indian Chronicles* (Chicago: Loyola University Press, 1969). See also Joseph Donnelly, S.J., translator, *Wilderness Kingdom: Indian Life in the Rocky Mountains, 1840–1847. The Journals & Paintings of Nicolas Point, S.J.* (New York: Holt, Rinehart and Winston, 1967). Another member of De Smet's original cadre of Jesuits to the Oregon country is Gloria Ricci Lothrop, translator and editor of Gregory Mengarini, S.J., *Recollections of the Flathead Missions* (Glendale, California: Arthur H. Clark, 1977). The story of the 1841 wagon train is in John Bidwell, *A Journey to California in 1841; The First Emigrant Party to California by Wagon Trail: The Journey of John Bidwell* (Berkeley: Friends of Bancroft Library, 1964). Sr. Leititia Mary Lyons has done good work in *Francis Norbert Blanchet and the Founding of the Oregon Missions (1838–1848)* (Washington, D.C.: Catholic University of America Press, 1940).

The Osage Indians and their Kansas mission are seen in John Joseph Mathews, *The Osages* (Norman: University of Oklahoma Press, 1961). See also Sister Mary Paul Fitzgerald, "Osage Mission, A Factor in the Making of Kansas," *Mid-America* 19 (July 1937): 182–96. See also Frank A. Mullin, "Father De Smet and the Potawatomie Indian Missions," *Iowa Journal of History and Politics* 23 (April 1925): 169–78.

The Flatheads and their missions are seen in John Fahey, *The Flathead Indians* (Norman: University of Oklahoma Press, 1973). Two publications provide insight into De Smet's missions in the Pacific Northwest: Lucylle Evans, *St. Mary's in the Rocky Mountains* (Stevensville, Montana: Montana Creative Consultants, 1976), and William L. Davis, S.J., *A History of St. Ignatius Missions* (Spokane, Washington: C. W. Hill Printing Co., 1945). See also Edwin V. O'Hara, "De Smet in the Oregon Country," *Quarterly of the Oregon Historical Society* 10 (September 1909): 239–62.

For De Smet's trek across the forty-ninth parallel in search of the Blackfeet, see Robert V. McGuinness, "The Missionary Journey of Father De Smet," *Alberta Historical Quarterly* 15 (Spring 1967): 12–19.

For De Smet's relations with the Sioux, see Louis Pfaller, O.S.B., *Father De Smet in Dakota* (Richardton, North Dakota: Assumption Abbey Press, 1962), and his editing of "The Galpin Journal: Dramatic Record of an Odyssey of Peace," *Montana: The Magazine of Western History* 18 (April 1968): 2–23. See also Robert M. Utley, *The Indian Frontier of the American West* (Albuquerque: University of New Mexico Press, 1984), and *The Lance and the Shield* (New York: Henry Holt, 1993). See also Ray H. Mattison, "Indian Missions and Missionaries on the Upper Missouri to 1900," *Nebraska History* 38 (June 1957): 127–54. Regarding the Sitting Bull episode in 1868, see "Statement of the Rev. P. J. De Smet, S.J., of his Reception by and Council with the Hostile Uncpapa Indians," *Papers Relating to Talks and Councils Held with the Indians in Dakota and Montana Territories in the Years 1866–1869* (Washington, D.C.: Government Printing Office, 1910), 108–13. Useful as a companion to De Smet's own letters, see Gilbert J. Garraghan, S.J., "Father De Smet's Sioux Peace Missions of 1868 and the Journal of Charles Galpin," *Mid-America* 13 (October 1930): 141–63.

David M. Brumbach wrote an excellent thesis that brings clarity and perspective to De Smet's complex financial dealings in, "Peter John De

Smet, S.J.: Fundraiser and Promoter of Missions" (Ph.D. diss., Washington State University, 1992). For the reservation system as a solution to the Indian question, see Robert A. Trennert, *Alternative to Extinction: Federal Indian Policy and the Beginnings of the Reservation System* (Philadelphia: Temple University Press, 1975). For the Grant Peace policy, see Peter J. Rahill, *The Catholic Indian Missions and Grant's Peace Policy, 1870–1884* (Washington, D.C.: Catholic University of America Press, 1953).

The Mormon War is best treated in Norman F. Furniss, *The Mormon Conflict: 1850–1859* (New Haven: Yale University Press, 1960) and George R. Adams, "General William Selby Harney: Frontier Soldier" (Ph.D. diss., University of Arizona, 1983). For the role of the Society of Jesus in the Coeur d'Alene War of 1858, see Robert Ignatius Burns, S.J., *The Jesuits and the Indian Wars of the Northwest* (New Haven: Yale University Press, 1966; Moscow, Idaho: University of Idaho Press, 1986).

Index

Accolti, Michael (Jesuit missionary), 75, 86, 129, 140
Albeni Falls, 79, 83, 84
American Board of Commissioners for Foreign Missions, 20
American Fur Company, 26, 31, 34, 38–41, 44, 62, 105, 115, 120, 130, 132, 168, 206. *See also* Chouteau, Charles
Annals of the Propagation of the Faith, 43
Anticatholicism, 4, 145–46. *See also* Know-Nothings
Applegate, Jesse, 64
Arapaho Indians, 133, 137
Arikara Indians, 41, 104, 105, 131, 133, 175, 188–90, 202, 217, 239. *See also* Fort Berthold
Assiniboin Indians, 131, 133, 134, 216; Assiniboins of the Forest, 89, 90
Association of the Propagation of the Faith, 120, 122, 123, 126, 141
Astoria, Ore., 71
Athabasca Pass, 95, 96
Athabasca River, 94
Atlantic Ocean. *See* Travels of De Smet, on oceans
Augur, Gen. Christopher C., 219

Badlands, Dak., 194, 220
Bailey, Edwin, 172

Baltimore, Md., 3, 8, 9, 17, 64, 109, 168
Baptism(s), by De Smet. *See* Indian converts, by De Smet
Barclay, Forbes, 72
Bartleson, John, 45
Bay of Kalispels, 84, 85
Bear River, Utah, 45
Bears, 11, 39, 89, 103, 104, 142, 164, 170
Beaverhead River, 37, 47, 59
Beckx, Peter, 143, 151, 166, 167, 169, 171, 176; and Rocky Mountain Mission, 144; combines Oregon and California missions, 144, 152; separates Oregon and California missions, 152
Belgium, 3, 17, 22, 26, 33, 75, 76, 88, 113, 120, 141, 184, 186, 233, 238; De Smet in, 14, 15, 65, 67, 142, 196, 197, 229, 235; Order of Leopold conferred by, 197
Bellevue, Nebr., 115, 118
Benton, Randolph, 146
Benton, Sen. Thomas Hart, 146
Biddle, Nicholas, 9, 39
Bidwell, John, 44–47
Big Face (Flathead), 36, 38, 45, 47, 64
Big Hole River, 59
Bighorn (steamboat), 209, 210
Bighorn River, 39, 219
Big Lake (Blackfeet), 103

Biledot, Peter, 75
Birnie, James, 71, 72
Bison. *See* Buffalo
Bitterroot Valley, 48–51, 53, 59,
  75, 82, 99, 129, 161. *See also*
  Saint Mary's Indian Mission
  (Flathead Indians)
Blackfeet Indians, 19, 37, 41, 48,
  49, 54, 60, 62, 77, 81, 88, 91–
  93, 100, 101, 114, 115, 140, 148,
  179, 203, 216, 232, 241; De
  Smet as missionary to, 86,
  89, 91; and intertribal peace,
  59, 85, 92, 102, 103, 106. *See
  also* Saint Peter's Indian Mis-
  sion (Blackfeet)
Blackfeet Sioux Indians, 41, 49,
  115, 173
Black Hills, 118
Black Moon (Hunkpapa), 223,
  224
Black Robe (Indian name for
  De Smet), 36
Blair, Congressman Frank P.,
  171
Blanchet, Archbishop Francis
  N., 38, 44, 57, 66, 67, 72, 73,
  79, 97, 109, 110, 183
Boat Encampment, 95, 96
Bogy, Lewis V. (Commis-
  sioner of Indian Affairs), 205,
  208
Bonaparte, Napoleon, 3, 14, 35,
  52
Boston, Mass., 3, 19, 64
Bow River, 89
Bozeman Pass, 39, 100
Bozeman Trail, 207, 208, 210,
  226
Bravest of the Brave (Flathead),
  46, 47
Bridger, Jim, 133, 217
Brown, B. Gratz, 133, 134

Browning, O. H., 207
Brulé Sioux Indians, 115, 118,
  147, 173, 185, 192, 210, 218, 224
Buffalo, 22, 27, 33, 36, 39, 40,
  46, 48, 89, 93, 105, 116, 120,
  132, 134, 135, 144, 164, 170, 183,
  189, 199, 201, 202, 219, 223,
  241; hunts, 37, 59, 78, 80, 81,
  100, 103, 135, 213, 226
Bull Run, Battle of (Manasas
  Jct.), De Smet witness to, 168
Bureau of Indian Affairs, 169,
  174
Burnett, Peter H., 64

Calispel Mountain, 79
Calumet. *See* Peace pipe
Campbell, Colin, 116, 118
Campbell, Robert, 133
Canada. *See* Assiniboin Indians,
  Assiniboins of the Forest;
  Fort Alexander; Fort Assini-
  boin; Fort Augustus; Fort
  Jasper; Forty-ninth parallel;
  Oregon country, joint oc-
  cupation of; Travels of De
  Smet, in Canadian Rockies;
  Rocky Mountain House;
  Travels of De Smet, on Ca-
  nadian prairies
Canoes. *See* Travels of De
  Smet, on Missouri River
  canoes
Cape Disappointment, 69–71
Cape Horn, De Smet around, 68
Catholic Indian missions, and
  Grant Indian policy, 231–33,
  236, 244
Catholic ladder, 64
Catlin, George, 113
Cayuse Indians, and Whitman
  massacre, 140
Chambers, A. B., 133

Chaplain of U.S. Army, De
    Smet as, 147–49, 166, 171; in
    Coeur d'Alene War, 151–60;
    in Utah Expedition, 147–49
Charles (Flathead), 51, 52, 55,
    56, 58, 59, 101, 102
Cheyenne Indians, 34, 133, 134,
    219
Cheyenne River, 118
Chicago, De Smet in, 146, 209,
    230
Chile, De Smet in, 68
Chinook Indians, 20, 72
Chittenden, Hiram M., 243
Chouteau, Charles, 168, 171, 172,
    176, 177, 187, 193, 206, 240. See
    also American Fur Company
Church of Jesus Christ of
    Latter-day Saints, 105, 146,
    149; De Smet is critical of,
    147, 148
Cincinnati, Ohio, 146, 196, 226;
    De Smet in, 64, 121
City of Dublin (ship), 229
City of New York (ship), 233
City of Paris (ship), 236
Civil War, 168, 171; Jesuits and
    Draft Act of 1863, 175, 179,
    194–96. See also Bull Run,
    Battle of; Lincoln, President
    Abraham
Claessens, William (Jesuit mis-
    sionary), 43, 48, 53, 82, 180
Clark, William, 13, 37
Clark Fork River, 51, 52, 83, 86
Clatsop Indians, 71
Coeur d'Alene Indians, 55, 72,
    77, 80, 108, 153, 155–59, 182,
    232; promised a mission, 59.
    See also Coeur d'Alene Indian
    War; Coeur d'Alene Mission
    of the Sacred Heart of Jesus;
    Point, Nicolas

Coeur d'Alene Indian War, 153,
    183; De Smet and, 155–60. See
    also Coeur d'Alene Indians
Coeur d'Alene Lake, 58, 77, 81,
    182
Coeur d'Alene Mission of the
    Sacred Heart of Jesus, 77,
    80, 83, 84, 157, 207; De Smet
    at, 156–58, 163, 182. See also
    Coeur d'Alene Indians; Saint
    Joseph's Indian Mission
    (Coeur d'Alenes)
Coeur d'Alene River, 163, 182
Columbia (ship), 5
Columbia (steamboat), 219
Columbia Lake, 88, 89
Columbia Plateau Indians, 19,
    20, 139, 158, 159, 240. See also
    Coeur d'Alene Indians; Flat-
    head Indians; Kalispel
    Indians
Columbia River, 19, 20, 50, 52,
    55, 56, 58, 62, 75, 87, 89, 95–
    98, 110, 123, 163, 182, 183, 206,
    217; crossing the bar at, 68–
    72, 106; De Smet at source
    of, 88. See also Dalles, The;
    Fort Vancouver; Hudson's
    Bay Company, barges; Oka-
    nogan Dalles; Travels of De
    Smet, on Pacific Northwest
    rivers
Colville Road, 79
Comanche Indians, 163, 164, 167
Confederate States of America,
    168. See also Civil War
Congiato, Nicholas (Jesuit
    missionary), 152, 155, 164,
    166
Connor, John C., 235, 236
Council Bluffs, Iowa, 21, 22,
    25–30, 36, 41–43, 105, 115,
    119, 147, 238; See also Saint

Joseph's Indian Mission
(Potawatomi)
Crow Indians, 39, 66, 92, 131,
133, 134, 177, 178, 192, 213; De
Smet visits, 40, 60, 61; and
Flatheads, 100–103
Cuelenbroeck, Blondeel Van,
170
Culbertson, Alexander, 132, 217

Dakota Sioux, 114. *See also* San-
tee Sioux Indians
Dalles, The (of the Columbia
River), 98, 182–83
Delano, Columbus, 231, 232,
236
De Meester, Peter, 233
Demers, Modeste, 38, 57, 66
Dendermonde (Termonde),
Belgium, 3–6
Denig, Edwin T., 216
De Smet (steamboat), 236, 237
De Smet, Charles (brother), 4,
5, 23, 145
De Smet, Francis (brother), 23,
88, 89, 145, 183
De Smet, Josse (father), 4, 5, 8,
14, 122
De Smet, Paul (nephew), 146
De Smet, Peter John: American
citizen, 14; author and publicist, 169, 200, 205, 238, 239,
240; as cartographer, 81, 82,
113, 145, 241; criticism of, 78,
108–10, 127–30, 166, 167, 176,
215, 216, 241, 244; death, 237;
education as a Jesuit, 5, 7, 10,
11, 21; as ethnographer, 240;
faith in God, 39, 40, 47, 51,
62, 83, 84, 86, 92, 109; health
of, 14, 15, 29, 30, 33, 75, 98,
119, 126, 130, 131, 144, 179, 183–
85, 196, 197, 215, 220–22, 227–

30, 236; and Indian lan-
guages, 27, 35, 92; love of
family, 4, 5, 17, 143, 183, 198,
229; nearly reassigned to
Holland, 141; nominated to
be bishop, 66, 67; personality, 11, 12, 26, 30, 167, 244;
physical description, 3, 4, 11,
126; public speaker, 27, 142; as
scientist, 26, 27; withdrawal
from Jesuits, 15, 16; as writer,
64, 113, 120, 132; youth, 3, 4.
See also Black Robe; Chaplain of U.S. Army, De Smet
as; Federal government envoy to Indians, De Smet as;
Federal government funds,
use of by De Smet; Fund-
raising, by De Smet; Indian
converts, by De Smet; "Indian Question" for De Smet;
Indians, understanding and
misunderstanding, by De
Smet; Intertribal peace-
maker, De Smet as; Procurator, De Smet as; Recruiting
for missions, by De Smet;
Souvenirs, given by De Smet;
Travels of De Smet; Writings
by De Smet
De Velder, Jean Baptiste, 35,
40–42
De Vos, Peter (Jesuit missionary), 63–65, 72, 75–78, 80, 81,
84, 107, 108
De Voto, Bernard, 243
Deynoodt, Francois, assembles De Smet's writings, 235,
236
Dogs, 22, 23, 34, 90, 93, 97, 134,
170, 189, 202
Dole, W. P., 185, 186, 193, 194
Douglas, James, 72

Drips, Andrew, 31, 32, 217
Du Bourg, Bishop Louis William, 8, 13

Eagle Woman (Mrs. Charles Galpin), 220, 222
Elet, John A., 113, 114, 116, 121, 124, 125, 128, 130, 140, 141, 244
Emile (steamboat), 172
England, 15, 33, 87, 196, 229, 233
Ermantinger, Frank, 46, 51, 95
Euro-American civilization, for Indians, 61, 99, 162, 238, 242
Europe, 4, 5, 7, 9, 14, 16, 17, 36, 58, 64–67, 75, 77, 80, 89, 108, 112–14, 123, 141–45, 150, 166, 167, 171, 181, 184, 196, 198, 229, 233, 236, 239, 240

Federal government envoy to Indians: De Smet as, 127, 171, 239, 241; to Coeur d'Alene Indians, 151, 155–60; to Sioux Indians, 183–94, 198–99, 208–15, 217
Federal government funds: De Smet presses claims for, 169, 170, 196; for Indian missions, 12, 25, 169, 170; use of by De Smet, 127, 165, 171, 183, 185, 186, 209, 217, 218
Fifth Baltimore Council, 66
Fitzpatrick, Thomas, 44–46, 105, 133, 136, 137
Flathead Indians, 39, 42, 66, 80, 81, 84, 86, 92, 106, 108, 115, 116, 118, 138–40, 148, 153, 157–59, 181, 185, 238, 241; and Crow Indian war, 100–103; first visit to by De Smet, 34–40, 43, 64, 125; loss of piety, 140; piety of, 37, 47, 49, 54,

109, 125, 129; second visit to by De Smet, 45–49, 53–55, 58–61, 64; seek Jesuit missionaries, 18–21, 29–31. *See also* Saint Mary's Indian Mission (Flathead Indians); Saint Ignatius Indian Mission (Flathead Indians)
Florissant, Mo., 10, 11, 13, 17, 18, 121, 131, 237
Food: in Indian camps, 22, 27, 34, 90, 134, 135; on the trail, 53, 103, 105, 119, 132, 164, 226; in British Canada, 89, 93, 94. *See also* Buffalo; Dogs
Fort Alexander, 40
Fort Assiniboin, 94
Fort Augustus, 93
Fort Benton, 167, 168, 171, 177, 178, 199, 206; De Smet at, 103, 164, 172, 173, 179, 203
Fort Berthold, 104, 172, 175–77; De Smet at, 188, 190–93, 202, 203; plans for Indian mission and school at, 174, 194, 199, 230. *See also* Arikara Indians; Mandan Indians
Fort Buford, 207, 213, 228
Fort C.F. Smith, 214
Fort Clark, 41
Fort Colville, 44, 50, 52, 53, 55, 59, 73, 78–80, 85, 86, 95, 97, 98
Fort Hall, 46, 47, 51, 64, 73, 95
Fort Jasper, 94
Fort Kearny, 136, 214
Fort Laramie, 131–33, 138, 139, 207, 218, 219, 226, 227
Fort Laramie council (1851), 127, 130, 131, 137, 140, 141, 149, 162, 173, 241; De Smet at, 133–35. *See also* Horse Creek, Nebr.
Fort Leavenworth, 18, 22, 137,

149, 219; De Smet at, 22, 148, 214, 215
Fort Pierre, 41, 126, 131, 173, 185; De Smet at, 105, 116
Fort Randall, 199; plans for Indian mission and school at, 230, 231
Fort Rice, 193, 207, 215, 218, 224, 225, 228; De Smet at, 213, 219, 220, 226, 227
Fort Ridgely, 174
Fort Stevenson, 230
Fort Sully, 185, 187, 207, 213; De Smet at, 202. See also Old Fort Sully
Fort Thompson, 210
Fort Union, 39–40, 103, 127, 136, 138, 141, 207, 216; De Smet at, 41, 61, 62, 104, 131, 132, 202, 213
Fort Vancouver, 20, 38, 44, 51, 55, 64, 67, 87, 95, 97, 123, 151, 157, 179, 206; De Smet at, 56–58, 72, 73, 75, 85, 153, 155, 159–63, 183
Fort Vermilion, 41, 105
Fort Walla Walla, 44, 73, 75, 76, 80, 98, 153, 155, 156, 182; De Smet at, 58, 78, 79, 159
Forty-ninth parallel, 97, 161
Four Horns (Hunkpapa), 221, 223
Francis Xavier (Flathead), 45, 46
Fraser, Colin, 94
Frémont, John Charles, 26
Fulton (ship), 141
Fundraising, by De Smet, 8, 44, 64, 106, 111, 122–25, 181, 239, 240; fundraising in Europe, 14, 16, 66, 67, 112, 114, 141–43, 166, 170, 171, 196, 197, 229, 233, 235; fundraising in America, 42, 43, 168, 230

Gabriel (Cree), 61, 101
Gaes, John Anthony, 215
Gall (Hunkpapa), 225, 227, 228
Galpin, Charles, 217, 218, 219; accompanies De Smet to Sioux, 220–26. See also Eagle Woman
Garreau, Pierre, 188, 203
Gaucher, Pierre (Iroquois), 28, 30, 34, 36
Gazzoli, Gregory (Jesuit missionary), 156, 166, 182
Georgetown College, 5, 7
Gerard, Frederick, 188, 217
Geyer, Charles A., 26, 27
Ghent, Bel., 4, 15
Giorda, Joseph (Jesuit missionary), 166, 180, 203
Gious, Alex, 210
Gold: in California, 109, 123, 129, 140; at Colville, 153; in Idaho and Montana, 182, 203, 207
Government funds. See Federal government funds
Graham (steamboat), 213
Grand Couteau, La. See Saint Charles College
Grand River Agency, S.Dak., 230, 231, 233, 235, 236
Grant, Pres. Ulysses S., and Indian policy, 230–33, 236, 244
Great Plains, 31, 33, 113, 115, 118, 120, 121, 126, 127, 130, 159, 164, 170, 179, 185, 198, 200, 208, 214, 227; condition and potential, 131, 149–51, 162. See also Travels of De Smet, on Great Plains
Great Powder River Council, 223–25
Green River, Wyo., 30, 31, 38, 44, 67, 105; De Smet at rendezvous, 34, 35, 45

Gros Ventres Indians, 133, 177, 188, 202
Guidon (steamboat), 209, 210

Harney, Gen. William S., 177; in Coeur d'Alene Indian War, 151–60; and De Smet, 161–63, 237; commanding Utah Expedition, 146–49; on Indian Peace Commission, 218, 219, 226, 227
Harriote, J. E., 91, 92, 95
Hell Gate, 48, 59, 64, 180
Hell Gate Treaty (1855), 181
Henderson, Sen. John B., 219
Hoecken, Adrian (Jesuit missionary), 63, 64, 72, 76, 82, 84, 85, 126, 128, 166, 243
Hoecken, Christian (Jesuit missionary), 41, 128, 130, 131
Holland. See Netherlands, De Smet in
Horse Creek, Nebr., 133, 135. See also Fort Laramie council
Howard (steamboat), 21
Hudson's Bay Company, 20, 44, 50–53, 56, 71, 86, 87, 89, 91, 93, 206; barges on Columbia River, 55, 58, 75, 87, 95–98; supplies for Jesuits, 46, 72, 73, 111, 123; annual brigade, 94, 95. See also Ermantinger, Frank; McLoughlin, John; Ogden, Peter Skene; and various posts
Huet, Charles (Jesuit missionary), 43, 48, 53, 77
Hughes, Archbishop John, 87, 111
Hunkpapa Sioux Indians, 115, 118, 173, 187, 198, 207, 219, 220, 226; meet De Smet at Powder River, 221–25. See also Sitting Bull

Huybrechts, Francis (Jesuit missionary), 157
Hyde, George, 241

Immigrants (Europe), predict success on Great Plains, 150
Imoda, Camillus (Jesuit missionary), 179
Indian converts, by De Smet, 23, 34, 36, 47, 52–54, 65, 69, 80, 81, 85, 86, 89, 92, 93, 105, 106, 108, 118, 127, 188–90, 238, 241. See also De Smet, Peter John, faith in God
Indian missions. See various Indian missions.
Indian Missions in the United States of America, under the Care of the Missouri Province of the Society of Jesus, The, 43
Indian policy. See "Indian Question," for De Smet
"Indian Question," for De Smet, 120, 150, 151; advice to Indians, 162, 219, 224; critical of whites, 37, 42, 87, 98, 136, 202, 205, 208, 211, 217, 231; role of missionaries, 99, 121, 212, 214, 242, 243; role of reservations, 87, 131, 161, 162, 241. See also Euro-American civilization, for Indians; Indians, understanding and misunderstanding, by De Smet; Intertribal peacemaker, De Smet as
Indians, understanding and misunderstanding, by De Smet, 12, 50, 54, 55, 61, 86, 100, 103, 108, 109, 118, 128–30, 135, 238, 240, 242
Indian Territory, 141
Infatigable (ship), 67–73, 86, 123

Intertribal peacemaker, De
  Smet as, 27, 28, 92, 100, 101,
  103
Iowa Indians, 22, 23
Iroquois Indians, 18–20, 96

Jackson, Pres. Andrew, 18
Jackson Hole, 35
Jefferson, Pres. Thomas, 8
Jefferson River, 37, 59
Jesuits. See Society of Jesus
Johnson, Pres. Andrew, 214
Joset, Joseph (Jesuit mission-
  ary), 78, 82, 107, 129, 139, 140,
  180, 244

Kalispel Indians, 51, 52, 55, 72,
  75, 76, 78–80, 83–85, 109, 110,
  128, 158, 159, 181, 241. See also
  Albeni Falls; Saint Ignatius
  Indian Mission (Kalispel);
  Saint Michael's Indian Mis-
  sion (Kalispel)
Kamiakin (Yakima), 159, 160
Kansas Territory, 162; need for
  renewal of missions in, 141
Kaw River, 44
Kearney, Stephen Watts, 23
Keller, Joseph, 176
Kettle Falls of Columbia River,
  53, 55
Kettle Indians, 53
Kickapoo Indian Mission,
  Kans., 18, 19, 31, 169
Killdeer Mountain, battle of,
  194
Kipp, James, 41
Know-Nothings, 145, 146, 148,
  244
Kohlmann, Anthony, 5
Kootenai Indians, 55, 158, 181
Kootenai River, 88, 161
Kuppens, Francis, 233, 235

La Barge, Joseph, 131, 172, 206,
  236, 240
Lakota Sioux, 115, 131, 147, 173,
  174, 176, 185, 187, 188, 190–94,
  202, 220. See also Blackfeet
  Sioux Indians; Brulé Sioux
  Indians; Dakota Sioux;
  Hunkpapa Sioux Indians;
  Miniconjous Sioux Indians;
  Sans Arc Sioux Indians; Two
  Kettles Sioux Indians
Latta, Samuel N., 171, 174, 175
Lee, Daniel, 20, 65, 73
Lee, Jason, 20, 65, 73
Letters and Sketches with a Nar-
  rative of a Year's Residence
  among the Indian Tribes
  of the Rocky Mountains, 64–
  66. See also Writings by De
  Smet
Lewis, Meriwether, 37
Lewis and Clark Expedition, 9,
  39
Lincoln, Pres. Abraham, 168,
  169, 174, 243
Linton, Moses, 165, 177, 232
Liquor. See Whiskey
Little Crow (Santee Sioux),
  174
Lizette (mule), 51, 82
London, Eng., 94, 111, 122, 123
Louisiana Purchase territory, 3,
  8, 9
Louisville, Ky., 10, 64
Loyola, Ignatius, 7, 70, 72, 82,
  85, 132; and fund raising, 143;
  and letter writing, 44

McDonald, Archibald, 53
MacGean, James B. (Jesuit missionary), 63, 64, 76
McLoughlin, John, 51, 52, 55, 57,
  72, 73, 75, 123

Mandan Indians, 41, 131, 133, 175, 188, 189, 202, 217, 239. See also Fort Berthold

Manifest Destiny, 150

Mankato, Minn., 174

Man Who Strikes the Ree (Yankton), 187, 189, 207, 209, 210, 218

Maps, by De Smet, 127, 134, 145, 217, 241. See also De Smet, Peter John, as cartographer

Maréchal, Archbishop Ambrose, 8

Martin, W. T. (Irish physician), 176, 177, 179, 182, 183

Maryland Province of the Society of Jesus, 7, 8; and Missouri Mission, 9, 10, 13; separate from Missouri Mission, 12

Mazelli, John (Jesuit missionary), 23

Meagher, Gen. Thomas, 203

Mechelin, Bel., 3, 4

Medicine Lodge Creek, Kans., 214

Mengarini, Gregory (Jesuit missionary), 43, 46, 48, 58, 59, 75, 77, 78, 80, 83, 129

Methodist Church, 20, 65, 73, 98, 232, 233

Mexican War, 150

Miége, Bishop John, 141, 143

Military Road. See Mullan Road

Milk River, Mont., 179, 181; confrontation with Oglala Sioux, 177, 178, 191

Milwaukee, Wis., De Smet in, 146, 230

Miniconjou Sioux Indians, 115, 173, 187, 210

Minnesota River, 114

Minnetaree Indians, 131

Minor (steamboat), 203

Mississippi River, 9, 168

Missouri, 8; in Civil War, 168, 169. See also Travels of De Smet, in Missouri

Missouri Mission of the Society of Jesus, 14–18, 21, 25, 31; becomes Missouri Vice-Province, 42; established, 10, 11; growth and responsibilities of, 13, 17, 18; separated from Maryland Province, 12. See also Florissant, Mo.; Maryland Province of the Society of Jesus; Missouri Vice-Province of the Society of Jesus

Missouri Province of the Society of Jesus, 205, 215, 216, 233; created, 184; De Smet writing history of, 230

Missouri River, 11, 21, 22, 25–27, 37, 38, 42, 48, 62, 88, 106, 115, 119, 127, 217, 226; De Smet, essay on, 103, 200; Indian unrest on, 173, 176, 179, 198, 202, 206. See also Steamboats, on Missouri River; Three Forks of Missouri River; Travels of De Smet, on Missouri River canoes

Missouri Vice-Province of the Society of Jesus, 76, 107, 111, 125, 140, 143, 151, 166, 167, 169; becomes Missouri Province, 184; created, 42; De Smet as socius and procurator, 121, 122, 124, 126, 138, 141, 144, 175. See also Fundraising, by De Smet; Missouri Mission of the Society of Jesus; Missouri Province of the Society of

Jesus; Rocky Mountain Mission of the Society of Jesus
Mitchell, David D., 127, 132–34, 136
Montana Territory, 173, 176; De Smet nominated to be bishop of, 198
Morgan, Henry Lewis, 171
Mormons. *See* Church of Jesus Christ of Latter-day Saints
Mossvelde, Charles Van (nephew), 169, 196
Mousse, Ignace la (Iroquois), 18, 19, 45
Mousse, Young Ignace la (Iroquois), 29–31, 61
Mullan Road, 180, 181
Murphy, William Stack, 141, 148, 151, 167, 169

Native Americans. *See* Federal government envoy to Indians, De Smet as; Indian converts, by De Smet; "Indian Question," for De Smet; Indians, understanding and misunderstanding, by De Smet; Intertribal peacemaker, De Smet as
Nauvoo, Ill., 147
Nebraska City, Nebr., 136
Nellie Rogers (steamboat), 176–78, 181
Nerinckx, Charles (missionary), 3–5
Netherlands, De Smet in, 4, 65, 67, 141, 196
New Indian Sketches, 183, 200
New Orleans, 43, 64, 107
New York, N.Y., 16, 64, 67, 111, 114, 151, 168, 183, 206
Nez Perce Indians, 36, 49, 82,

163; and Crow Indian war, 100–102
Nicholas (Blackfeet), 102
Nicollet, Joseph N., 26
Niobrara River, 118
Nobili, John (Jesuit missionary), 86, 97, 126
No Neck (Hunkpapa), 223
North Platte River, 33. *See also* Platte River
Notre Dame de Namur, sisters of, 67, 70, 72, 73, 75

Oceana (ship), 43
Ogden, Peter Skene, 55, 86–88, 95
Oglala Sioux Indians, 115, 118, 185, 192, 207, 208, 210, 214, 218; at Milk River, 177, 178
Ohio River, 9, 10, 43
Okanogan Dalles (of Columbia River), 56, 97
Old Fort Sully, De Smet at, 211–13. *See also* Fort Sully
Omaha, Nebr., 209, 215; De Smet in, 164, 187, 219, 229
Omaha Indians, 27
Omega (steamboat), 62
Ontario (steamboat), 199–203
Oregon country, 19, 38, 43, 44, 50–52, 57, 58, 60, 63–67, 73, 75, 81, 85–87, 94, 99, 103, 109, 111, 114, 115, 122, 124, 128, 129, 139–41, 238, 240
Oregon Mission of the Society of Jesus, 166–68, 171, 237; created, 144; De Smet as procurator for, 166–68, 173, 176, 186, 199, 206, 207; separated from California, 152. *See also* Missouri Vice-Province of the Society of Jesus; Rocky

Mountain Mission of the Society of Jesus
Oregon Missions and Travels over the Rocky Mountains in 1845–46, 112, 113
Oregon Trail, 98, 127, 132, 133, 136, 137, 149
Osage Indians, 12, 184, 196
Oto Indians, 23
Owen, John, 128, 160

Pacific Northwest, 20, 38, 48–50, 52, 60, 63. *See also* Oregon country; Travels of De Smet, in Pacific Northwest mountains; Travels of De Smet, on Pacific Northwest rivers
Pacific Ocean, travels of De Smet, 67, 68
Panken, Ignatius, 230
Paraguay reductions, 48–50, 57, 85, 99, 139. *See also* Reduction concept
Paris, France, 113, 114, 124; De Smet in, 141, 143, 196
Parker, Ely S., 211, 214, 233
Parker, Samuel, 20
Pawnee Indians, 27
Peace Commission of 1868, 219–27
Peacemaker. *See* Intertribal peacemaker, De Smet as
Peace pipe, 27, 223, 240
Peacock (ship), 68, 69
Pend Oreille Indians, 36, 49, 158, 159, 181
Pend Oreille Lake, 51
Pend Oreille River, 55, 79, 83, 84
Peru, De Smet in, 68
Philadelphia, Pa., 3, 5, 42, 64, 177

Picotte, Joseph, 210
Pierre's Hole, 34, 35
Pittsburgh, Pa., De Smet in, 9, 43, 64
Platte River, 45, 64, 131, 219, 226; De Smet describes, 149, 150. *See also* North Platte River; South Platte River
Pleasonton, Alfred, 157, 158
Point, Nicolas (Jesuit missionary), 43, 46, 52, 64, 76, 77, 82, 86, 99, 101, 107, 108, 113, 140, 216; and the Blackfeet Indians, 59, 85, 102, 103; and Coeur d'Alene Indians, 59, 60, 72, 80; and Flathead Indians, 48–50, 53, 78, 81, 100
Ponca Indians, De Smet visits, 116
Pope Clement XIV, 7
Pope Gregory XVI, 66
Pope Paul III, 7
Portland, Oreg., De Smet in, 160, 183
Potawatomi Indians, 21, 31, 37, 41, 43, 105, 137, 238; De Smet as missionary to, in Iowa, 23, 25–29; in Kansas, 169, 184, 196, 230, 232, 239. *See also* Saint Joseph's Indian Mission (Potawatomi); and Saint Mary's Indian Mission, Kansas (Potawatomi)
Powder River, 219, 221, 226
Précis Historiques, De Smet writes essays for, 138, 144, 183, 184, 205, 215, 216, 228. *See also* Terwecoren, Edward
Procurator, De Smet as, 239, 240; for Missouri Vice-Province, 138, 141, 144; for Oregon Mission, 144, 166, 173, 176, 186, 199, 206, 207

Promoting missions, by De Smet. *See* Fundraising, by De Smet; Writings by De Smet

Puget Sound, 58, 87

Quebec, 38, 66, 95

Railroads, 209, 210, 219, 231
Ravalli, Anthony (Jesuit missionary), 129
Recruiting for missions, by De Smet, 15, 67, 114, 192, 240
Red Cloud (Oglala Sioux), 207, 208, 214, 215
Red Fish (Oglala Sioux), 192
Red Fish, son of (Oglala Sioux), 178
Reduction concept, 63, 76–78, 80, 81, 84, 100, 106, 109, 125, 162, 163. *See also* Paraguay reductions
Rencontre, Alexander, 210
Rencontre, Zephyr, 217
Reservations, Indian. *See* "Indian Question," for De Smet
Revolutions of 1848 (Europe), encourages immigration, 150
Richardson, Alfred T., 243
Rocky Mountain House, De Smet at, 91, 92
Rocky Mountain Mission of the Society of Jesus, 57, 59, 63, 65, 67, 121, 124, 138, 139, 238, 239, 243; created, 43; De Smet dismissed from, 107, 239, 243, 244; personnel matters in, 76–78, 80, 81, 99, 106–108, 239; procurator for, 111, 121–23; renamed Oregon Mission, 144; separated from Missouri Vice-Province, 111, 125, 140; *See also* Fundraising, by De Smet; Missouri Vice-Province of the Society of Jesus; Oregon Mission of the Society of Jesus; Roothaan, John, complaints against De Smet

Rocky Mountains, 18–20, 29–31, 33, 35, 41–43, 45, 49, 51, 59, 62, 66, 76, 87, 89, 90, 94, 95, 105, 108, 110, 113, 115, 118, 120, 124, 125, 136, 145, 159, 161, 185, 197, 237. *See also* Travels of De Smet, in Rocky Mountains

Rome, Italy, 33, 66, 67, 76, 114, 124, 141, 143, 170, 196, 197
Roothaan, John, 15, 16, 63, 66, 67, 76, 77, 86, 99, 111, 114, 122, 126, 141, 148, 151, 170, 206; complaints against De Smet, 107–10, 124, 125, 128–30, 138–40
Rosalie (sister), 23, 82, 236
Rosebud River, 40
Rowand, John, 93, 95
Running Antelope (Brulé Sioux), 224

Sacred Heart Indian Mission. *See* Coeur d'Alene Mission of the Sacred Heart of Jesus
St. Ange (steamboat), 130–32
Saint Charles College (Louisiana), 50, 60, 76, 77
Saint Francis Regis Indian Mission (Chewelah Indians), 85
Saint Francis Regis Indian Seminary (Florissant, Mo.), 12, 13, 18, 21
Saint Francis Xavier Mission (Willamette Valley), 73, 75, 77, 97, 110
Saint Ignatius. *See* Loyola, Ignatius

Saint Ignatius Indian Mission (Flathead Indians), 158, 159, 163, 164, 179–82, 206. *See also* Flathead Indians; Saint Mary's Indian Mission (Flathead Indians)

Saint Ignatius Indian Mission (Kalispel), 93, 128; De Smet at, 85. *See also* Kalispel Indians; Saint Michael's Indian Mission (Kalispel)

Saint Joe River, 58, 78, 81, 82

Saint Joseph, Mo., 119, 186

Saint Joseph's Indian Mission (Coeur d'Alene), 78, 82. *See also* Coeur d'Alene Indians

Saint Joseph's Indian Mission (Potawatomi), 23, 25, 28–30, 41, 80, 105. *See also* Potawatomi Indians; Saint Mary's Indian Mission, Kansas (Potawatomi)

Saint Louis, Mo., 8–10, 14, 16–21, 28–30, 38, 41, 42, 47, 58, 59, 61, 62, 67, 72, 76, 77, 99, 100, 103, 105–107, 113, 116, 119, 127, 128, 130, 132, 136, 137, 143, 144, 146, 151, 163, 164, 168, 169, 171, 175–77, 179, 181, 183, 184, 186, 189, 194, 196, 199, 205, 209, 215, 229, 230, 239; anti-catholic sentiment of, 145; funeral for De Smet, 237

Saint Louis University, 13, 17, 42, 107, 114, 121, 137; De Smet at, 138, 145, 151, 168, 169, 181, 184, 215, 229, 230

Saint Mary's Indian Mission (Flathead Indians), 63, 64, 72, 76, 82–84, 99, 100, 102, 158; established, 48–50, 53, 109; supplies for, 52, 53, 55, 57, 75. *See also* Flathead Indians;

Mengarini, Gregory; Point, Nicolas; Saint Ignatius Indian Mission (Flathead Indians)

Saint Mary's Indian Mission, Kansas (Potawatomi), 137, 169, 227; corruption of Indians at, 229, 230. *See also* Potawatomi Indians; Saint Joseph's Indian Mission (Potawatomi)

Saint Michael's Indian Mission (Kalispel), 72, 75, 76, 78; De Smet at, 79, 83, 84. *See also* Kalispel Indians; Saint Ignatius Indian Mission (Kalispel)

Saint Paul Indian Mission (Kettle Indians), 85

Saint Paul's Mission (Willamette Valley), 57, 72, 73

St. Peter (steamboat), 26, 27

Saint Peter's Indian Mission (Blackfeet), 173, 179, 180, 203. *See also* Blackfeet Indians

Saint Stanislaus (Florissant, Mo.), 17, 70

Salt Lake City, Utah, 105, 147–49

Sanborn, John B., 219, 226, 227

San Francisco, Calif., 87, 206; De Smet in, 153, 183

Sans Arc Sioux Indians, 115, 173, 187

Santee Sioux Indians, 114, 174, 176, 191, 194, 213; *See also* Lakota Sioux

Saskatchewan River, 91

Second Baltimore Council, 17, 18

Selkirk Mountains, 88

Shawneetown, Ill., 10

Sherman, William T., 218, 219

Shoshone Indians, 35
Sibley, General Henry H., 174
Sioux City, Iowa, 209, 210, 237
Sioux Indians, 21, 116, 120, 125, 134, 167, 171, 175, 183, 186, 192, 202, 213, 219, 227, 241; defined, 115; first impression of by De Smet, 118; incident at Fort Berthold, 190; incident at Milk River, 177, 178; plans for Jesuit mission and school, 114, 119, 170, 173, 194, 198, 199; restlessness and war, 173, 174, 176, 179, 185, 198, 207. See also Grand River Agency, S.Dak.; Lakota Sioux
Sitting Bull, 198, 207, 215, 219, 228, 235; councils with De Smet, 222–25
Smith, Joseph, 147
Snake River, 20, 35, 36, 46, 47, 55, 58
Soaring Eagle (Mandan), 189
Society of Jesus, 15, 16, 19, 42, 44, 57, 70, 82, 99, 111, 113, 123–25, 143, 175, 194, 216, 218, 232, 238, 243; history of, 7, 8; principle of accommodation, 17, 18, 50
Soda Springs, 45, 46
Soderini, Tiberio (Jesuit missionary), 78, 84, 99, 110
Sopranis, Felix, 166
South Pass, 34, 45
South Platte River, 135, 149
Souvenirs, given by De Smet, 143, 183
Spalding, Henry, vilifies the Jesuits, 140
Specht, Joseph (Jesuit missionary), 43, 48, 53, 82
Spokane Desert. See Travels of De Smet, on Spokane Desert

Spokane Indians, 153, 155, 159
Spokane River, 55, 77
Spread Eagle (steamboat), 171, 172, 174
Stanley, Gen. David S., 226, 227
Stanton, Edwin M. (Secretary of War), 194, 195
Steamboats, on Missouri River, 25, 28, 31, 43, 61–63, 145, 164, 168, 173, 176, 179, 186, 203, 206, 215, 227, 236, 237; De Smet on, 21–23, 26, 27, 62, 106, 107, 115, 119, 130–32, 137, 171, 172, 174, 176–78, 181, 187, 188, 199, 200–203, 205, 209, 210, 213, 219, 220. See also various steamboats
Stellam (Coeur d'Alene), 77, 80
Stephen Watts Kearney, 23
Steptoe, Edward, 153
Stevens, Isaac I., 181; asks De Smet to assist him, 148; makes Indian treaties, 152, 153
Sully, General Alfred, 174, 185, 186, 214; and Sioux, 191–94, 211, 212; mellows toward De Smet, 199, 206
Sylvie (niece), 82, 126

Tappan, S. F., 219
Taylor, Nathaniel G. (Commissioner of Indian Affairs), 219
Ten Commandments, 34, 37, 52
Terry, Gen. Alfred, 219, 226, 227
Terwecoren, Edward, 138, 184, 205, 215, 216, 228. See also Précis Historiques
Teton Sioux Indians. See Lakota Sioux; Sioux Indians
Three Forks of Missouri River, 37, 38, 47, 59, 60

Tobacco, as traditional Indian gift, 34, 220–22
Travels of De Smet, 62, 106, 137, 165, 238, 240; on Canadian prairies, 93, 94; in Canadian Rockies, 89, 91, 94–96; Plains, 31, 32, 45, 115, 116, 131, 220, 221; in Missouri, 11, 29, 42; on Missouri River canoes, 28, 41, 61, 103–105, 119, 166; on oceans, 15, 67, 68, 229, 235, 240; in Pacific Northwest mountains, 50, 51, 53, 58, 59, 80, 84, 85, 88, 156, 158, 159, 163, 164, 182; in Rocky Mountains, 33–35, 45, 46, 51; on Pacific Northwest rivers, 55, 56, 58, 61, 72, 75, 82, 83, 86, 96, 97, 182, 183; on Spokane Desert, 58, 78, 79, 163; on Yellowstone Desert, 39, 40, 60–62, 101, 132. *See also* De Smet, Peter John, faith in God; Food; Steamboats, on Missouri River, De Smet on
Treaties, with Indians, 217, 226, 227; Isaac Stevens's treaties, 152, 160
Turin Province of Society of Jesus, responsibility for North American Jesuit Indian missions, 144, 152
Two Bears (Yanktonai Sioux), 224, 233
Two Kettles Sioux Indians, 115, 173, 187, 210, 220

Umatilla Indians, 163
United States Exploring Expedition, 69
Utah Expedition, 146–49, 151, 162, 183

Utah Territory, 146
Ute Indians, 35

Van de Velde, James, 107, 128
Van Quickenborne, Charles (Jesuit missionary), 9, 10, 12, 13
Vercruysse, Louis, 156
Verhaegen, Peter, 14, 21, 23, 29–31, 33, 37, 38, 42–44, 47, 63, 76, 78, 138
Vermilion River, 26, 115
Verreydt, Felix (Jesuit missionary), 23, 41
Victor (Flathead), 101
Victoria, Vancouver Island, De Smet in, 183

Walla Walla, Wash., 20, 65, 183; growth of, 182. *See also* Fort Walla Walla
Wallula, Wash., 182, 183
Washington, D.C., 137, 146, 170, 175, 215; De Smet in, 64, 168, 169, 183, 194–96, 208, 232; Indians as visitors to, 207–209
Washington Territory, 166
Weed, Thorlow, 175, 194, 243
Western Emigration Society, 44, 45
Western Mission and Missionaries, 183
Westport, Mo., 31–34, 42–44, 49, 64, 67, 76, 105, 137
Wheeling, W.Va., 9
Whiskey, 23–26, 28, 60, 121, 230
White Man Pass, 89
White Marsh, Md., 7–9
White Parfleche (Arikara), 189
White River, 118
Whitman, Marcus, 20, 64, 65, 140
Willamette Valley, Oreg., 20,

38, 46, 57, 62, 66, 73, 75, 87, 97, 110, 129, 140
Wilmington (steamboat), 22, 23
Wolves, 11, 22, 39, 41, 97, 164
Wright, George, 153, 155, 156, 160
Writings by De Smet, 33, 43, 45, 63, 66, 88, 89, 108, 111–13, 116, 126, 128, 129, 138, 144, 183, 205, 228. *See also Précis Historiques*

Yakima Indians, 159, 163
Yankton Agency, 209, 210; De Smet at, 203–205; Jesuit Indian mission proposed, 199, 207, 208
Yanktonai Sioux Indians, 114, 210, 220; peace council with, 191, 192
Yankton Sioux Indians, 26–28, 114, 115, 174, 185, 187, 204, 205, 239
Yellowstone (steamboat), 186–88, 193
Yellowstone Desert, 213. *See also* Travels of De Smet, on Yellowstone Desert
Yellowstone National Park, 217
Yellowstone River, 38, 39, 100, 194, 217, 221
Yellowstone Valley, 219, 221
Young, Brigham, 105, 146; De Smet's opinion of, 147; Harney's opinion of, 148